TAILORING HEALTH MESSAGES

CUSTOMIZING COMMUNICATION
WITH COMPUTER TECHNOLOGY

D1125745

LEA'S COMMUNICATION SERIES
Jennings Bryant/Dolf Zillmann, General Editors

For a complete list of other titles in LEA's Communication Series, please contact Lawrence Erlbaum Associates, Publishers.

TAILORING HEALTH MESSAGES

CUSTOMIZING COMMUNICATION WITH COMPUTER TECHNOLOGY

MATTHEW KREUTER
HEALTH COMMUNICATION RESEARCH LABORATORY
SAINT LOUIS UNIVERSITY

DAVID FARRELL
PEOPLE DESIGNS, DURHAM, NC

LAURA OLEVITCH
HEALTH COMMUNICATION RESEARCH LABORATORY
SAINT LOUIS UNIVERSITY

LAURA BRENNAN
SAINT LOUIS UNIVERSITY

WITH A FOREWORD BY
BARBARA K. RIMER

2000

LAWRENCE ERLBAUM ASSOCIATES, PUBLISHERS
Mahwah, New Jersey   London

The final camera copy for this work was prepared by the authors, and therefore the publisher takes no responsibility for consistency or correctness of typographical style. However, this arrangement helps to make publication of this kind of scholarship possible.

Lawrence Erlbaum Associates, Inc., Publishers
10 Industrial Avenue
Mahwah, New Jersey 07430

Layout, design, and cover by Dawn Bucholtz

ISBN 0-8058-3386-2 (cloth)
ISBN 0-8058-3387-0 (pbk.)

Books published by Lawrence Erlbaum Associates are printed on acid-free paper, and their bindings are chosen for strength and durability.

Printed in the United States of America
10   9   8   7   6   5   4   3   2   1

Contents

Acknowledgments

We express our sincere gratitude to our close colleage at the Health Communication Research Laboratory, Dawn Bucholtz, who worked tirelessly on the design and layout of this book. We also thank Heather Jacobsen of the Health Communication Research Laboratory, Nicole Lezin of Cole Communication in Atlanta, GA, and Kristin Trangsrud of People Designs in Durham, NC, who each provided thoughtful and thorough reviews of earlier drafts of the book.

We would also like to recognize three of our research partners in tailored communication whose work has provided not just examples shared in the book, but has also the inspiration to write the book in the first place. Drs. Marci Campbell, University of North Carolina at Chapel Hill, and Celette Skinner, Duke University, contributed pioneering research to the study of tailored health communication, and remain highly valued friends and collaborators today. We appreciate their constant willingness to share their ideas and respond to ours. Lastly, this book would never have been written without the influence and guidance of Dr. Vic Strecher, University of Michigan. Dr. Strecher first introduced us to the idea of tailoring health messages over a decade ago, and provided the resources and environment necessary for us and other to begin making this new possibility a reality. His innovative thinking in computer interactive health communication continues to inspire researchers and practitioners worldwide.

Authors

Matthew Kreuter, PhD, MPH, is associate professor and Director of the Health Communication Research Laboratory at the Saint Louis University School of Public Health. He has been actively involved in developing and testing tailored health communication programs since 1990, including programs promoting alcoholism recovery, cancer and cardiovascular disease screening, childhood immunization and injury prevention, dietary change, medication compliance, occupational safety and health, smoking cessation, weight management, and women's health. Dr. Kreuter's research has been funded by the Agency for Health Care Policy and Research, Centers for Disease Control and Prevention, National Cancer Institute, National Institute of Child Health and Human Development, National Institute on Occupational Safety and Health, and the Susan G. Komen Breast Cancer Foundation.

David Farrell, MPH, has been involved in tailored health communication programs since the methodology was first used for public health communication. He founded and is currently President of People Designs, a design and materials development firm specializing in one–of–a–kind educational materials for health and human service programs. With People Designs, he provides technical assistance in planning and implementing tailored health communication programs, designs tailored materials, and produces tailored feedback for dozens of programs throughout the United States. His tailoring interests include designing individualized communication, and development of tailored feedback production tools and processes.

Laura Olevitch, MS, RD, is Assistant Director of the Health Communication Research Laboratory at the Saint Louis University School of Public Health. She is a registered dietitian and holds a Master of Science Degree in nutrition from Case Western Reserve University. Ms. Olevitch's background includes working with patients living with chronic diseases such as diabetes, heart disease, and end stage renal disease to promote dietary change and medication and treatment compliance. She has been involved in tailored health communication since the mid–1990s, specializing in: program planning, background research, questionnaire development, tailored message writing, and formative evaluation. She has developed numerous tailored health education programs on topics ranging from weight management to injury prevention.

Laura Brennan is a research assistant at the Saint Louis University School of Public Health. She is currently working on a masters degree in Public Health and doctorate in Health Services Research. Ms. Brennan worked at the Health Communications Research Laboratory for 3 years helping to design, develop, and evaluate tailored health communication programs, with an emphasis on writing and testing tailored message algorithms.

Foreword

It is more than a pleasure, it is an honor to write the Foreword for Tailoring Health Messages. It has been obvious for some time that there is a great hunger among researchers, clinicians, and other health practitioners to learn about tailored health communications and to acquire the skills needed to produce them. But until now, the tools to enable greater dissemination have been lacking. Tailoring Health Messages fills an important void by providing a scholarly how-to resource that will be as valuable to researchers as it will be to practitioners. The book is incredibly readable. In fact, I was so fascinated that I read it in one sitting.

Tailored health communication is part of the larger field of health communication. Communication is central to effective, quality health care, from primary prevention to survivorship. Communication empowers people; it can raise awareness of health problems and recommended actions, and give people the health information they need to make informed decisions. The Science Panel on Interactive Communications and Health (Henderson, 1999) has concluded that few other health–related interventions have the potential of interactive health communications to simultaneously improve health outcomes, decrease health care costs, and enhance consumer satisfaction.

The communications environment is changing so dramatically that it has been called a communications revolution. Perhaps, the best example of this is the astronomical growth of the Internet. More than 40 million people now use the Internet for a variety of purposes, ranging from e–mail access to Medline and other library retrieval services, online support and delivery of personalized, individualized services. In the future, more and more health communication programs are likely to be delivered online.

Tailoring Health Messages comes at an important point in history. The burgeoning communications revolution offers an ever–increasing array of tools for communication, including interactive CD–ROMs, the Internet, interactive kiosks, wireless pagers, and personal digital assistants. Parallel trends have made powerful computing available at the desktop. In the business world, mass customization has become a way of life. Who has not received a personalized mailing with one's name and perhaps other information emblazoned on the front of it? People have come to expect individualized communications as a consequence of the trend toward mass customization in U.S. society.

Where once health educators and other behavioral scientists relied on generic materials designed to reach as many people as possible, the growing evidence base of tailored communications shows that print and electronic communications created for individuals based on information specific to them can result in significant positive outcomes across a range of health problems and conditions. There are now more than 30 controlled studies of tailored health communications that demonstrate significant main effects or interactions on behaviors such as smoking, diet, and exercise. But tailored communications also are being used in complex areas of health behavior. These include decision making about difficult topics, such as genetic testing for susceptibility to cancer and use of hormone replacement therapy (Annals of Behavioral Medicine, 1999). Converging trends in business, health, and computing augur that in the future there will be even greater opportunities to deliver individualized health messages. Given the growth of the evidence base, it now is appropriate to disseminate tailored strategies more widely.

Health educators and others must be poised to develop and deliver state–of–the–science tailored health communications. This book will help them. The "how–to" aspects of this work are especially noteworthy. The focus on the nuts and bolts of tailoring is a unique part of this book. For most people, tailoring has been a black box. This book takes readers inside the black box and shows us how to create design templates to produce tailored communications, how to develop message libraries, and how to operationalize the messages by creating algorithms, and finally, how to evaluate. This information is just what people need! One of the particular values of Tailoring Health Messages is that it puts tailoring into its larger context as part of health communication. But it also takes the reader through the key steps necessary to design tailored communications.

Matt Kreuter and David Farrell were ideally suited to author the first comprehensive text on tailored health communications. Not only were they among the first practitioners of the art and science of tailoring health communications, but they have continued to advance the frontiers of tailored health communications. Laura Olevitch and Laura Brennan are important additions to the author team. Moreover, the authors and their book blend rigorous scientific methodology with a creative, even exuberant, approach to communication. Tailoring Health Messages is a ground-breaking contribution and should be read by all who want to communicate more effectively about health.

Barbara K. Rimer

Director

Division of Cancer Control and

Population Sciences

National Cancer Institute

CHAPTER 1

What Is Tailored Communication?

Imagine opening your morning newspaper to find a cover story reporting the latest developments in your company's industry and providing an analysis of how those developments might affect your work environment and your paycheck. Inside the paper, the sports pages are full with in–depth stories about your favorite players and teams from across the country, and all your favorite comic strips are presented. The financial section focuses on your personal investments, and the weather forecast includes a 5–day outlook for your next business destination. The paper offers feature stories about your favorite hobbies and a review of the latest CD recorded by your favorite artist. Even the advertisements are right for you—a shoe sale at the mall and discount tires at the auto repair shop. It's as if the paper were written specifically for you!

Futuristic fantasy? Not really. Customizing the types of news and advertising a person receives is already quite common via electronic media, such as the World Wide Web, and is becoming more widespread in many forms of print media. It's easy to see how news information can be quickly customized to a specific individual. Because most news information is routinely gathered and reported by existing organizations, it can simply be partitioned for distribution and used in many different ways. But how does this process of customization apply to personal health issues?

Let's say you have an appointment to see your doctor about your high blood cholesterol level. In the past, your doctor has monitored your cholesterol and has lectured you about taking your medication, avoiding fatty foods, and getting more exercise. But today's visit is different. Your doctor gives you the same advice, but at the same time hands you a set of printed materials and tells you to read them. She says, "These have been created just for you and will help you make the changes we've talked about to manage your cholesterol." As you begin reading the materials, you're amazed at how closely they relate to the specific ways *you* are working to manage your cholesterol. One section reads:

> Since you're the person who usually does the grocery shopping for your family, you're in a great position to control the kinds of food that come into your home. The next time you're at the store, try to do most of your shopping on the outside aisles. That's where you'll find healthier foods like fresh fruits and vegetables, whole grain breads, skim milk, and lean cuts of meat. And remember to read the nutrition labels on foods to be sure you're choosing a low–fat option—you haven't been doing this lately.

On another page you read:

> It's clear that your family members don't like the taste of lower fat foods and haven't been very supportive of your efforts to eat healthier. That's why it's important for you to try some of the new recipes listed below. They're all Mexican and Italian dishes like the ones your family enjoys, they taste great, but they have only a few grams of fat per serving.

Adjacent to the recipe cards is yet another message. It reads:

> It seems like the cold weather has been keeping you from walking every day like you had hoped to in your physical activity plan. Did you know that many of the local malls open early in the winter for walkers? Crestwood Mall is the one closest to your house, and it opens for walking at 6:30 every morning. Mall walking might also help with your recent lack of motivation. You've been struggling with exercise because your walking partner moved away, and this might be a way for you to meet some new people, and not feel like you're exercising alone.

Below that is a new section that reads:

> Also, the upset stomach you've been experiencing could be a side effect of the cholesterol lowering medication you're taking. Fortunately, there are several things you can do to prevent it. First, avoid taking your medication on an empty stomach. If you still feel queasy, try taking an antacid tablet before taking your pill, but most importantly, keep taking your medication. It looks like your cholesterol levels are starting to come down, and we want to make sure it stays that way.

Both of these examples—the newspaper and the cholesterol management materials—illustrate how information can be customized, or tailored, to meet the unique needs, interests, and concerns of a specific individual. Although both examples may sound innovative, the basic approach they use is not new at all. Effective teachers, physicians, real estate agents, stock brokers, salespersons, and even hair stylists identify a client's needs through observation and inquiry and use that information to customize solutions.

In the area of health promotion, individual counseling for improved nutrition, physical activity, smoking cessation, stress management, weight control, and other health–related behaviors is also based on this approach. Counselors ask questions, patients provide answers, and the counselors use that information to determine the most appropriate course of action for that particular individual, given his or her unique life circumstances.

The interpersonal contact, interactivity, and immediate feedback that can be provided in one–on–one counseling make this approach especially desirable. However, the impact of such counseling on the health of populations is limited by cost and by the relatively small number of individuals who can be reached by an even smaller number of trained professionals. That's why tailored health communication, such as the cholesterol management materials described in the second example, are so appealing. With the use of computers, it is possible to generate highly customized health messages on a mass scale, reaching many members of a large and diverse population almost instantaneously. In a recent series of well–designed studies, such computer–generated materials tailored to the unique needs and interests of individual subjects have been shown to be more effective than conventional health communication approaches in helping some patients quit smoking (Prochaska, DiClemente, Velicer, & Rossi, 1993; Strecher et al., 1994), reduce their dietary fat intake (Brug, Steenhaus, van Assema, & de Vries, 1996; Campbell et al., 1994), increase levels of physical activity (Bull, Kreuter & Scharff, 1999; Kreuter & Strecher, 1996; Marcus et al., 1998), and get mammograms (Skinner, Strecher, & Hospers, 1994), cholesterol tests (Kreuter & Strecher, 1996), and childhood immunizations (Kreuter, Vehige, & McGuire, 1996).

The purpose of this book is to introduce the concept of tailoring health messages, present the theoretical rationale and empirical evidence that support using this approach, and describe the steps one must take to create and deliver programs that provide tailored health messages. As with any innovation in the early stages of diffusion (Rogers, 1983), tailored message programs have been used by just a handful of pioneers to date, and mostly within the context of research studies. Given the growing evidence supporting tailored interventions as a promising approach to health promotion, students, practitioners, and researchers in health science and communication disciplines should understand the approach and consider the opportunities it presents for enhancing their work.

Tailoring and Related Concepts

The distinctions between tailored, targeted, personalized, and other forms of health communication are important ones, yet the terms have too often been used interchangeably in health communication and behavior change research literature (Davis, Cummings, Rimer, Sciandra, & Stone, 1992; Drossaert, Boer, & Seydel, 1996; Eakin et al., 1998; Morgan et al., 1996; Pasick, 1997; Rimer & Orleans, 1994). Given that research findings suggest there can be significant differences in the relative effectiveness of these approaches (Skinner, Campbell, Rimer, Curry, & Prochaska, in press), there is a clear need to standardize terminology. If apples are always compared to oranges, understanding is obscured. Furthermore, the comparative value of different health promotion programs and communication–based interventions cannot be fairly evaluated.

Traditionally, health education materials have been generic, and have aimed to provide as much information as possible within a single health communication, without considering any specific characteristics of prospective consumers (Strecher, Rimer, & Monaco, 1989). Generic materials typically aspire to be all things to all people, providing a single comprehensive set of information about a specific content area. In using generic materials, it is not necessarily assumed that all people have the same informational needs, but rather that individuals can and will sift through the parts of these materials that do not apply to them in order to find and consume those that do. Can you imagine a real estate agent saying to a prospective home buyer, "Here's a street map of our entire city. By going up and down all the streets, you're sure to find something that meets your needs"? A few motivated buyers might use this approach and find the right home, but many more would give up before then, or never start because the burden seemed too great. Alternatively, the agent could have targeted particular neighborhoods for the buyer to explore or even provided the address of one specific home that had all the qualities the buyer was looking for. Either of these alternative approaches—targeted or tailored— would greatly reduce the burden placed on the buyer.

Targeted health education materials are those materials intended to reach some specific subgroup of the general population, usually based on a set of demographic characteristics shared by its members. The use of targeted materials is based on principles of "market segmentation," which aim to find the right kinds of consumers for a particular product or service (Zimmerman et al., 1994). In health promotion, this approach might lead to creating a self–help smoking cessation manual especially for older adults (Rimer et al, 1994), or breast and cervical cancer screening materials for midlife or older women ("Pathways to Freedom," 1992). Although there is a sound public health rationale for using this approach—namely that certain health problems disproportionately affect certain populations—its effectiveness as a communication strategy is unclear. Implicit in the use of targeted health messages is the assumption that sufficient homogeneity exists among members of a demographically defined population to justify using one common approach to communicate with all of its members. In fact, this assumption is largely unfounded for some populations (Abad, Ramos, & Boyce, 1974; Bryant, 1982; Counsel on Scientific Affairs, 1991; Furino, 1991; Novello, Wise, & Kleinman, 1991; Strecher et al., 1989; Yankauer, 1987). Targeted communication is an incremental advance over the generic one–size–fits–all approach, and there is some evidence that such materials can contribute to individual behavior change (Davis et al., 1992; Gritz & Berman, 1989; Kristeller, Merriam, Ockene, Ockene, & Goldberg, 1993; Morgan et al., 1996; Peppers & Rogers, 1993; Rimer et al., 1994). However, targeted materials cannot address naturally occurring variations between individuals on important factors that are not demographic in nature.

Still, other materials are personalized at the rather superficial level of using some common personal identifier. *Personalization,* or using a person's name to draw attention to an otherwise generic message (Raphel, 1996; Snoddy, 1996) is a commonly used approach in direct–mail marketing (e.g., "Matthew W. Kreuter, you may have already won $2,500,000!"). This kind of nominally personalized communication is commonly used in mass mailings so that even a very low percentage of returns might generate a profit (Geller, 1997).

Both targeted and personalized communications base their messages on factors that are unique to individuals (e.g., age, race, name), but these factors alone provide little information about the cognitive and behavioral patterns that influence people's health–related decisions and actions. As a result, both approaches lack the depth of understanding that is often necessary in order to develop truly individualized strategies to address complex lifestyle behaviors. For example, which would be more useful to health educators developing a dietary change program: knowing the age, race, and sex of program participants or knowing about their specific dietary habits, cooking skills, and eating patterns? Tailoring health promotion materials allows one to build on the strengths of demographic, personal identification, and behavioral information, without being confined by the limitations inherent in using population–based demographic data alone.

Tailored health promotion materials are any combination of information and behavior change strategies intended to reach one specific person, based on characteristics that are unique to that person, related to the outcome of interest, and derived from an individual assessment (Kreuter, Lezin, Kreuter, & Green, 1998). The process of tailoring health messages is a lot like the process an actual tailor uses to make custom–fit clothing.

A tailor takes a customer's measurements, asks about preferences for fabric, color, and style, and uses this information to create a suit to fit that customer. Likewise, a tailored health communication program measures a participant's needs, interests, and concerns, and uses that information to create health messages and materials to fit that person. Like a cheap suit or a one–size–fits–all jacket, health promotion materials that aim to meet the needs of all people with a single message will seldom fit as nicely as individually tailored materials.

This definition of tailoring highlights the two features that set it apart from other commonly used approaches to health communication. It is *assessment–based*, and as a result its messages can be individual–focused. Figure 1.1 classifies different communication strategies along these two dimensions: (1) the extent to which an individual's characteristics have been assessed in order to drive the communication; and (2) the degree of individualization in the communication itself.

In general, it is expected that as the level of assessment increases, so would the degree of individualization in the content of the communication. Obviously, the more information one has about the intended recipient of the communication, the better equipped one is to create messages and materials individualized to that person's specific needs.

What's in a Name?

As if it's not enough to keep the differences straight among tailored, targeted, and personalized health messages, researchers and practitioners must also contend with a host of synonyms for tailoring that have recently emerged from business and industry. The term "mass customization" was coined by Stanley Davis in 1987 (Davis, 1987) to describe a more individualized approach to the production of consumer goods. This idea was more fully developed by Joseph Pine (1993) who described the opportunity and potential benefits to be gained in some industries by shifting away from systems of mass production toward *mass customization—* a more individualized process based on establishing and maintaining individual relationships with each customer. In advertising and marketing, similar approaches have been labeled "one–to–one," (Peppers & Rogers, 1993) "data–based" or "relationship" marketing, and "micromass communication" (Anonymous, 1997).

Importantly, whether creating health education materials, dress shoes, or marketing appeals, the process underlying each of these terms is fundamentally the same. It requires both an assessment of the individual

Figure 1.1

Classification of Five Approaches to Health Communication by Level of Assessment and Nature of Content.

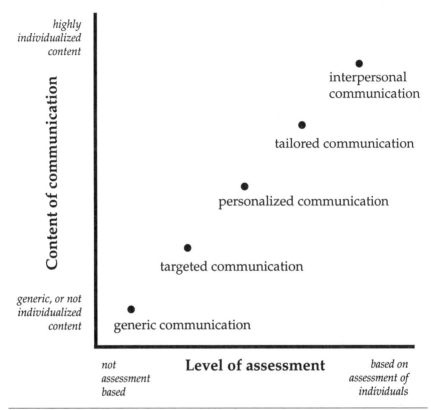

and a customized end product. Also shared across disciplines is the recognition that this approach has the potential to reach mass populations in an individualized fashion, but there are important differences as well. Foremost among these differences are the motives and objectives for tailoring, specifically the ways in which data obtained from an individual will be used. For example, it is clear that many financial and marketing applications of tailoring principles seek to use such data to exclude or "dump" unprofitable consumers from their business planning (Peppers & Rogers, 1997). Following this kind of profit motive is not consistent with meeting public health objectives. Rather than dumping individuals who appear less likely to adopt a specific behavior change, tailored health communication seeks to identify alternative approaches that might be better suited to that person's needs or abilities.

A Brief History of Health Communication: How Did We Arrive at Tailoring?

This section is not intended to be a comprehensive history of health communication or health education in the United States—either topic alone would easily a fill a book at least the size of this one. Rather, it is meant to give readers a brief review of major changes that have occurred in the 1900s in the ways health information has been communicated to populations. The pattern of evolution described in this section includes some adaptive and some less adaptive changes and helps us to understand how tailoring has emerged as the most recent advance in the field.

"Just the Facts, Ma'am"

During the first half of the 1900s, health education consisted largely of what was termed *health publicity* (Patterson & Roberts, 1951). The primary role of health educators in this era was to pass along information about health and diseases to populations at risk and to the general public. As Lemuel Shattuck had written almost a century earlier in his famous Report of the Sanitary Commission, there was a great need to:

> collect and diffuse by personal intercourse, public lectures, printed work, or otherwise, information to the end that among all persons the laws of health and life may be better understood, the causes of disease known and avoided, the term of life extended, the vital force and productive power increased, the greatest possible amount of physical and sanitary happiness enjoyed."(Patterson & Roberts, 1951, 21–22)

For the most part, this education took the form of presenting facts, dispelling myths, and giving directives for actions believed to enhance health or prevent disease (see Fig. 1.2). Implicit in this approach was the belief that changes in knowledge alone would lead to changes in behavior. As a result, information was poured on the public with the belief that more information would lead to greater changes. Much of this activity took place in school settings, where didactic teaching of health facts and recommended behaviors to school children was commonplace (see Fig. 1.3).

A Shift Toward Community

By the 1950s, increasing emphasis was being placed on working within communities to promote health and prevent disease. Health educators' traditional role as disseminators of information was not yielding the expected behavioral results, especially when their facts and recommendations were not clearly understood by the intended recipients or when they conflicted with cultural values and beliefs. A new role for health

Figure 1.2

Fact-Based Health Education.

educators as catalysts for change emerged, with community members viewed more as active participants in the change process than empty vessels to be filled with knowledge. As Ivah Everett Deering (1942, p. 26) wrote, "Those who have had a true part in making decisions will not see those decisions lightly set aside." To make health education efforts more effective, it was necessary to better understand the needs and values of those within a community and to find ways to help them achieve whatever measures would most benefit their health. This was clearly a shift toward a more interactive and assessment–based approach to health education and health communication. However, it was still unclear whether such an approach could reach all communities in need.

Reaching the Masses

The use of mass media campaigns in the United States to reach large populations with health messages can be traced back as far as 1721, when Reverend Cotton Mather reportedly distributed thousands of pamphlets throughout the town of Boston, promoting inoculation during a city–wide smallpox epidemic (Paisley, 1989). In 1995, television was reaching 95 million homes in the United States, or 98.3% of all households (U.S. Bureau of the Census, 1997). Where once three major networks

Figure 1.3

School-Based Health Education.

dominated television airwaves, by the late 1980s roughly three–quarters of households had access to 35 or more channels through cable television (Erickson, McKenna, & Romano, 1990). Radio and newspapers also reached large populations, but it was television that held the greatest allure for health educators.

Using the mass media as a vehicle for planned health promotion campaigns was appealing for at least three reasons. First, its broad reach promised to expose vast audiences to important health messages. From a public health perspective, even very modest rates of change in large populations can lead to meaningful reductions in disease. As Chapman (1985, 918) noted in critiquing different approaches to smoking cessation, "a 5% success rate among 10,000 people is over 33 times more efficient than the 30% success rate achieved by group work involving only 50 subjects." Second, mass media campaign planners could exercise control over which messages were shown to whom, and at what time. Third, mass media campaigns would provide high visibility for the health issues they were addressing (see Fig. 1.4), and thus help keep certain issues in the public's eye.

Figure 1.4

Mass Media Campaign.

It seems that many health educators had adopted what Larry Wallack (Wallack, Dorfman, Jernigan, & Themba, 1993)has since termed *the mass media fantasy*—the belief that all public health objectives could be achieved if we could only get the right message to the right person through the right channel at the right time. Excitement about the great potential of mass media campaigns seemed to mask some obvious limitations of this approach. For example, from a communication theory perspective, television offers only one–way communication with no feedback loop or opportunity for interaction (Warner, 1987). There were practical limitations as well, namely cost. It was expensive to produce materials of sufficiently high quality that they could stand out in what had become a busy and highly sophisticated media environment (Hammond, Freimuth, &

Morrison, 1987). Air time for campaign messages was also costly, and, as is true today, most public health agencies had limited budgets.

The alternative to paying for media coverage was to appeal to television stations and networks to air campaign messages as public service announcements (PSAs). This reduced the cost barrier to mass media health communication because radio and television stations are required to provide free air time for community and public service, even though these time slots have been increasingly filled with local promotional pieces (Dessart, 1990). Having limited resources also meant having limited control over the distribution and content of campaign messages. The good news was that one could get air time for free. The bad news was that radio and television stations would rarely fulfill this obligation during prime viewing hours because those time slots generated the most advertising revenue. As a result, most PSA campaign messages were played only sporadically and during odd hours, when far fewer listeners and viewers would be reached. Erickson and colleagues (Erickson et al., 1990) reported that only 30% to 40% of PSAs from the Office on Smoking and Health were aired between the hours of 5:00 p.m. and 11:00 p.m. Similarly, McKenna (McKenna & Romano, 1989) reported that 60% of PSAs from an anti–smoking campaign in New York were aired between midnight and 7 a.m. Finally, from an educational and behavior change perspective, it is unclear how much impact a 30–second message can have on complex lifestyle behaviors.

Right on Target

Unlike mass media campaigns that may reach a vast but undifferentiated audience, targeted communication programs seek to reach a more precisely defined population. Because many important public health problems disproportionately affect specific subgroups within the general population, we target those population subgroups for special programs or services. For example, homicide by gunshot disproportionately affects young African American males (Centers for Disease Control, 1987b). Motor vehicle crash injuries and fatalities are most common among younger drivers (U.S. Department of Transportation, 1987). Rates of screening for breast and cervical cancer are often lower among Hispanic women compared to White women (Centers for Disease Control, 1987a). Such patterns of injury and health–related behavior suggest that special efforts may be needed to address the health problems experienced by members of populations most affected. Not unlike community–focused approaches, the targeted approach to communication reflects recognition of the uniqueness of different populations. Yet although the public health rationale for targeting interventions is clear and justifiable, its effectiveness as a communication approach may be less so. As previously described in this chapter, it is assumed that a single approach can be used to reach a group of people who hold some (usually demographic) characteristic in common.

An Individual Focus

During the 1970s, researchers' ability to quantify more precisely the impact of various behavioral risk factors on mortality rates was combined with emerging computer technology to develop individualized health risk appraisals (HRAs). To participate in an HRA program, individuals typically complete an assessment to provide information about their health–related behaviors (e.g., smoking, seat belt use), health status indicators (e.g., blood pressure, cholesterol level), and other personal characteristics related to mortality risk (e.g., age, gender, weight, present disease status). This information is fed into a computer–based risk estimation algorithm that weights each of these factors according to its relative contribution to different disease states, establishes a health profile for each participant, and then looks at population mortality rates experienced by others of the same age and sex with a similar profile.

HRA is probably the most widely used health education tool for promoting individual behavior change (Becker & Janz, 1987; DeFriese & Fielding, 1990). By 1986, as many as 15 million Americans had participated in HRA or HRA–like programs in worksites, universities, community wellness programs, health fairs, and health care organizations (Schoenbach, 1987). A random sample survey of U.S. worksites showed that, in the late 1980s, HRA activities took place at nearly one third of all worksites (Fielding, 1989). HRA feedback appealed to individual users because its quantification of personal risk status was novel and interesting (see Fig. 1.5). That, in turn, appealed to employers and health care institutions, because it could provide a thumbnail sketch of the risk status and health promotion priorities, in aggregate, for members of a defined population. For some HRA users—though perhaps only the most highly motivated—this individualized feedback may have provided a "cue to action" (Becker, 1974) to reduce their risks.

The use of computers to batch process large amounts of HRA data and provide individualized feedback was a clear precursor of modern tailored communication. However, the designers of most HRA feedback apparently failed to consider some of the important lessons learned from past health education efforts. For example, risk information alone is seldom sufficient to help people change complex lifestyle behaviors. Although HRA feedback may have provided some new information to users initially,

Figure 1.5

HRA Feedback.

```
Example1                                                            Mon Jun 17 1991
Female  Age 48                                                         Version 4.0
                    ----------------------------------------------------
                   |   YOUR        NOW          TARGET       |  <-- Risks are elevated due to
                   |   RISK AGE:  68.40 years   60.25 years  |      diabetes and
                    ----------------------------------------------------   family breast cancer.
            THIS REPORT CONTAINS ESTIMATES DUE TO MISSING ITEMS, INCLUDING THE FOLLOWING:
Beer, Wine Coolers, Liquor.

Many serious injuries and health problems can be prevented.  Your Health Risk Appraisal lists factors you can
change to lower your risk.  For causes of death that are not directly computable, the report uses the average risk
for persons of your age and sex.  More technical detail about the report is on page 2.
---------------------------------------------------------------------------------------------------
 MOST         | NUMBER OF DEATHS IN NEXT 10
 COMMON CAUSES| YEARS FOR 1000 WOMEN AGE 48
 OF DEATH     |                                      MODIFIABLE RISK FACTORS
              |  YOUR              POPULATION
              |  GROUP   TARGET     AVERAGE
--------------------------------------------------------------------------------------------------
 Heart Attack          104      22        6      Avoid Tobacco Use, Blood Pressure, HDL Level, Weight
 Breast Cancer          43      43        6      A Low-Fat Diet and Regular Exams Might Reduce Risk
 Stroke                 19       5        2      Avoid Tobacco Use, Blood Pressure
 Diabetes Mellitus      18      18        1      Control Your Weight and Follow Your Doctor's Advice
 Lung Cancer            12       7        5      Avoid Tobacco Use
 Kidney Failure          2       2       <1
 Emphysema/Bronchitis    2      <1        1      Avoid Tobacco Use
 Colon Cancer           2*       2*       2      A High-Fiber and Low-Fat Diet Might Reduce Risk
 Ovary Cancer           1*       1*       1      Get Regular Exams
 Esophagus Cancer        1      <1       <1      Avoid Tobacco Use
 Pancreas Cancer         1      <1        1      Avoid Tobacco Use
 Cirrhosis of Liver      1       1        1      Continue to Avoid Heavy Drinking

 All Other              21      19       22
 ---------------        ----    ----     ----       * = Average Value Used

 TOTAL:                227     121       47    Deaths in Next 10 Years Per 1,000 WOMEN, Age 48
---------------------------------------------------------------------------------------------------


    -------------------------------------------------------------------------------------------
 |    For Height 5'7" and Large Frame, 175 pounds is about 20% Overweight.  Desirable Weight Range:  139-153   |
    -------------------------------------------------------------------------------------------

 GOOD HABITS                       | TO IMPROVE YOUR RISK PROFILE:            RISK YEARS GAINED
 + Regular pap tests               | - Quit smoking                               2.09
 + Safe driving speed              | - Lower your blood pressure                  1.84
 + You don't use smokeless tobacco | - Improve HDL level                          1.38
                                   | - Lower your cholesterol                     1.17
                                   | - Bring your weight to desirable range       0.20
                                   | - Always wear your seat belts                0.02

```

its contents (i.e., showing the link between disease and a person's risk factors like smoking, diet, cholesterol, and blood pressure) have become so mainstream in the health–conscious media that its recommendations are likely to be more obvious than informative to most users today.

Despite HRA's pervasiveness, reviews of the research literature have found little evidence for HRA's efficacy in changing individual behavior (Beery et al., 1986; Schoenbach, 1987; Wagner, Beery, Schoenback, & Graham, 1982). One explanation for this apparent failure has been that HRA does not provide individuals with sufficient information about how to make the behavior changes it recommends. As described in Chapter 14, there is considerable potential for creating a second generation (enhanced HRA) that fortifies typical HRA feedback by adding tailored communicationto it for behavior change.

A Different Approach to Using the Mass Media

Despite the limitations of traditional mass media approaches to health communication (i.e., PSA and other campaigns), newspapers, radio, and television remain attractive as potentially powerful tools for reaching large populations. In contrast to planned campaigns that view the media primarily as a vehicle for delivering health messages, media advocacy recognizes that the media hold an important agenda–setting function in society. In other words, by attending to some issues and not others, the media help define what is important for viewers, listeners, and readers to think about (McCombs & Shaw, 1972). From this perspective, the mass media provide a means of social change by helping put certain public health issues on the agenda (Wallack et al., 1993). Media advocacy seeks to both "influence the selection of topics by the mass media and shape the debate about these topics" (Wallack et al., 1993, p. 73). A successfully implemented media advocacy campaign will capitalize on the credibility and reach of the mass media to meet objectives traditionally associated with community advocacy: increasing public awareness, shaping public opinion, marshaling resources, and building support for programs and policies.

As illustrated in Fig. 1.6, the objectives and processes for carrying out media advocacy are quite different from those of more traditional uses of the mass media. The skills needed for successful media advocacy are actually similar to those used in creating tailored health communication. Successful media advocates need to observe and assess new events and reporters' styles and preferences. They must then craft their appeals, messages, and stories in a way that will meet the needs of the media and at the same time address specific advocacy and public health objectives. This approach is especially appealing because it does not require a large production budget, and community groups can be trained to carry out media advocacy activities themselves. In this way, media advocacy brings together the advantages of the community–based educational programs discussed previously, but with the potential for broader reach.

Lay Media

Just as media advocacy provides community members with the skills to work directly with the mass media to promote social change, so too have other lay–based approaches to health communication emerged as viable tools. The term *lay media* refers to any media created by laypeople for

Figure 1.6

Differences in Objectives and Processes for Carrying Out Media Advocacy and Mass Media Campaigns (Wallack, 1993).

	Media advocacy	Media campaigns
Objectives	to change the social, physical, and political environment	to change individual behaviors
Basic strategy	provide community groups with skills to tell their own story in their own words	disseminate health messages from a centralized point
Underlying theories	agenda setting and message framing	behavioral science theories about changing individuals
Role of community members	valuable resources for promoting social change	passive recipeints of planned communication
Gaining access to the media	through the news room, demonstrating to reporters, producers and editors the importance and relevance of an issue	through the public affairs office, asking for PSA time, or though the advertising office, if resources allow

laypeople. This type of communication is conceived and produced by individuals without professional training or sanction, and is usually designed for consumption by small numbers of people. It is often produced by members of the community it is designed to serve. Common examples of lay media include church and neighborhood newsletters, support group literature, school newspapers, community action guides, certain World Wide Web sites (see Fig. 1.7), and video documentaries.

The relatively recent proliferation of lay media is due in part to the popularization of, and increased access to, publishing technology. Lower cost video equipment made available in the 1970s and the desktop publishing revolution of the 1980s have made it possible for individuals with little or no professional training in media production to possess and use the tools of professionals. At the same time, a heightened sense of identity among members of many subgroups and subcultures in American society has created an appetite for media that is specific to their communities. Taken together, these factors have created a new genre of media that fills a void left by professional producers and is less constrained by political and

Figure 1.7

Lay Media Health Education Materials.

moral ideologies that sometimes inhibit governments or large private organizations from producing appropriate media.

In recent years, lay media have been widely used to communicate health issues. Perhaps most notable among these are the HIV/AIDS materials—addressing topics from condom use to drug treatments for AIDS—developed by lay people and community–based organizations. Relative to the other health communication approaches discussed in this section, one might think of lay media as a kind of targeted communication, but one that is initiated and developed by members of the target group itself.

How has Tailoring Evolved from these Other Approaches?

Considering the lessons learned from previous approaches to health communication, what positive attributes of each would one want to retain in moving towards a new generation of health communication? First of all, one would want a communication strategy capable of recognizing and addressing the uniqueness of populations and individuals (like community approaches, targeted communication, HRA, and lay media). One would want an approach that actively engaged the target audience in the change process (like community approaches, media advocacy, and lay media), recognizing that only by conducting an individual assessment (like HRA) could the specific health concerns of different individuals be addressed. Lastly, the approach would have broad reach (like mass media campaigns) to maximize the number of people who could benefit from it.

At the same time, one would want to avoid the pitfalls that have compromised the effectiveness of previous approaches. Instead of providing people with only health facts or risk information (like the days of health publicity and later, HRA feedback), or selecting a single communication approach to use with a group of people just because they shared a particular skin color, gender, or age category (like targeting), one would look for an approach that could meet specific public health objectives without breaking the bank. Finally, the ideal approach would be something that has been proven to work—an approach with a sound theoretical rationale and empirical evidence to support its use.

Tailored health communication fits the bill. It is assessment–based at the level of the individual. As a result, the content of its communication can be highly individualized, going beyond risk status to develop personal plans to modify complex health–related behaviors by addressing motivation and beliefs. Yet at the same time, it is truly a population approach with a potentially limitless reach for highly individualized communication among large populations.

Why haven't these aspects of previous approaches to health communication been synthesized into one "best practice" before now? The reason is technology. Technology is the enabling factor in the emergence of tailored communication. Computer automation allows for the rapid processing of individual responses to an assessment and interpretation of those responses to determine which health messages from a large pre–existing library are most appropriate for each individual. Technology allows tailored communication programs to have broad reach and individual specificity, yet at relatively low costs. There is also a clear theoretical rationale and research evidence suggesting that tailoring is a promising approach (see chap. 2).

Questions and Concerns About Tailoring

It is ironic and somewhat unfortunate that in a book on tailoring we are unable to tailor its contents to the needs, interests, and concerns of each reader. But here's a chance for you to self–tailor the remainder of this chapter. Listed below are six of the most common questions and concerns we've heard expressed about tailored communication, and about its role in the broader context of public health education. We've addressed each concern based on our own experiences developing and implementing tailored communication programs. Here's the self–tailoring part: Read each of the paragraph headings. If that issue is not a question or concern you have about tailoring, skip it! Find just those issues that pique your interest, and focus on them.

Is "tailoring" just another fad that will pass in time?

This much we know for sure: The widespread use of computers and other communication and information technologies in all facets of everyday life is not a fad, nor is it likely to pass with time. According to former U.S. Surgeon General C. Everett Koop:

> cutting–edge technology, especially in communication and information transfer, will enable the greatest advances yet in public health. . . . A generation of children raised on video games will probably be more attuned to health messages coming from interactive videos than from lectures by the school nurse (Koop. 1995, p. 760)

New applications for technology are constantly being found. Existing applications are evolving and improving or being replaced by superior ones.

Tailored communication is one such application. It allows us to better meet the communication demands of public health education, and its use is still being refined and improved. Tailored communication certainly will not be the only application of technology to health communication and health education. Ultimately, it may not even be the best one. But it seems likely that computers and other communication technologies will play a greater, not lesser, role in health communication in the future.

You're trying to replace people with computers; you're trying to replace counselors.

If imitation is indeed the highest form of flattery, then counselors should feel flattered by the emergence of tailored communication programs. Tailored communication follows a typical counseling–type approach. Both consist of an assessment phase, a data processing phase, and a feedback phase, but that's where the similarities end. In tailored communication programs, both the assessment questions and feedback materials must be predetermined and thus have defined limits. This is not true for counseling. More importantly, although the assessment–feedback structure of tailoring programs makes them somewhat interactive, they don't come close to approximating the interactivity, intimacy, and immediacy of interpersonal communication. Tailoring should be viewed as complementary to the counseling activities of health educators and others—a potentially powerful tool to enhance their work, not replace it.

Because tailoring is focused on the individual, it perpetuates "blaming the victim."

Victim–blaming ideology—the belief that a health or social problem, deficiency, or defect lies primarily within the individual (Ryan, 1971) —usually leads to the development of programs aimed at correcting those deficiencies or simply dismissing the problem as something that should be self–corrected. Intervention approaches like this that promote individual change in the absence of broader environmental change are often labeled as "victim blaming."

Does tailored communication fall into this category? It depends on how it is used. Take the example of childhood lead poisoning. A tailored communication program to help address this problem might focus on promoting the kinds of household cleaning practices a family could routinely engage in to remove excess lead dust from their home and thus reduce their child's level of exposure. But perhaps in some such homes, the landlord refuses to perform necessary abatement procedures to remove lead–based paint from walls and ceilings, or perhaps the source of lead is ambient lead particles from nearby lead mining.

In either case, providing only a tailored communication program about house cleaning without addressing other causes of the problem would indeed be victim blaming and an inappropriate use of tailoring. Ideally, one would use tailoring as an educational intervention in conjunction with lead testing, abatement, and treatment programs, while promoting policy measures designed to increase accountability of property owners and environmental responsibility among local industry. As with any educational or communication–based intervention, it is best to view tailoring as one part of a more comprehensive intervention strategy.

How might tailoring fit into a more community-based or environmental intervention approach?

Imagine a tailored communication program designed to help reduce the incidence of falls and the consequent injuries among an older adult population. One approach might be to assess older adults' home environments.

Are there stairs inside or outside the home? Do the stairs have hand rails and traction strips? Who is responsible for snow removal at the home? Are there traction strips in the bathtub or shower? Are there small rugs or carpets in the home that are not tacked down? Are there wires or cords laying across the floors or in passageways? Is it necessary for the resident to stand on a stool to reach some cupboards? Given this information, what kind of tailored feedback would you provide to participants? One approach might be to simply tell participants what they needed to fix to make their homes more fall–proof. Though straightforward enough, many residents may lack the means or ability to undertake such home improvements. An alternative would be to use the tailored messages to link participants with social service organizations, churches, or other resources in the community that could actually provide specific services or repairs for them at low or no cost. The latter approach illustrates how tailored programs could be integrated into a broader community–based program, without inappropriately (and unrealistically) placing full responsibility on the individual home owner.

Most practitioners won't have the skills or resources to do tailored communication.

In truth, most practitioners are already tailoring their educational approaches to some extent. The real issue here is whether or not they have the technological know–how to create tailored programs. This book lays out a step–by–step approach to developing tailored communication programs that we believe the vast majority of practitioners will have the skills to follow. As for resources, creating these programs from scratch can be a time–consuming endeavor, especially if the scope of the project is large. However, premade but modifiable tailoring programs and tailoring software are now available to make the process both faster and easier (see chap. 11).

Computers are too impersonal; most people won't respond well to tailoring.

In using tailored print communication, the computer processing and feedback creation is almost always invisible to program participants. All they know is that they completed an assessment and received feedback based on that assessment. In fact, they are probably more likely to view the feedback as coming from their doctor, employer, insurer, or whoever is running the program than they are to see it as coming from a computer. As illustrated in detail in chapter 9, the tailored messages themselves are anything but impersonal.

A Focus on Printed Materials

Importantly, the process of tailoring can result in many different kinds of final products. Just as a tailor would follow the same basic steps in preparing to custom make a jacket, skirt, or trousers, a tailored message program could take the form of a World Wide Web site, an interactive computer kiosk in a doctor's office, a videotape mailed to the participant's home, telephone counseling, a printed newsletter, or any number of other executions. This book focuses on tailored print communication. We have chosen this focus because more is known about print tailoring than other forms of tailored communication and because print tailoring is available to more people now.

Although even print tailoring is quite new, its effectiveness has been evaluated in a number of well–designed, long–term, and large scale research studies. Since 1993, evidence has been accumulating that tailored print communication is a promising approach (Skinner et al., in press). Moreover, because many tailored health communication programs have now been developed and implemented, we have a much clearer under-standing than we did even 5 years ago of the steps and processes involved in creating tailored print materials and implementing tailored message programs.

It's exciting to see that tailoring principles are also being applied to more advanced technologies, such as interactive multimedia and World Wide Web programming. These technologies have several obvious advantages over print tailoring and other traditional kinds of health education materials. First, they are less dependent on user literacy and, thus, may be useful in reaching some high risk populations. Second, they not only allow for vicarious learning through the modeling of healthy behaviors, but they can actually allow users to select a particular "model" who they feel similar to or believe to be credible. Third, because the technology is interactive, it is more engaging than one–way communication, and it can still produce a tangible product for users to take with them, such as a printed tailored letter, behavior change plan, or even a tailored videotape.

Although a number of interactive multimedia programs have been developed for health promotion purposes (Skinner, Siegfried, Kegeler, & Strecher, 1993), there remains a dearth of rigorously designed studies assessing their effectiveness. From a more practical standpoint, it is not at all clear that a majority of health education practitioners presently have the means to develop such programs. Furthermore, although access to electronic media, such as the World Wide Web, is growing, it is hardly universal and not at all representative of the general population. A 1997 Business Week/Harris poll found that 85% of Internet users are White, and 42% have annual incomes over $50,000 (Hof, 1997). Only 6% are African American, and only 12% earn less than $15,000 per year, including students.

Unlike some of these more advanced technologies, print tailoring is not just a possibility for the near future, it is already here. People don't even need access to a computer to benefit from it. Tailored print communication programs are being used today, not only in health and medicine, but also in publishing, marketing, and advertising. The technology needed to tailor print materials is fully developed and widely available. We believe this book will give readers the know–how to use existing technologies to create effective print tailored communication programs. Chapter 2 describes the theoretical rationale and empirical evidence supporting the use of tailored health communication. The remaining chapters describe a step–by–step approach to creating tailoring programs.

CHAPTER 2

Why Tailor Health Information?

The general concept of tailoring has a certain intuitive appeal. Given a choice between products, services, and information that are made either specifically for you or for no one in particular, most people would probably choose the former. But is there more to recommend tailoring than simply passing the "common sense" test? In this chapter four major reasons for tailoring health information are presented: a theoretical rationale, a public health rationale, a behavioral rationale, and empirical evidence gathered from first generation studies of tailored health communication.

Theoretical Rationale for Tailoring

Theories of information processing have been especially useful in explaining why tailored health communication may be more effective that nontailored approaches. For example, Petty and Cacioppo's (1981a) elaboration likelihood model (ELM) suggests that people are more likely to process information thoughtfully if they perceive it to be personally relevant. The ELM is based on the assumption that under many circumstances people are active information processors. They think about messages carefully, relate them to other information they have encountered in the past, and consider the messages in the context of their own life experience. Studies of information processing have shown that messages that are processed in this way (i.e., "elaborated" on) tend to be retained for a longer period of time and are more likely to lead to permanent attitude change (Petty, Cacioppo, Strathman, & Priester, 1994).

The rationale for using a tailored approach to health communication, inferred from ELM, can be summarized in a five–step logic sequence (Strecher & Kreuter, 1999):

1. By tailoring materials, superfluous information is eliminated.

2. The information that remains is more personally relevant to the recipient.

3. People pay more attention to information they perceive as personally relevant.

4. Personally relevant information that is attended to is more likely to lead to thoughtful consideration of factors that could facilitate or hinder behavior change.

5. When information specifically tailored to the unique needs of an individual is attended to and thoughtfully processed, it will be more useful than nontailored information in helping the person enact desired behavioral changes.

Several well–designed randomized studies have reported findings consistent with these expectations. For example, compared to nontailored messages, tailored messages appear to be more likely to:

- Catch attention (Kreuter, Bull, Clark, & Oswald, in press);

- Be read and remembered (Brug, Glanz, Van Assema, Kok, & Van Breukelen, 1998; Brug, Steenhaus, van Assema, & de Vries, 1996; Campbell et al., 1994; Skinner, Strecher & Hospers, 1994);

- Be saved (Brug et al., 1996);

- Be discussed with others (Brug et al., 1998; Brug et al., 1996);

- Be perceived by readers as interesting (Brug et al., 1998; Brug et al., 1996; Skinner et al., 1994);

- Be perceived by readers as personally relevant (Brug et al., 1998; Brug et al., 1996; Bull, Kreuter, & Scharff, in press); and,

- Be perceived by readers as having been written especially for them (Brug et al., 1996).

At the same time, however, it is generally not expected that greater message recall and higher ratings of personal relevance alone would explain subsequent changes in complex health–related behaviors. More plausibly, and in accordance with the ELM, health messages that are per-ceived as personally relevant should be more likely to stimulate thoughtful and thorough consideration of a proposed behavior change. For example, tailored materials might promote more issue–relevant thinking, more self–assessment, and even modify a person's intentions to take action.

To learn whether this ELM–based explanation of tailoring effects is valid, Kreuter and colleagues (Kreuter et al., in press) conducted a study among 198 overweight men and women who were randomly assigned to receive one of three different types of printed weight–loss information: (a) materials that were computer–generated and tailored to the individual, (b) standard preprinted materials from the American Heart Association (AHA), or, (c) computer generated materials containing the same content as the AHA materials but formatted to look identical to the tailored materials (Kreuter et al., in press). Follow–up surveys administered immediately after participants received their weight–loss materials and one month later looked for differences across study groups in the ways participants processed the weight–loss materials. Specifically, the study examined people's elaborations in the form of *cognitive responses*—thoughts and ideas listed by study participants immediately after receiving and reading their weight–loss materials. This thought–listing method is commonly used to identify thoughts and ideas generated by different types of messages and by different types of people under different conditions (Cacioppo, Harkins, & Petty, 1981; Petty & Cacioppo, 1981b)

The findings show that compared to participants in either of the two nontailored groups, those who received tailored weight–loss materials listed significantly more (a) positive thoughts about the materials, (b) positive thoughts reflecting a personal connection to the materials, (c) positive thoughts indicating self–assessment took place, and (d) positive thoughts indicating intention to make behavioral changes. These findings suggest that by tailoring health information to each individual's unique needs, the likelihood that it will be thoughtfully considered by the recipient can be greatly improved and can even stimulate important prebehavioral changes such as self–assessment and intention.

How is this kind of information processing related to behavioral change? According to the ELM, when cognitive responses are specific and behavioral implications are straightforward (i.e., few intervening events), a relationship between cognitive and behavioral responses is found (Petty & Cacioppo, 1981b). Data from the aforementioned study support this hypothesis as well. In the study, both the intention to try behavioral recommendations for weight loss and the number of suggestions actually tried were significantly correlated with certain cognitions. Furthermore, among participants in the tailored message group, those who generated more favorable thoughts were significantly more likely to make behavioral changes than those who generated fewer favorable thoughts. In other words, participants who received tailored messages on weight loss and generated more thoughts about those materials were more likely to make changes in weight–loss behaviors than were those who received tailored messages but generated fewer thoughts. These findings suggest that certain cognitions may be important mediating factors in the relationship between tailored communication and behavioral outcomes.

Summarizing this theoretical rationale, tailored communication trims the fat—cutting out all information that is not pertinent to the individual recipient. What remains is only that information that the person has identified as being important. As such, tailored messages are able to address the specific concerns, interests, and needs of an individual person. As described in theories of information processing such as ELM, the person is more likely to attend to the information and thoughtfully consider it because it is seen as more personally relevant. When the person's attention is captured and elaboration begins, health messages have a better opportunity to influence the person's awareness, knowledge, attitudes, beliefs, or behaviors.

Public Health Rationale for Tailoring

Public health has been defined as:

> What we, as a society, do collectively to assure the conditions for people to be healthy. (Institute of Medicine, 1988);

> The combination of sciences, skills, and beliefs that are directed to the maintenance and improvement of the health of all the people through collective or social actions. (Last, 1988); and,

> Protection from hazards that are rooted outside the individual . . . embracing a wide range of community health services that affect large numbers of people. (Turshen, 1989)

In contrast to a traditional medical model of health in which individual patients go to a doctor when they are sick and doctors try to alleviate whatever symptoms or disease the patient presents, public health is more interested in the health status of populations than individuals and is more interested in preventing disease from occurring rather than treating or curing it after the fact (Scutchfield & Keck, 1997).

In addition to its focus on population–based prevention, public health emphasizes that its programs and services should be designed to meet the unique needs of the populations affected (Green & Kreuter, 1991), recognizes the value of interactive and individualized learning experiences in changing behavior (Street & Rimal, 1997), and is generally cost–conscious (Institute of Medicine, 1988). Until recently, few public health education approaches could truly claim to combine assessment–based planning, broad population–wide reach, and interactive learning experiences in a single, cost–effective package. But computer–tailored health communication has demonstrated the promise of doing just that. It is a potentially powerful tool of the public health educator to be incorporated into comprehensive programs of health promotion, disease prevention, and disease management.

Tailored health communication programs that are computer–based are less constrained by volume or capacity limitations than some other educational approaches. Whereas an individual educator or an ongoing outreach program might reach a handful of people each day, a computer tailoring program can process information from 10,000 people as easily and almost as quickly as it can process information from one individual. Moreover, it can generate health information that is distinct and personally relevant for each of those 10,000 people. Consequently, it may be that the traditional public health approach of using mass media to disseminate health information is eventually supplanted by micro–mass media (Anonymous, 1997) or mass customization (Davis, 1987; Pine, 1993). This allows the fine–tuning of tailored message content to individuals' needs but on the scale of mass communication. From a public health perspective, even modest results from a program with broad reach can result in significant population health benefits (Chapman, 1985).

Behavioral Rationale for Tailoring

Consider the following example of a simple tailored health communication program designed to encourage women over age 50 to get annual mammograms for early detection of breast cancer. The tailoring program might include messages addressing barriers to mammography, beliefs about cancer in general, risk of breast cancer due to family history, other breast cancer risk factors, family support for breast cancer screening, and information on local health–care organizations that provide mammograms. Within the program, a multitude of messages would exist to address each of these topics, even though participants would receive only those messages that pertained to them. For example, there might be 16 messages that each address a different barrier to mammography, 18 different messages addressing beliefs about cancer in general, 12 messages for women with different levels of family history of breast cancer, 24 different messages about other risk factors and perceived susceptibility to breast cancer, 8 different messages about getting family members to support routine screening, and 16 different messages identifying the nearest health–care provider that performs mammograms. By asking women to answer questions about each of these five topics, we could determine which specific message or messages from each group would be most appropriate for that person and select only those messages. Note that from these five questions we could create at least 10.6 million different combinations of the 94 total messages (i.e., unique permutations of 16 + 18 + 12 + 24 + 8 + 16 messages, assuming only one message from each section is selected). In his 1993 book, *Mass Customization: The New Frontier in Business Competition,* Joseph Pine likened this phenomenon to a child playing with Lego® building blocks (Pine, 1993). Although there is a discrete number of blocks to play with, an almost infinite number of objects can be created because all blocks have been designed to fit together regardless of size, shape, or color.

Many tailored message programs are considerably more complex than the example above, easily generating hundreds of millions of different possible message combinations for even a short printed communication. Being *able* to generate millions of different message combinations is one thing, but *needing* to do so is another. In the previous example, if the process of tailoring were truly necessary to encourage women to seek mammograms, it must assumed that only 1 of these 10.6 million combinations would be exactly right for any given woman. Is that a reasonable assumption? If it were, it would expected for there to be substantial variation across individuals in factors known to be associated with mammography use. In other words, if all women shared roughly the same beliefs, barriers, levels of social support, risk factors, and family history, then one single communication could probably adequately address their needs. However, if different women have very different beliefs and concerns, a tailored approach might be more appropriate.

To test this assumption, we examined data from the *Change of Heart* study, a large randomized trial of the effectiveness of tailored health messages, conducted among adult primary care patients in southeastern Missouri (Kreuter, Brennan, Lukwago, Scharff, & Wadud, 1997). In the first set of analyses, we looked at responses to a baseline questionnaire from 882 patients to see the extent of variation that existed among several factors known to influence a person's likelihood of increasing levels of physical activity, reducing dietary fat consumption, and quitting smoking. In nearly all cases, there was a considerable range of responses provided. For example, when asked to identify the main reason they wanted to increase their level of physical activity, 44% of patients said "to improve my health," 28% said "to control my weight," 20% said "to look and feel better," and 8% said "to help relieve stress." Similar patterns of variation were also found for factors influencing diet and smoking behaviors (see Table 2.1). These findings suggest that individuals probably vary considerably in their status on important factors known to influence health–related behavior change. As such, message tailoring is indicated to adequately address each person's unique needs and concerns.

In the second set of analyses, we sought to determine how many people would get a truly unique set of messages if everyone received tailored health information. To do this, we examined data from the intervention portion of the same study described previously. In the study,

Table 2.1

Variation in Factors Associated with Health–Related Behavioral Change Among Participants in Change of Heart Study.

Increasing Physical Inactivity

Main reasons for wanting to increase levels of physical activity (n=562)		Barriers that would prevent you from increasing physical activity* (n=571)		Preferred type of physical activity or activity of daily living** (n=562)	
improve my health	(44%)	lack of time	(47%)	aerobic type exercise	(41%)
control my weight	(28%)	bad or extreme weather	(40%)	yard work	(19%)
look and feel better	(20%)	no one to exercise with	(20%)	work around the home	(16%)
help relieve stress	(8%)	equipment is expensive	(10%)	strengthening exercises	(10%)
				sports	(8%)

Reducing Dietary Fat Consumption

Level of support you'd receive from others in your home (n=843)		Barriers that would prevent you from reducing dietary fat intake* (n=781)		Responsibility for food shopping and preparation in my home (n=854)	
very supportive	(50%)	high fat foods tast good	(31%)	I shop, I prepare	(67%)
somewhat supportive	(28%)	low fat foods cost more	(14%)	I don't do either	(20%)
unsupportive	(10%)	my family won't change	(13%)	I shop, don't prepare	(7%)
I live alone	(11%)	it's too much trouble	(7%)	I prepare, don't shop	(6%)

Quitting Smoking

Main reasons for wanting to quit smoking** (n=117)		Barriers that would prevent you from quitting smoking* (n=127)		Level of physiologic dependence on nicotene (n=180)	
improve my health	(55%)	stress	(58%)		
look and feel better	(10%)	fear of weight gain	(36%)	highly dependent	(49%)
protect family's health	(8%)	I don't think I can do it	(30%)	dependent	(28%)
save money	(7%)	nothing/ don't know	(20%)	less dependent	(23%)
take control of my life	(7%)				

* Participants could identify more than one barrier, thus percentages do not total 100.
** Response choices selected by fewer than 5% of patients are not listed.

patients received health information according to their risk status. In other words, smokers received information on quitting, those eating a high–fat diet received information on reducing fat intake, and those who were physically inactive received information on increasing physical activity. By random assignment, patients received information that was either individually tailored and personalized, generic and personalized, or generic and nonpersonalized (see definitions in chap. 1). For this set of analyses, we imposed algorithms from the tailored and personalized intervention on baseline data collected from all patients regardless of which study group they had been assigned to, just as if they would have received the tailored intervention.

Findings showed that among 190 smokers, 186 (98%) would have received a different combination of the 1,272 different possible combinations of smoking cessation messages. For the materials promoting reduced dietary fat intake and increased physical activity, rates of uniqueness were 86% and 78%, respectively (see Fig. 2.1). These data suggest that, for at least some behaviors, patients in this population vary considerably in their status on important predictors of behavior change, thus reinforcing the need for more individualized approaches to intervention. This fundamental principle of tailoring—the assumption of variation in the target population and in their target behaviors—is discussed in greater detail in chapter 4. A clear understanding of both types of variation is invaluable in planning tailored health communication programs.

Empirical Evidence for Tailoring Effects

The earliest investigations of computer–tailored health communication were undertaken in the late 1980s. The number of published studies and tailoring researchers grew steadily throughout the 1990s. In 1999, Skinner et al. published the first scientific review of tailoring research in the *Annals of Behavioral Medicine*, concluding that "tailored print communications demonstrate an enhanced ability to attract notice and readership . . . are more effective than non–tailored communications for influencing health behavior change . . . (and) can be an important adjunct to other intervention components" (Skinner, Campbell, Rimer, Curry, & Prochaska, in press). In this section, we will present empirical evidence in support of tailored communication by summarizing selected studies from this first generation of tailoring research. For a more detailed treatment of the research designs, methodology, and interventions used in these trials, we direct readers to the review article by Skinner et al. (in press), and to the individual studies cited in this chapter.

Figure 2.1

Percentage of Patients in Change of Heart Study Who Would Have Received a Combination of Tailored Messages No Other Patient Received for Smoking Cessation, Dietary Fat Consumption, Physical Activity, and Nutrition Label Reading.

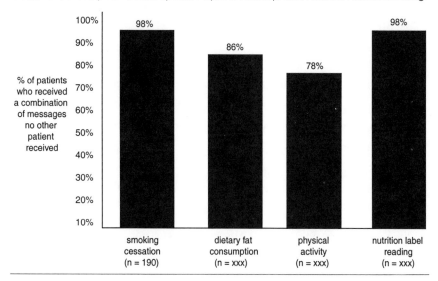

Studies of tailored print communication conducted to date can be classified into four general categories based on the main comparisons of interest. These categories include studies exploring the effects of:

1. tailored versus nontailored health information;
2. tailored health information versus other types of interventions;
3. tailored health information as part of a more comprehensive intervention strategy, and;
4. different variations in tailored health information compared to one another.

Studies from each of these categories are described in the following.

Studies of Tailored vs. Nontailored Health Information

The most fundamental research question involving computer–tailored health communication is simply, "Does it work better than nontailored communication?" Accordingly, this is the question that has received the most attention from researchers to date. Studies have compared the effects of tailored and nontailored print materials on the following outcomes:

- Dietary change (Brinberg & Axelson, 1990; Brug et al., 1998; Brug et al., 1996; Campbell et al., 1994; Campbell et al., in review; Kreuter, 1997);

- Smoking cessation (Brennan, Kreuter, Caburnay, & Wilshire, 1998; Dijkstra, De Vries, & Roijackers, 1998b; Orleans, Boyd, Noll, Crosette, & Glassman, 1996; Shiffman, Gitchell, & Strecher, 1997; Strecher et al., 1994);

- Physical activity (Bull et al., 1999; Kreuter & Strecher, 1996; Marcus et al., 1998);

- Mammography (Meldrum et al., 1994; Skinner et al., 1994);

- Weight control (Kreuter et al., in press);

- Cholesterol screening (Kreuter & Strecher, 1996); and,

- Nutrition label reading (Kreuter et al., 1997).

Most of these studies followed a similar, pretest–posttest randomized trial design. In the studies, participants completed some form of behavioral assessment questionnaire, then were randomly assigned to receive health– and behavior–change information that was either tailored based on their answers or nontailored. After a follow–up period, the questionnaire was readministered and analyses were conducted to look for differences in behavioral and other outcomes across study groups.

As an example, in one of the earliest studies of tailoring, Skinner et al. (Skinner et al., 1994) compared the effects of tailored and nontailored physician letters on rates of mammography among adult primary care patients in North Carolina. Tailored letters were customized based on variables from the Health Belief Model; perceived barriers, perceived benefits (Becker, 1974) and the Transtheoretical Model; stage of mammography adoption (Prochaska & DiClemente, 1983), and included graphics tailored to a woman's age and race. Figure 2.2 shows a sample tailored physician letter used in the study. Nontailored letters were similar in appearance but contained generic mammography information derived from U.S. Public Health Service materials on cancer prevention. At a 3 month follow–up, women in the tailored letter group were significantly more likely to remember receiving their letters compared to those in the nontailored group, and to have read most or all of the materials. Among lower income and African–American women, the tailored letters also led to significantly greater movement toward the action and maintenance stages of mammography use.

In two separate trials testing the effects of tailored print materials on smoking cessation, Strecher et al. (1994) found significantly higher quit rates among light to moderate smokers who received a two–page tailored

Figure 2.2

Sample Tailored Letter from Skinner, et al, 1993.

Mammography

"I've had a mammogram, but it was over two years ago. Since I'm in my 40's, I know I should be checked every 2 years. I've thought about having another mammogram, but I just haven't done it yet."

What Are The Facts?

Most women surveyed know that *breast cancer has a good chance of being cured if it is found early*, when it's just getting started, and that mammograms are the best way of finding breast cancer early. In fact, *mammograms can detect breast cancers much smaller than the hand can feel.* They know that regular mammograms are so important they could save your life.

Many patients in our survey had their last mammogram more than two years ago. It's now time for them to have another mammogram. They may be thinking about having another one but they haven't done it yet. Has it been more than two years since *your* last mammogram? Since breast cancer can develop at any time, you should be checked again soon.

Any Roadblocks?

You may have heard that mammograms are very expensive. While it's true that certain facilities charge high rates, there are places in the area where mammograms are not expensive. Also, more and more health insurance plans are covering the cost of mammograms. *Don't let the cost hold you back.*

Some women may not think mammography is important because they get physical breast exams by their doctors. Since a breast exam *and* a mammogram is much more likely to find breast cancer than an exam alone, a breast exam should not be considered a substitute for mammography.

Having regular screening mammograms is very important and *could save your life.* That's why the National Cancer Institute and the American Cancer Society recommend getting regular mammograms.

Can it happen to you?

Almost every woman thinks, "I'm not going to get breast cancer". But studies show that one in every ten women in the U.S. (10%) will get breast cancer sometime during her life.

So, the thing to do is to get regular mammograms -- just like regular pap smears -- either to find out you don't have breast cancer or to find it early while there's a good chance for a cure. If you've had a mammogram, that's a great start. But it may be time for you to have another one. If you've thought about having another mammogram, please go ahead and call our office to arrange for an appointment or to get more information (542-2731).

Chatham Family Physicians   Route 5, Box 7   Pittsboro, North Carolina   27312

letter compared to smokers who received nontailored letters of the same length. There were no differences in quit rates for heavier smokers. In the study, tailored letters were based on smokers' motives for quitting, perceived barriers to quitting, addiction to nicotine, past quit attempts,

Figure 2.3

Sample Tailored Quit Smoking Letter from Strecher, et al, 1994.

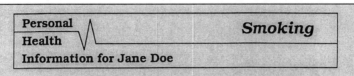

In the survey you filled out, you told us you'd like to quit smoking to set a good example for your family. We think that's great! Did you know that three out of four teenagers who smoke cigarettes have at least one parent who smokes? You can be a good role model for your family by quitting smoking now.

Clearing the air...
As you know, smoking increases your risk of many diseases. The longer you stay off cigarettes the lower these risks get. Quitting smoking helps your lungs work better and increases your energy level. It also improves your sense of taste and smell, eliminates your cough, and reduces your chances of getting wrinkles at an early age.

Weigh the benefits...
You told us you're worried about gaining weight if you quit smoking. Some people do gain weight after quitting, but many do not. The average weight gain after quitting is just 5 pounds -- that's about as much as most of us gain each year during the holidays!
Nicotine, a chemical found in all cigarettes, makes your body burn calories faster than is normal. So during the first few months after quitting smoking, you'll need to find other ways to burn these calories. For most people, 15 minutes of brisk walking each day will be more than enough to keep the extra weight off. Walking not only keeps your weight down, but also helps you relieve stress and gives you more energy.

Many smokers crave sweets right after quitting. You can satisfy your cravings without gaining weight by having plenty of sugarless candy and gum nearby after you quit. Carry a package of small breath mints with you everywhere -- they only have about one calorie each, and they keep your hands and mouth busy with something other than cigarettes.
If you've tried to quit before but failed, take heart! Almost every smoker has tried to quit at least once. In fact, successful quitters usually fail a

"I want to quit smoking to set a good example for my family."

few times along the way. Think about situations that tempt you to smoke. Then think about different ways you can handle these situations without smoking. Having such a plan will increase your chances of successfully quitting. Quitting smoking is difficult, but with a great deal of effort you will succeed.

Partners in
Prevention

perceived health risks of continued smoking, and perceived benefits of quitting (see Fig. 2.3). Nontailored quitting materials were derived from a generic quit–smoking pamphlet printed by a national not–for–profit health organization. The findings that tailored messages work better for lighter smokers (who are probably less addicted to nicotine than heavier smokers) suggest that information alone might be sufficient to address the behavioral and social aspects of smoking but probably cannot overcome a physiologic dependence. It might be expected, therefore, that if tailored messages were combined with nicotine replacement therapy, such as that delivered via a transdermal patch or gum, similar effects might also be obtained among heavier smokers.

A more recent study of 3,807 smokers trying to quit using Nicorette® gum set out to answer this question. Smokers using Nicorette gum enrolled in the study by answering a series of questions about their smoking behavior and were then randomly assigned to receive either the Committed Quitters (CQ) tailored personal support plan materials or a self–help quit–smoking booklet. At a 6–month follow–up, smokers who had received the tailored CQ materials were significantly more likely to quit smoking (28–day continuous abstinence) than those who received the nontailored booklet (Shiffman et al., 1997).

In the earliest tailoring studies, message tailoring and personalization (i.e., putting a person's name on materials) were frequently comingled without any attempt to identify the unique contributions of each. If personalization alone were found to be effective, customized communication programs would be less costly to develop. The Change of Heart study examined the relative effectiveness of printed behavior–change materials that were either tailored and personalized (TAP), generic and personalized (GAP), or generic but not personalized (GNP) in reducing heart–disease risk factors among adult patients from four family medicine clinics in southeastern Missouri. While in the waiting room of their doctor's office, patients completed a brief behavioral assessment of their tobacco use, diet (intake of fat, fruits, vegetables, and fiber), and physical activity. Each patient was randomly assigned to one of the study groups or to a usual care, no–intervention control group (CONTROL). Tailored materials were based on patients' stage of readiness to change each behavior, perceived barriers to changing, and reasons for wanting to change (see Fig. 2.4). At a 3–month follow–up, patients who received TAP materials were more likely than those receiving GAP or GNP materials to rate them as "applying specifically to me"(Kreuter, 1997). In general, the TAP materials also led to greater change than GAP, GNP, or CONTROL materials in the areas of smoking cessation, physical activities of daily living (Bull & Jamrozik, 1998), new use of nutrition labels, and reduced dietary fat consumption (Kreuter et al., 1997).

An alternative application of tailoring principles for promoting smoking cessation is to match smokers to the quitting program that best fits their needs. For example, rather than use each smoker's behavioral profile to create individually tailored messages, use the same information to match

Figure 2.4

Sample Tailored Nutrition Materials from Kreuter, et al, 1998.

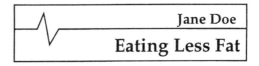

Jane Doe

Eating Less Fat

As part of the survey you filled out in your doctor's office, you answered a series of questions about how often you eat certain foods. Using your answers to these questions, we were able to estimate the amount of fat you eat. As the chart below shows, your diet is probably too high in fat.

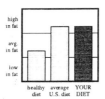

Your score for fat was 24. Check the table below to see where your score ranks. The good news is, you can make changes now to reduce the amount of fat you eat. You're not thinking about eating less fat now, but you may in the future. The information on this page can help you get started when you are ready to make changes in your diet.

Score	It means you are...
< 17	making the best low fat food choices
18-21	making good low fat food choices
22-24	eating a typical American diet, too high in fat
25+	eating a diet quite high in fat

Why eat less fat?

You said concern about future health problems might make you think about starting to eat less fat. A diet too high in fat may seem harmless now, but over time can lead to serious health problems and weight gain.

A high fat diet may seem harmless now...

Studies by medical and nutrition experts have found that eating a low fat diet can reduce a person's risk of heart disease, high blood pressure, diabetes, and certain types of cancer.

You're not thinking about eating less fat now, but that may change in the future. If it does, you'll find eating more whole grains, fresh fruits, and vegetables will help you cut fat and control your weight, too. When you're ready, you can do it!

Choices, choices...

Foods with 3 or fewer grams of fat per serving are considered low in fat. Here's a list of some low fat foods, and the grams of fat in each. You don't have to limit yourself to this list, just try to include items like these more often. Note any foods you enjoy on this list , and try to eat them more often in the future.

3 pancakes (4 inch round)	3g
cup of soup (broth based)	3g
broiled fish (3 oz.)	3g
skinless chicken breast	3g
spanish rice (1 cup)	3g
flour tortilla (6 inch round)	3g
graham crackers (3 crackers)	3g
vanilla wafers (6 cookies)	3g
oatmeal (1 cup)	2g
bagel (3 inch round)	2g
animal crackers (10 cookies)	2g
pasta (1 cup)	1g
white rice (1 cup)	1g
mashed potatoes (1/2 cup)	1g
corn tortilla (6 inch round)	1g
frozen yogurt (1/2 cup)	1g
apple sauce (1/2 cup)	1g
english muffin	1g
bran cereal (1/2 cup)	1g
baked potato	0g
corn on the cob (1 ear)	0g
kidney beans (1/2 cup)	0g
banana	0g
air popped popcorn (1 cup)	0g
apple	0g
orange	0g
angel food cake (1 piece)	0g
pudding (with skim milk)	0g
zucchini (1/2 cup)	0g
jello (1/2 cup)	0g
broccoli (1/2 cup)	0g
carrots (1/2 cup)	0g
pretzels (1 oz.)	0g
fruit juice (1 cup)	0g
nonfat yogurt (8oz.)	0g
skim milk (8 oz.)	0g

each smoker to a cessation program that is best suited to address his or her needs. In this study conducted by Brennan, et al. (Brennan et al., 1998), 272 adult smokers were randomly assigned to receive either a tailored letter inviting them to try quitting smoking with a local program selected just for them because it addressed more of their quitting needs than any other program, or a letter inviting them to try quitting smoking with any 1 of 6 different local cessation programs. The key portion of the tailored letter read:

> In the last few weeks, we have closely examined your smoking patterns, your reasons for wanting to quit, and your concerns about quitting. In all, we looked at 46 different aspects of your smoking! Then we tried to find the quit smoking program that addressed the greatest number of your personal quitting needs. The program that best matched your needs is called "Freedom From Smoking." It deals with 86% of the quitting issues that will be important to you—that's more than any other program did!

> Based on the information you gave us, we believe Freedom From Smoking can help you quit for good. Quitting is never easy, but we think this is the right program for you. If you want to try quitting smoking with the Freedom From Smoking program, please call us at (314) 977–9999, and we will make arrangements to enroll you in the program and pay for your participation.

In contrast, the equivalent portion of the non–tailored letter read:

> In the last few weeks, we have identified six different quit smoking programs that would be available to you in the St. Louis area. Three of them are "self–help" quitting programs and three are "group" quitting programs. These six programs are listed below.

> (six programs listed by name and type)

> If you would like to try quitting smoking with any of these programs, we will pay for your enrollment in that program. Just call us at (314) 977–9999, and we will make arrangements to enroll you in the program and pay for your participation.

The decision rules that guided program matching were based on behavioral characteristics of smokers (as measured using a self–administered questionnaire) and attributes of the six cessation programs (as identified through an expert review; Brennan et al., 1997). Smokers who received the tailored matching letter were more than twice as likely to accept the invitation to try quitting as were those receiving the self–selection letter. At a 3–month follow–up, the smokers who received the tailored letter were more likely to have quit smoking and to rate their cessation program as "a very good fit" (Brennan et al., 1998).

Other studies not described in detail here have shown that tailored messages are more effective than nontailored messages in helping individuals eat less fat (Brug et al., 1996; Campbell et al., 1994), increase fruit and vegetable consumption (Brug et al., 1998; Campbell et al., 1999), quit smoking (Dijkstra et al., 1998b; Orleans et al., 1996), increase physical activity (Bull et al., 1999; Kreuter & Strecher, 1996; Marcus et al., 1998), and increase intentions to change and actual changes in weight–control behaviors (Kreuter et al., in press).

Studies of Tailored Health Information Versus Other Types of Interventions

Although the use of health risk appraisal (HRA) is widespread (DeFriese & Fielding, 1990; Fielding, 1989), there is little evidence to support its effectiveness as a behavioral intervention. Because risk information alone (i.e., that provided by HRAs) is seldom sufficient to promote changes in complex lifestyle behaviors (Becker, 1974; Fishbein & Azjen, 1975; Weinstein, 1988), Kreuter and Strecher (1996) examined the effects of adding computer–tailored behavior change materials to typical HRA feedback. In a large sample of adult primary care patients, those who received the enhanced HRA feedback were 18% more likely to change a risky behavior than were those who received typical HRA feedback or those who received no feedback at all. The study also examined effects of tailored materials on patients' perception of their own health risks and found that tailored materials were significantly more effective than nontailored materials or usual care in correcting inaccuracies in patients' perceived personal risk of cancer and stroke (Kreuter & Strecher, 1995).

Studies of Tailored Health Information as Part of a More Comprehensive Intervention

Curry, Wahner, and Grothaus (1990) tested the relative and combined effects of computer–tailored feedback and financial incentives as adjuncts to a self–help booklet designed to help smokers quit. In the study, adult smokers in an HMO setting were randomly assigned to receive either: (a) a self–help quitting booklet; (b) the booklet plus computer–tailored motivational feedback; (c) the booklet plus a financial incentive, or; (d) the booklet, tailored feedback, and a financial incentive. The tailored materials were customized to each person's smoking history, past quit attempts, and reasons for wanting to quit. Results showed that a significant advantage was gained by adding tailored feedback to the self–help booklet. Smokers in this study group had higher rates of quitting than the other three groups at both 3– and 12–month follow–up assessments.

In a similarly designed study, Prochaska, DiClemente, Velicer, and Rossi (1993) randomly assigned adult smokers to receive either:

• Three different self–help quit–smoking booklets with a description of which one was most appropriate for which stage of readiness to quit smoking;

- A self–help quit–smoking booklet targeted to each patient's stage of readiness to quit with additional booklets for later stages;

- The stage–targeted manuals plus three computer–tailored printed reports addressing the smoker's stage of readiness and the corresponding processes of change; or,

- The stage–targeted materials, computer–tailored reports, and three telephone–counseling sessions reinforcing the content of the tailored reports (Prochaska et al., 1993).

The computer tailored reports were customized based on each smoker's stage of readiness to quit smoking. The study reassessed participants' smoking status at 6–, 12–, 18–, and 24–month follow–up. After 18 months, the highest rates of cessation were found among smokers who received stage–targeted self–help manuals plus tailored reports. Prochaska et al. (1993) concluded that this combination was superior to either standard or targeted self–help materials alone and probably more cost–effective than using live telephone counselors.

Studies of Different Types of Tailored Materials Compared to Each Other

As described previously, the first 10 years of research on tailored health communication has focused primarily on establishing the effectiveness of tailoring relative to more conventional approaches to health education and health communication, but a second wave of studies is now being undertaken that promises to advance the field even further. Among these, the work of Kreuter et al. (in press)—discussed in the "theoretical rationale" section of this chapter—has addressed the question of how tailoring achieves these effects (Kreuter et al., in press). Recently, the first studies have been published that examine the relative effectiveness of different kinds of tailored messages. For example, Dijkstra et al., (1998b) randomly assigned smokers to receive quit–smoking materials that were either tailored on the outcomes of smoking cessation, tailored on coping skills needed for quitting, or to a no–intervention control group (Dijkstra, De Vries, & Roijackers, 1998a). As the authors hypothesized, the outcome–focused tailoring improved smokers' expected outcomes more than the control group, and the skill–focused tailoring increased smokers' self–efficacy more than the control group. Comparing the two tailoring groups, the outcome–focused materials led to more positive outcome expectations than did the skill–focused materials, but the latter did not lead to greater self–efficacy than the former.

Summary

In a growing number of well–designed studies addressing a range of health related behaviors and other outcomes, tailored health communication materials outperform nontailored materials. Evidence from a few studies also suggests that adding tailoring to other interventions (e.g., HRA feedback, self–change booklets) can enhance the effectiveness of those approaches. Finally, there is some very early evidence that specific psychosocial outcomes, such as health–related beliefs and expectations, can be modified by intentionally tailoring messages in a certain fashion. Considered alongside the theoretical, public health, and behavioral rationale for tailoring, findings from these early studies of tailored communication provide a strong justification for the continued use and investigation of this approach.

As our understanding of how and why tailored health communication works is further refined, we can expect that methods of tailoring will also become more sophisticated. This may yield new and innovative approaches to tailoring unforeseen today. Furthermore, as future research reveals additional keys to tailoring effectiveness, the efficiency of this approach should be maximized.

CHAPTER 3

An Overview of the Tailoring Process

This chapter introduces a conceptual model to guide readers through the nine major steps of developing and implementing a tailored health communication program (see Fig. 3.1). The model has evolved since 1989, constantly being refined and updated to reflect lessons we have learned while creating and conducting dozens of tailored programs. We believe it provides a simple and straightforward organizing framework that can easily be adapted to fit a wide variety of tailoring situations.

Like most program-planning models, it begins with a diagnostic phase (Green & Kreuter, 1991). In Step 1, *Analyzing the Health Problem*, the objective is to learn as much as possible about the health outcome of interest. For example, if we are creating a tailored health communication program to help promote breast-feeding among new mothers, we need to know all there is to know about the factors that influence a woman's decision whether to breast-feed. These factors might include the woman's beliefs, values, concerns, motivation, social support, family norms, and a range of lifestyle factors. Only when these factors are clearly identified and well understood can they be accurately measured and then adequately addressed by tailored messages.

In Step 2, *Developing a Program Framework*, an outline is created to describe all the parts of the tailored health communication program. In our breast-feeding program, the first communication to mothers might address any misconceptions they have about the health benefits of breast-feeding for both the mother and baby. A second communication might suggest solutions for situations when mothers find it difficult or embarrassing to breast–feed. A third could help them talk to their friends and relatives about breast–feeding. This step defines the broad subject matter to be addressed at each point in the program.

To address each of these topics in a tailored fashion, it is necessary to gather information about that topic directly from program participants—

Figure 3.1

The Tailoring Process.

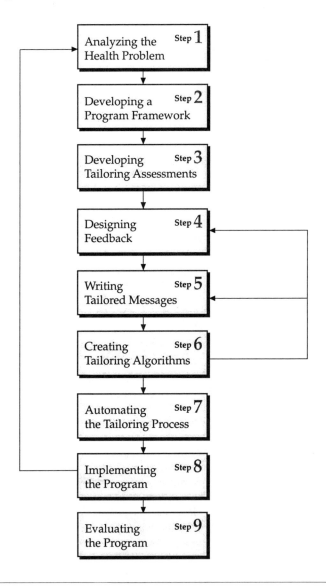

in this case, the mothers themselves. Step 3, Developing Tailoring Assessments, involves creating the assessment tools that will be used to collect this information.

In Step 4, *Designing Tailored Feedback*, decisions are made about how the tailored messages will look and how they will be presented to program participants. These decisions are hardly arbitrary. Rather, they are based on a solid understanding of the needs and preferences of intended recipients and the nature of the health problem being addressed.

If a jockey is only as good as the horse he's riding, then a tailored health communication program is only as good as the actual messages provided to participants. An attractive design and vivid colors might catch a reader's attention, but that alone will almost never be sufficient to bring about changes in complex lifestyle behaviors.

In Step 5, *Writing Tailored Messages*, the actual content of the communication is finally created. Here, a large library of different messages is created such that all possible responses to questions in the tailoring assessment can be adequately addressed by some message or combination of messages. Great care and planning is taken to determine the most appropriate communication approach, tone, and information for each message.

The messages in this library are then formally linked to the tailoring assessment in Step 6, *Creating Tailoring Algorithms*. These algorithms are logic statements or decision rules that specify which messages should be given to which participants under which circumstances. Algorithms are also the primary basis for conducting Step 7, *Automating the Tailoring Process*. In this step, the algorithms are translated into a computer program that automatically performs the final tailoring tasks. This computer program will match participants' answers with specific tailored messages and place those messages into the final feedback format.

In Step 8, *Implementing the Program*, the tailored health communication program is actually put into use, and in Step 9, *Evaluating the Program*, the program's effectiveness is systematically examined.

This chapter provides a brief introduction to the main activities conducted in each of these nine steps. Chapters 4 to 13 describe each of the steps in much greater detail. We caution that, although Fig. 3.1 depicts the development process as a linear model, its real–life use sometimes requires conducting multiple steps at once and permits starting some later steps before all earlier steps have been completed.

Step 1: Analyzing the Health Problem

As with planning any health promotion program, it is essential to understand the determinants of the problem one is seeking to address (Green

& Kreuter, 1991). Consider the metaphor of tailored messages being like custom–made or tailored clothing. For a clothier, the key measurements will vary depending on what kind of garment is being made. Sleeve length, shoulder breadth, and chest circumference might be the important variables for making a jacket, and measures of waist and inseam are needed to make a pair of trousers. The same is true for tailoring health communication materials: The key measurements, or determinants, vary depending on the outcome of interest. For example, a tailored program to help participants quit smoking may need to assess their readiness to quit (Prochaska & DiClemente, 1983), addiction to nicotine (Fagerstrom, 1978), and self–efficacy for quitting (Bandura, 1977).Tailored materials promoting breast cancer screening might focus on a woman's perceived susceptibility to breast cancer (Becker, 1974), beliefs about mammography, and perceived barriers to getting a mammogram (Abrams et al., 1996).

Program planning models such as PRECEDE/PROCEED (Green & Kreuter, 1991) provide a useful framework from which to analyze health problems in a systematic way. Prominent theories of health–related behavior change, for example, the Transtheoretical Model (Prochaska & DiClemente, 1988), Health Belief Model (Becker, 1974), self–efficacy and social learning theories (Bandura, 1977; Strecher, DeVellis, Becker, & Rosenstock, 1986), and Relapse Prevention Theory (Marlatt, 1985) also suggest important constructs to consider for many behavioral health problems. Finally, reviewing the research literature for correlates of behavior change in cross sectional studies and for effective health promotion strategies in intervention studies can help generate ideas about other determinants. This process should yield a list of candidate factors to be considered as key determinants of the outcome of interest. It should also provide information about the population and health problem that will be useful in developing the rest of the tailored intervention. This step is explained in detail in chapter 4.

Step 2: Developing a Program Framework

Any good intervention will have a guiding plan—a "blueprint" that planners can turn to and follow as they build the intervention. Like an architect's blueprint, a tailored health communication program blueprint has two levels: a big–picture view of the intervention and a detailed description of each intervention component.

In an architect's blueprint, the big–picture view shows the main pieces of the structure—the landscape, buildings, and rooms. In a tailored health communication program blueprint, the big–picture view shows the points at which we collect data from program participants and the points at which we provide them with tailored feedback. In an architect's blueprint, the detailed view describes the special characteristics of each piece of the structure (e.g., the size and shape of the rooms and the distance and relationship to other rooms). It also explains the different parts that each piece is made of—the building materials and the specifications for their assembly. The detailed view for a tailored health communication program blueprint describes each of the assessment and feedback pieces of the program. For each assessment, the program blueprint explains what information should be gathered (what do we need to know about an individual in order to provide him or her with appropriate tailored messages?) and the method of assessment (phone, paper and pencil, website, etc.). For each set of tailored feedback to be provided, the program blueprint explains the educational goal, messages to be presented, and the design and feel of the feedback.

Once the program blueprint has been developed, we begin the detailed task of constructing the specific pieces of the tailoring intervention (Steps 3–7). A well–developed and comprehensive program blueprint helps to focus this process and make it easier to complete.

Step 3: Developing Tailoring Assessments

Tailored materials are assessment based. Although some data used for tailoring may be obtained from existing databases, such as a patient's computerized medical record, in most cases a questionnaire or survey must be developed to measure a person's status on the key determinants identified in Step 1. A tailoring assessment tool may be self–administered, administered by an interviewer, or even by an interactive computer program or on a World Wide Web site. Whatever the format, a distinguishing characteristic is the closed–ended nature of the questions. In order to create all possible tailored messages before the assessment takes place, the response choices to each question must be known. Because of this, a major task in developing the assessment tool is determining which response choices will accompany each assessment question. The objective here is to develop concise surveys that collect all needed data but will not be a burden for individuals to complete. Pre–testing assessments with members of the target population is essential for refining questions and response choices to achieve the appropriate balance of comprehensiveness and conciseness. This step is explained in detail in chapter 6.

Step 4: Designing Feedback

Now attention is turned to the way in which messages are presented to the reader—the *format* of the printed communication. In this step, an outline is created that describes the technical and design characteristics of the communication. This outline is called a *feedback template* and will serve as a valuable guide for developing both the computer program (see Step 7) and message content (see Step 4). The feedback template will clearly indicate the relation between different messages that may appear in the same tailored communication and the relationship of each message to the communication piece as a whole. The feedback template accomplishes this by:

- Specifying the physical characteristics of each communication (e.g., a four–page newsletter with an attached refrigerator poster), the general feel of each (e.g., fun or professional), and the length, number, and size of pages;

- Indicating the location and size of each message on each page;

- Describing any preprinted components of each page (i.e., items that are not tailored, and thus can be preprinted before tailored items are added); and,

- Describing the textual and graphic characteristics of each message, including typeface, text organization, and graphic style. (chap. 7 describes this step in detail.)

Step 5: Writing Tailored Messages

When writing tailored health messages, no assumptions need to be made about the type of person who might receive a given message because it is already known who the message is being written for. In other words, tailored messages will always address whatever problems and issues a particular individual has identified as relevant for himself or herself. From a practical standpoint, this means hundreds or even thousands of different text messages and graphics may need to be created in order to address all possible needs of any population. To stay organized when developing all these messages, it is important to follow a structured approach.

Message development begins by defining and describing the unique characteristics of each message. These characteristics include the key points to be made, the writing style and tone to be used, the communication approach to be taken, and the communication objectives to be achieved. This information serves the same purpose as an outline for a paper or a speech—it organizes the main ideas from which the final product will be created. When these detailed message descriptions are completed, one can begin writing the actual tailored messages.

Writing good tailored messages demands more than just creativity, it requires effectively translating the background research, appropriate theories, and message descriptions into meaningful action steps for the recipient. Messages should be creative and interesting, but also clear, specific, and useful in helping the recipient enact the desired changes. Chapters 8 and 9 describe the message development process in detail.

Step 6: Creating Tailoring Algorithms

By the time this step is reached, the tailoring assessments, feedback templates, and tailored messages should all be reasonably well–developed. It is now necessary to link these pieces together. Tailored algorithms provide the decision rules for these linkages.

Algorithm development begins by coding the assessment questionnaire and the individual messages. Each question on the assessment is given a variable name and each response option for that question is assigned a corresponding value. All possible values for each question are noted and described. At the same time, each message space on the feedback template is given a variable name, and each tailored message is assigned a value corresponding to that variable name.

From here, algorithms are written that link specific responses to each assessment question with the corresponding message or messages from the tailored message library. These algorithms are sometimes referred to as *pseudo–code*, a series of logical statements—"if this, then that." This pseudo–code is later used to write the computer program (see Step 7) that automates the linking process. (Chapt. 10 describes the process of creating tailoring algorithms in detail.)

Step 7: Automating the Tailoring Processes

In Step 7, the more technical and, for many health practitioners, the most foreign aspect of a tailored health communication is addressed—developing the computer programs that automate the process of assembling and printing tailored feedback. Creating computer programs for tailoring can, indeed, be a highly technical process and will often be passed on to other individuals or organizations with specialized technical skills and resources. However, it is important that intervention planners and those developing the less–technical portions of the intervention also be involved in the process of developing the computer program. In fact, many people discover that the overall programming process is relatively simple although the programming tools and skills can be complex.

Creating a computerized tailoring program involves turning the basic algorithms developed in Step 6 into linear program logic, then turning that logic into a computer program. The first step—translating algorithms into programming logic—is often referred to as program design. The developer is literally designing a program, just as an architect designs a building. The components of the program are identified and described, and the processes by which those components work together (i.e., the logic) are detailed.

In the second step—turning the logic into the computer program— software and programming languages are used to build a program according to the design. Building a program may involve writing program code (what is traditionally thought of as "programming"), assembling existing specific–function programs or program pieces together into a larger program that performs all the functions we have designed, or simply using a dedicated tailoring program. The specific strategies to be used are determined by the complexity and special needs of each tailored intervention. Chapter 11 describes this development process and the many options currently available for developing programs.

Step 8: Implementing the Program

Implementing a tailored health communication program is similar to carrying out any other type of educational or communication–based intervention. There are, however, key factors that make a tailored intervention unique. The fact that a tailored intervention is data–driven requires that steps be taken to ensure data accuracy and timeliness of feedback production and delivery. The one–of–a–kind premise behind tailored print materials (i.e., that each individual's feedback will be different) requires careful review of and quality control over the production process.

Our approach divides implementation into five major components:

1. Preparation consists of all the steps that must be taken ahead of time to ensure accuracy and timeliness.

2. Data collection and processing includes tasks related to collecting, cleaning, and storing data to be used for tailoring.

3. Feedback production steps take data that have been collected and stored and use them to produce individually tailored feedback.

4. Feedback delivery involves the timely dissemination of tailored feedback to recipients.

5. Quality control functions are integrated throughout the process and are essential to an intervention that produces a unique set of tailored feedback for each recipient.

(The implementation process is described in detail in chap. 12.)

Step 9: Evaluating the Program

A tailored communication program can be evaluated on at least three levels: process, impact, and outcome. In a process evaluation, the focus is on measuring the extent to which the tailored intervention reaches the target population. An impact evaluation seeks to determine reactions of the population to the tailored intervention (e.g., whether it was comprehensible, interesting, or personally relevant). Outcome evaluation looks at the effect of the tailored intervention on the health problem or health related behavior being addressed (e.g., whether it resulted in behavior change). In evaluating tailored communication programs, we generally want to know (a) how much of the information was read, saved, remembered, and shared with others; (b) perceived relevance, credibility, and attractiveness of the information to recipients; and (c) whether the information was understood, thoughtfully considered, and acted on. (These and other evaluation outcomes and methodologies are discussed in chap. 13.)

Summary

The model introduced in this chapter was designed to be general enough to apply to many different types of tailoring interventions but not so general that its recommendations were vague and difficult to follow. As a result, the way this model looks when put to use in developing any given tailored communication program may be slightly different with each intervention than it looks here. Some interventions require more or less attention to certain steps, and the order of completing steps are dictated as much by real world imperatives as by the model itself. As we present these same nine steps in detail in the following chapters, we identify areas where each step and all of its substeps can be modified—tailored, as it were—to meet the needs of specific interventions.

CHAPTER 4

Background Research: Understanding the Health Problem and Target Population

The first step in developing a tailored health communication program is to conduct background research to fully understand the nature of the health problem to be addressed and important characteristics of the population to be served. The ultimate objective is to identify those factors most likely to influence a person's motivation or ability to make whatever changes in health or behavior are necessary to accomplish the program's goals. Once this set of factors has been identified, it is possible to measure an individual's status on each of them and, subsequently, tailor messages to each person's unique needs based on this information. In other words, the factors identified during background research are the basis for the tailored messages. Thus, if background research is incomplete or misses the mark, it will seriously compromise the effectiveness of the tailored health communication program that follows. This chapter describes a systematic process for gathering information about health problems and populations and explains how to use this information to select the most important factors to be addressed in a tailored health communication program.

Understanding the Health Problem or Behavior to be Addressed

Consider again the basic metaphor of tailored communication: that individualized health messages are created in much the same way as custom–made clothing. In order to custom-make any garment, a tailor must first obtain certain measurements from the customer. Importantly, these measurements will vary depending on what kind of garment is being made. For example, measurements of sleeve length, shoulder breadth, and chest circumference are required to custom-make a jacket, but waist, inseam, and outseam are needed to custom-make a pair of trousers. The same is true for tailored health communication programs: The key measurements will vary depending on the health or behavioral changes being promoted. To illustrate this point, imagine creating a tailored health communication program to help smokers try quitting. The first step is to identify those factors that have the greatest influence on a smoker's motivation and ability to quit—the "key measurements" for quitting smoking. After following the steps described in this chapter, it might be decided that these factors include a smoker's stage of readiness to quit (Prochaska & DiClemente, 1988), level of addiction to nicotine (Fagerstrom, 1978), and level of confidence in their ability to quit (Bandura, 1977). If these background research findings are sound, the factors identified will be closely related to the outcome of quitting smoking. They will not, however, be related to a different outcome, like getting a mammogram for early detection of breast cancer. Thus, to create a tailored health communication program to promote mammography, one would almost certainly identify a different set of key measurements.

In this portion of chapter 4, we describe how to identify the key measurements or *determinants* of a health problem to be addressed in a tailored health communication program. As discussed in later chapters, once the determinants of a given health or behavioral outcome have been identified, a questionnaire or other assessment tool can be designed to measure each person's status on these determinants (see chap. 6). Then tailored messages can be created to address each person's unique set of answers to the assessment questions (see chap. 8 and 9), but first, one has to know what to measure.

Analyzing Health Problems to Identify Determinants of Change

Program planning models, such as PRECEDE/PROCEED (Green & Kreuter, 1991), provide a useful framework for analyzing health problems in a systematic way. As described elsewhere (Skinner & Kreuter, 1997), this model helps identify factors that influence people's decisions and actions about their health. It suggests that health behaviors are influenced by three specific types of factors: predisposing, enabling, and reinforcing factors. *Predisposing* factors facilitate or hinder a person's motivation to change and include knowledge, attitudes, values, and beliefs. *Enabling* factors support or hinder a person's efforts to make the desired behavior change and include skills, resources, and barriers. *Reinforcing* factors encourage or discourage continuation of the desired behavior and include rewards, punishment, or any other feedback received from others following adoption of the behavior.

Consider the following application of the model to understand the problem of low immunization rates among preschool children. Lack of knowledge about the recommended intervals for childhood immunization and the perception that immunization is not important are factors that might predispose parents not to have their child immunized (Keane et al., 1993; Langkamp & Langhough, 1993; Lannon et al., 1995; Lieu et al., 1994; National Vaccine Advisory Committee, 1992; Salsberry, Nickel, & Mitch, 1993). Lack of time and transportation, as well as health-care system factors, such as inaccessibility of services, limited clinic hours, and restrictive policies (e.g., immunization by appointment only) are *nonenabling* factors or barriers to immunization compliance (Abbotts & Osborn, 1993; Bobo, Gale, Thapa, & Wassilak, 1993; Brenzel & Claquin, 1994; Lannon et al., 1995; Oeffinger, Roaten, Hitchcock, & Oeffinger, 1992; Orenstein, Atkinson, Mason, & Bernier, 1990; Weese & Krauss, 1995; Wood, Halfon, Sherbourne, & Grabowsky, 1994; Zimmerman et al., 1996). Finally, dissatisfaction with clinic care and prolonged crying by the baby after receiving shots are disincentives to immunize a child, thus reinforcing noncompliance. From a PRECEDE/PROCEED perspective, these factors would make it less likely that a child would be immunized, which would increase the child's likelihood of contracting a preventable illness, which would adversely affect the quality of life for the parents and child (see Fig. 4.1).

A tailored health communication program would seek to interrupt this downward spiral by measuring each of these determinants of childhood immunization among individual families and addressing whichever of them were especially problematic. For example, parents' beliefs about immunizations can influence their decisions and efforts to get their child immunized, therefore a tailored communication program might ask parents how strongly they agree or disagree with statements like the following:

- My child is perfectly healthy, so he doesn't need to get immunized.
- None of my other children were fully immunized, and they're just fine today.
- Nobody gets measles anymore, and if they do, modern medicine can fix it.

Figure 4.1

PRECEDE/PROCEED Model and Non–adherence with Immunization Recommendations (Street, 1997).

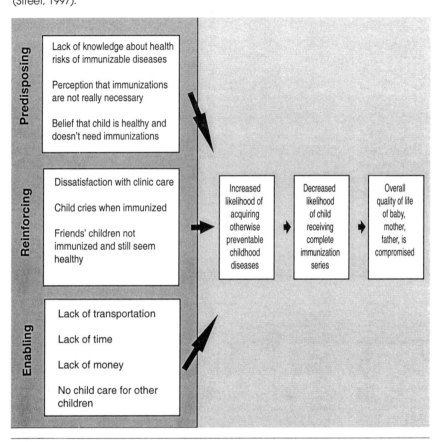

We would certainly communicate differently to a person who strongly agreed with these statements compared to a person who disagreed with them.

But how do you know which predisposing, enabling, and reinforcing factors might influence a given health problem or behavior? In the previous example, how did we know which specific beliefs and misconceptions existed, and how important each was to childhood immunization? There are three main strategies for finding this information: (1) reviewing applicable theories and models; (2) reviewing previous research; and, (3) collecting original data. Each of these is discussed in the following.

Reviewing Applicable Theories and Models

In the social and behavioral sciences there are many well–established and empirically supported theories and models that explain health–related behavior change. Theories such as the Transtheoretical Model (Prochaska, DiClemente, & Norcross, 1992), Health Belief Model (Becker, 1974; Janz & Becker, 1984), Social Cognitive Theory (Bandura, 1977), Theory of Reasoned Action (Fishbein & Azjen, 1975), and Relapse Prevention Theory (Marlatt, 1985) are all intuitive and clear, with well–defined constructs. In general, these theories and others spell out a set of conditions under which some health–related action is most likely to occur. They point out the ways in which a person's thoughts, beliefs, motives, expectations, present habits, and past experiences can influence their decisions and actions. They also explain how social and environmental factors (i.e., a person's social network and the resources in his or her community) can affect health. In doing so, these theories give us a framework for analyzing and understanding specific factors that might be related to a given health behavior. Thus, background research for any tailored health communication program seeking to change behavior should always consider which constructs, if any, from theories of health behavior change apply to the problem.

In order to use a theory to help us understand the nature of a health behavior, we need to know three things: (1) What does the theory tell us about the behavior change process? (2) What constructs from the theory are important in predicting behavior change? (3) What kinds of health problems is the theory best suited to explain?

As an example, this type of information is summarized in Table 4.1a and 4.2b for two of the five aforementioned theories—the Health Belief Model and Transtheoretical Model. For those wishing to learn more about theories of health–related behavior change, more comprehensive theory summaries are provided in Kreuter et al. (Kreuter, Lezin, Kreuter, & Green, 1998) and Skinner and Kreuter (1997). Although these are not the only useful theories to draw on, they are among the most commonly used in health behavior research and health promotion and health communication programs.

Reviewing Previous Research

Background research may begin with a review of the work others have done addressing the same topic or health problem. Much of this can be accomplished by reviewing scientific journals that publish studies from

Table 4.1a

Overview of Health Belief Model.

<table>
<tr><td colspan="2" align="center">Health Belief Model (Becker, 1974; Janz, 1984)</td></tr>
<tr><td>What does it tell us about the behavior change process?</td><td>Behavior change is most likely to occur when a person views some behavior as posing a personal risk, and perceives there to be more benefits than obstacles to changing the behavior.</td></tr>
<tr><td>What constructs are important in predicting behavior change?</td><td>Perceived susceptibility: a person's beliefs about their own susceptibility to health or other problems as a result of some behavior</td></tr>
<tr><td></td><td>Perceived severity: a person's beliefs about how severe the negative consequences of that behavior would be</td></tr>
<tr><td></td><td>Perceived benefits: expectations about benefits or other positive rewards that would be gained as a result of changing the behavior</td></tr>
<tr><td></td><td>Perceived barriers: concerns about factors that would make it difficult for them to make the behavior change</td></tr>
<tr><td>What kinds of health problems is it best suited to explain?</td><td>When members of the target population are unaware of or unconcerned about the health problem you are addressing (i.e., they have low perceived susceptibility and severity), the health belief model may be helpful in describing the problem and generating tailored messages to address it. It is also helpful when members of the target population see little reason to adopt recommended changes (i.e., there are few perceived benefits) and identify lots of reasons that would keep them from making the change (i.e., perceived barriers).</td></tr>
</table>

the social and behavioral sciences, public health, medicine, nursing, health education, health communication, and other health science disciplines. When reviewing the published research literature for the purpose of building a better tailored health communication program, look for four types of studies:

- literature reviews or health agency reports that summarize the results of many different studies on the topic of interest;

- cross–sectional studies or surveys that have measured factors related to the topic;

Table 4.1b

Overview of Transtheoretical Model.

Transtheoretical Model, or "Stages of Change" (Prochaska, 1992)	
What does it tell us about the behavior change process?	Behavior change is an ongoing process in which people move through a series of "stages" from not thinking about making a behavioral change to actually changing the behavior and maintaining it.
	Stages
What constructs are important in predicting behavior change?	Pre-contemplation: individuals who are not thinking about changing
	Contemplation: individuals who are thinking about changing
	Preparation: individuals who are planning to change in the near future
	action: individuals who are in the process of changing
	Maintenance: individuals who are trying to maintain a change
What kinds of health problems is it best suited to explain?	The theory has been applied to a wide range of different health behaviors. It suggests that for many behaviors, not all people are equally ready to change at any point in time. Thus, different intervention strategies will be necessary to address the needs of individuals in different stages of readiness. By measuring readiness among program participants, health communication programs can tailor messages based on stage of change. This sort of stage-matched tailoring has been shown to be effective in interventions promoting smoking cessation (Prochaska, 1993) and physical activity (Marcus, 1998).

- qualitative research studies, such as focus group interviews, that report on individuals' concerns, beliefs, barriers, and knowledge about the topic; and,

- intervention studies that describe effective health education or health communication strategies addressing the topic.

Literature reviews summarize in concise fashion what has been learned from previous studies addressing a particular topic. As an example, let's revisit the case of childhood immunization described previously. Dozens of different studies have been conducted to help identify barriers to child-

---

Table 4.2

Barriers to Childhood Immunications, Based on the Institute of Medicine (IOM) (Institute of Medicine, 1994).

Barriers Within the Health Care System	Barriers in the Provider Setting	Personal and Cultural Barriers Related to Families
Lack of systematic information identifying children who need immunizations	Missed opportunities to immunize	Underestimation of the risk and severity of vaccine–preventable diseases
Lack of resources available to provide immunizations	Lack of access to a child's immunization records	Lack of understanding of the importance of immunization
Poor quality of care	Failure to review or inaccurate assessment of a child's immunization record	Concern about the safety and effectiveness of some vaccines
Limited hours		
Long waiting times	Weak ties between private health care providers and the larger health care community	Objections to immunization as "unnatural"
Mandatory appointments		Language barriers
High cost of immunization		Demographic and socio–economic characteristics
Low rates of reimbursement for providers		

---

hood immunization. If we wanted a quick overview of those factors that consistently appeared to be important, a good review article or summary report would probably serve us better than reading 20 to 30 independent studies. Table 4.2 summarizes the conclusions from one such review, "Overcoming Barriers to Immunization," a workshop summary published by the Institute of Medicine (Institute of Medicine, 1994). Clearly this listing of different system, setting, and personal barriers could focus the efforts of a tailored health communication program planner.

For many research topics—especially newer ones—literature reviews have not yet been conducted. In other cases, literature reviews may not be current, lacking information from important studies published more recently. In these cases, *cross–sectional studies* or surveys will often provide valuable information for planning tailored communication programs. Specifically, studies that report on the prevalence of certain beliefs, attitudes, or barriers among populations similar to the one with which you will be working would be helpful. For example, if you were developing a tailored communication program to promote breast-cancer knowledge, awareness, and prevention among African–American women, a literature search of recent studies might yield articles like the one from Skinner et

Table 4.3

Selected Knowledge and Attitudes about Breast Cancer, Based on Skinner et al. (1998).

Questionnaire Item	% of women answering correctly
Do women with breast cancer almost always have to have their breast removed?	55%
Are women with larger breasts more likely to get breast cancer than women with smaller breasts?	55%
Are older women more likely to get breast cancer than younger women?	52%
Can touching, fondling, or squeezing the breasts lead to breast cancer?	44%
Are women who have close relatives with breast cancer more likely to get it themselves?	27%
Can bumping or bruising the breast lead to breast cancer?	18%

al. (1998), summarized in Table 4.3. These selected findings from older African–American women in urban St. Louis, Missouri, would provide valuable insight into possible reasons why some women might be less likely to engage in cancer prevention activities like mammography.

Findings from *qualitative research studies* using focus groups, individual interviews, or observational data collection methods can also provide valuable information. These studies typically involve fewer subjects and, thus, are less representative of the larger population but have the major advantage of gathering large amounts of rich data(Krueger, 1994; Patton, 1980). Many times, the purpose of these studies is to identify issues that might be examined in greater detail in subsequent larger research projects or to gather information that will be used to shape a program or intervention. As it applies to tailoring, if one were developing a communication program to prevent childhood obesity in a Native-American population, one might draw on qualitative research such as that conducted by Gittelsohn et al. (Gittelsohn et al., 1998). Based on information gathered from observation, interviews, and surveys, they were able to classify risk behaviors for obesity as high, moderate, or low priorities for intervention. The high-priority behaviors are listed in Table 4.4 .

Finally, *intervention studies* can demonstrate which factors, if addressed, lead to the kinds of change one seeks to accomplish. For example, Thomas, Cahill, and Santilli, developed and tested a computer adventure game, "Life Challenge," designed to help youth at increased

---

Table 4.4

High Priority Obesity Risk Behaviors Among Native American Children, Based on Gittelsohn et al. (1998).

High Priority Risk Behavior	Potential site for intervention	Potential focus of intervention
Few family-based activities (especially outside the home)	Home	Physical activity
Children watch a lot of TV	Home	Physical activity
Little home-based role modeling for physical activity	Home	Physical activity
Drinking a lot of sugar drinks at home, in community	Home	Diet
Eating high fat foods at home meals	Home	Diet
Parents encourage children to finish all their food	Home	Diet
Not enough physical activities for children in school	School	Physical activity
A lot of TV watching in class	School	Physical activity
Eating high fat foods at school meals	School	Diet
Eating seconds of high fat foods at school	School	Diet

---

risk for HIV/AIDS, negotiate safe sex with their sex partners (1997). "Life Challenge" draws heavily on concepts and constructs from Bandura's (Bandura, 1977; Strecher, DeVellis, Becker, & Rosenstock, 1986) self efficacy theory. For example, the game seeks to build players' confidence in their own ability to negotiate effectively (i.e., self efficacy) by identifying difficult negotiation situations and providing opportunities to practice negotiation skills in those settings by recording and playing back their own responses on the computer (i.e., behavioral rehearsal, vicarious learning). At key decision points in the game, four peers appear on the screen to provide advice and sample lines for the player to try (i.e., modeling). In a preliminary field test involving 324 youths who played the game, the following findings were reported:

- 81% recorded a response that was coded as turning down sex;
- 93% asked their partner to use a condom or dental dam;
- 85% continued negotiating condom use even when their partner resisted an initial request;

- significant prepost learning gains occurred for four items related to knowledge about condom use; and,

- significant prepost gains occurred in self–efficacy for safe sex negotiation.

From the standpoint of tailored communication, the fact that this program appears to have influenced safe sex negotiation behavior by building self–efficacy is important information. It tells us that self–efficacy may be an important and changeable factor that should be addressed if we seek to intervene effectively on safe sex negotiation. As such, it should receive serious consideration for inclusion in our tailoring program.

Studies published in scientific journals are not the only forms of research one can access in gathering information for the planning stages of developing a tailored health communication program. Most large cities, counties, and states also routinely collect health information, such as the Behavioral Risk Factor Surveillance System (Stein, Lederman, & Shea, 1993) and make it available to the public (Kreuter & Scharff, 1999). Other surveys and polls not completed for scientific purposes can also provide useful information. As when reviewing any data, always consider possible motives of the sources and the methods used to select respondents and collect the data.

Collecting Original Data

In most instances, one needs to collect at least some new information about the problem to supplement what has been learned from other studies. An elaborately designed research project is not necessary to do this. The amount of time and resources available will largely dictate what can be accomplished. Remember though, the more comprehensively one understands determinants of the problems, the better the tailored communication program will be. If the key determinants of change are not identified, they cannot be measured or addressed in tailored messages.

For those who are already quite familiar with the health problem being addressed, observations and experiences will be one of the most valuable resources. It is useful to think about what one has seen and what members of the target population have revealed about the health problem of interest. Write it down. This list can serve as the foundation of background research.

At least as important as the experiences of researchers and practitioners are the experiences and ideas of members of the target population.

No one knows better than they do what is affecting a person's health and behavior. Conduct interviews—formal or informal, group or individual—to learn more about the problem and the population.

Prioritizing Among the Determinants

This background-research process should yield a list of candidate factors to be considered as key determinants of the outcome of interest. Once a list has been created, it must be determined which of these factors should be addressed in the tailoring program. One might ask, why not just use all of the determinants that were identified in the background research? If unlimited resources were available and all determinants were equally important, we could justify such a decision. However, this is rarely the case. Thus, for efficiency's sake, we hope to identify those determinants that are most likely to lead to the kind of health or behavior change being sought and that are most amenable to change via a communication–based approach like tailoring. To do this, we can use a 2 by 2 matrix of "importance" by "changeability," as first described by Green and Kreuter (1991). As shown in Table. 4.5, this matrix allows for determinants to be classified as high or low on changeability and high or low on importance. Each potential determinant is classified in the matrix on the basis of two questions: (1) "If this factor is changed, how important would that be in helping the person adopt or achieve the desired outcome?" (i.e., importance); and (2) "How amenable to change would this factor be in response to a communication–based intervention such as tailoring?" (i.e., changeability).

Table 4.5

Prioritization Matrix of Importance by Changeability.

		Importance	
		High	Low
Changeability	High		
	Low		

How does one know how important or changeable a determinant is? One way to find out is to go back to the library. Published research can be reviewed to learn what others have found to be the most important factors related to the outcome of interest. In particular, look for intervention research studies that have examined the relative strength of different variables in predicting behavior change. Intervention research will also help show what kinds of factors are modifiable in minimal contact interventions. It may also help to seek the advice of someone with recognized expertise in the content area to sort out the potential determinants that have been identified. Perhaps most importantly, factors that are not changeable via a tailored communication program must be identified at the outset.

When all determinants have been classified into one of the four cells of the matrix, decisions can be made about which determinants to keep. As a rule, it is best to include those factors classified into the "high–high" cell (i.e., high importance and high changeability). There is also some value in including factors classified as "high changeability, less important." Addressing these factors in tailored messages will help build participants' self–efficacy because participants are more likely to experience success in changing them. This increased self–efficacy sometimes translates into increased effort or persistence for more difficult tasks later (Bandura, 1977; Strecher et al., 1986). Tailored interventions will be most efficient and cost effective when this process identifies the fewest number of determinants that predict the greatest amount of change in the outcome of interest.

A Note on Changeability

Just because a particular determinant is not changeable via a communication–based intervention does not mean that it cannot or should not be addressed in a tailored health communication program. But family history is not changeable. There is nothing a tailored message can do to reverse the fact that a woman's mother or sister has previously been diagnosed with breast cancer. However, knowing that a woman has a family history of breast cancer may be very important information to use in a tailored communication program. For example, special messages might be developed for such women, emphasizing the added importance of performing regular breast self–exams and getting yearly mammograms. Thus, although we cannot hope to change certain important determinants, we can still use information about those determinants to make other tailored messages more effective.

Table 4.6

Summary of Background Research Findings on Relapse Prevention Among Recovering Alcoholics.

Factors Increasing the Likelihood of Relapse Among Recovering Alcoholics		
Individual Factors	**Situational Factors**	**Physiological Factors**
Negative emotional states Frustration, anger, anxiety, depression, boredom, loneliness, fatigue, shame, jealousy, fear, hatred, sadness, stress	**Social pressure** Direct coercion to drink alcohol Socializing with other people who drink	**Dependence on alcohol** More alcohol cravings Stronger conditioning to drinking-related cues
Lack of coping skills Low self-efficacy for coping with high-risk drinking situations No effective responses to high-risk drinking situations	**Lack of social support** Lack of a social network, and/or a supporting "partner" Members of social network continue to drink alcohol No abstinence-specific support from others Any interpersonal conflict	**Genetic predisposition** Increased likelihood of alcoholism
	Alcohol-related cues Special events where drinking is the norm (e.g., weddings, funerals, holidays) Significant dates (e.g., anniversaries) People who drink or former drinking partners Any physical or social setting associated with drinking	

Summary of Background Research on the Health or Behavioral Problem

Findings from the background research and prioritization exercise should be summarized in a final report or similar document. At a minimum, this document should include a list of those factors deemed important and/or changeable, and thus to be addressed by the tailored health communication program. In later stages of the planning process, assessment questions are developed to measure these factors and tailored messages written to address each different possible response. Table 4.6 shows a summary page from background research efforts in planning a tailored health communication program to prevent relapse among recovering alcoholics (Doorway to Recovery, 1995). Note that this summary has grouped the determinants into categories. It distinguishes between individual factors (i.e., cognitive and affective determinants that lie within the individual), situational factors (i.e., determinants that lie within the social and physical environment), and physiological factors (i.e., determinants with a biological or similar basis). Furthermore, within each of these broad categories, similar types of factors are grouped together. Although category headings will likely be different for any given health outcome, this type of classification system can help organize findings from background research so that later steps in the development process are simplified.

Understanding the Population to be Served

Just as we want to understand as much as possible about the health or behavioral problem and its determinants, we also want to learn about the population that will be receiving the tailored communication program. Having such information will help us to communicate more effectively with program participants. As described at the beginning of this chapter, the process of tailoring health messages is like that of tailoring clothing— some key measurements have to be obtained before one can begin. In the previous section on understanding the health or behavioral problem to be addressed, the key measurements were factors that influenced the outcome of interest. However, if this were the only type of information gathered, it would be like a clothing tailor taking a customer's waist, inseam, and outseam measurements to make a pair of trousers, but not asking about the preferred style, color, or fabric. The pants would fit well, but might never be worn if the tailor used inappropriate colors, style, or fabric. Tailored communication must not only address the right health and behavioral variables, but do so in a way that recognizes and builds on other important characteristics of the study population that vary from individual to individual.

For example, imagine creating a tailored health communication program designed to help cigarette smokers get ready to quit. Part of the program provides each participant with reasons to quit that are highly personally relevant. Two such reasons might be to protect the health of other family members living in the same home and setting a good example for children in the home. At the most basic level, one needs to know if there are other people living in the same home as the smoker because such messages would not be meaningful to a person who is living alone. But this information alone would not be enough. It would also be important to know who lives in the household with the smoker, whether any children live there, and, if so, what their ages are. By obtaining this more detailed information about each member of the target population, one could now provide a smoker with messages about the specific risks of passive smoking for their children under age 5, if that's who lives at home with them. Program materials could talk about the importance of positive role modeling for smokers who have older children living in their home. This is the level of specificity necessary to develop effective tailored health communication programs. It cannot be obtained without an understanding of key attributes of the intended audience.

Although the types of population characteristics of interest will likely vary based upon the health problem being addressed, we find that population profile research generally should address at least four areas: personal values, cultural norms, living patterns, and social networks.

Each of these is described in the following, with sample questions to ask and illustrations of how such information can be important in the construction of tailored messages. This information can be obtained from multiple sources, including individual and group interviews, direct and participant observation, questionnaires and surveys, and previous research.

Personal Values

A common mistake in creating any health–education or health–communication program is to assume that improved health is a primary value for people. Often, it is not. As Green and Kreuter (1991) noted, health is an instrumental, rather than an ultimate, value and is cherished primarily "because it serves other ends" (Green & Kreuter, 1991, p. 49). In other words, the presence or absence of health is most important because it determines the extent to which people can engage in and enjoy life activities they value most. The more a person's health status impairs their ability to pursue valued life activities, the more negative their perception of their own quality of life (QOL) (Ditto, Druley, Moore, Danks, & Smucker, 1996). At the same time, participation in valued life activities is positively associated with happiness, an important indicator of QOL (Mishra, 1992) and negatively associated with indicators of poor mental health

(Winefield & Cormack, 1986). If such values can be identified and measured, tailored communication programs can use this information to create more salient health messages.

To help identify personal values and beliefs held by members of the target population, one would want information such as:

- What is important to them?
- What are their highest priorities in life?
- What are their valued life activities?
- What motivates them?
- What are their fears and aspirations?

This information can be used in at least two ways. First, it can help shape the very nature of the program being developed. As an example, consider the tailored childhood immunization calendar program described in chapter 2. In this program, the target population was parents of children from birth to 2 years. What are the values and priorities for these parents? For many of them, their new baby is a high priority. They express this by spending time with the baby, cuddling the baby, singing to the baby, buying the baby gifts, showing the baby off to others, and adorning their homes and offices with pictures of the baby. Given this information, one way to make a childhood immunization program more appealing to new parents would be to offer them highly individualized educational materials that even included a picture of their baby. This is the approach that was ultimately used in the ABC Immunization Calendar® program, and was quite favorably received by new parents (Caburnay & Kreuter, 1998; Kreuter, Vehige, & McGuire, 1996).

A second way information on values and beliefs can be used is to indicate the need for specific tailored messages. For example, a typical motivational message about quitting smoking will focus, at least in part, on the reduced risks of lung cancer and heart disease and other smoking–related illnesses. But these health benefits might not be important to every smoker. Consider how such a message might be different if you knew what really mattered to each smoker. Here's how such a message might look for someone who reported that they were a devoted pet owner and that their pets were the greatest source of happiness in their lives:

> Anyone who has loved a pet has probably marveled at how human they can seem – the way they look at you, the affectionate greeting you get when you come home from work, and all the ways they find to make you laugh and smile. Animals are like humans in another way, too:

their lungs can be damaged by cigarette smoke. Can you imagine how much smoke the Marlboro Man's horse had to inhale? In truth, respiratory diseases in cats, dogs, and birds are nothing to laugh about. They complicate other routine problems, and are difficult to treat. Worst of all, a pet can't tell you that he or she is suffering. Your pets depend on you to help them stay healthy. If they could help you quit, they would do so in a heartbeat!

And here's a different version of the same type of message, but created for a person who indicated that their faith and religious beliefs were central to their quality of life:

"Let no man do to another what would be repugnant to himself." That's a Hindu saying, but it probably sounds familiar because some version of it is a part of many religions. In fact, scriptures from all religions contain spiritual messages urging us not to abuse our bodies or other people's bodies. There is no question that smoking damages your own body, and can affect the health and well being of those around you. The good news is that as a religious person, you have a powerful resource to draw upon in your struggle to quit smoking. Through prayer or talking to other members of your congregation, you can ask for the help you need to quit smoking. If you study scriptures as part of your worship, you may want to discuss this theme with others. You can search for inspiration from that source, and share your ideas with others.

It should be clear from these examples that knowing more about the values and beliefs of those who will be receiving the tailored communication materials is essential for developing appropriate program materials and messages.

Cultural Norms

Although no single definition of culture is universally accepted by social scientists, there is basic agreement that culture is learned, shared, and transmitted from one generation to the next and can be seen in a population's values, norms, practices, systems of meaning, ways of life, and other social regularities (Betancourt & Lopez, 1993; Herkovits, 1948; Hughes, Seidman, & Williams, 1993; Rohner, 1984). Triandis (1980) provided a more practical (i.e., measurable) formulation, identifying specific cultural elements such as familial roles, communication patterns, affective styles, values regarding personal control, individualism, collectivism, spirituality, and religiosity (Triandis et al., 1980). These culturally–based norms can have a significant effect on people's lives, including health–related beliefs and behaviors. For example, eating foods like fried fish and chicken, biscuits and gravy, and deep–fried vegetables can be an integral part of culture in many parts of the southeastern United States (Campbell et al., 1994).

Unfortunately, many of these foods are also high in fat and saturated fat, important factors in the development of heart disease and some types of cancer (Brownson, Remington, & Davis, 1993). A tailored health communication program to reduce these health risks might well promote dietary changes, including eating less of the kinds of foods aforementioned. However, program planners must recognize that by asking people to avoid these foods, you are actually asking them to give up part of their culture. These foods are inextricably linked to family reunions, community and church picnics, with family recipes that have been passed down through generations. They are deeply ingrained in the fabric of the culture. This does not mean it's useless to try to change dietary habits, but it does mean that any diet–related health communication to members of this population should reflect an understanding of the importance of these foods. Rather than asking people to give up these foods, ask them to restrict the frequency or quantity of these foods. Or, encourage them to eat these foods on special occasions but to avoid them at other times.

Traditional foods are just one of many cultural norms and values that can affect health communication programs. For example, the health practices of American farmers are said to follow a kind of agrarian philosophy that equates health with the ability to work (Kelsey, 1994). One possible consequence of this is that farmers may view preventive actions or other precautions as unnecessary as long as they are still able to work (Wadud, Kreuter, & Clarkson, 1998). Rather than attack or challenge these culturally based beliefs, health messages promoting prevention among farmers might build on on other cultural beliefs. For example, self reliance is also a highly prized value in agrarian philosophy. Thus, preventive health messages for farmers might focus on the fact that using protective equipment now will reduce their chances of being dependent on someone else later, should they become sick or unable to work.

In an ongoing tailored health communication study, Kreuter and colleagues are tailoring cancer prevention materials for urban African–American women on four culturally based constructs: religiosity, collectivism, ethnic identity, and perception of time. These constructs are prevalent in urban African–American populations (Akbar, 1991; Bergadaa, 1990; Boyd–Franklin, 1989; Graham, 1981; Hays, 1973; Klonoff & Landrine, 1996; Klonoff, Landrine, & Scott, 1995; Landrine & Klonoff, 1994, 1995, 1997; Leshan, 1952; Lozoff, Wolf, & Davis, 1984; Mandansky & Edlebrock, 1990; Nobles, 1991; White & Parham, 1990) and have been shown to be associated with health–related beliefs or practices (Brown & Segal, 1996; Brown & Gary, 1987; Jackson & Gurin, 1987; Klonoff & Landrine, 1996; Parker & Calhoun, 1996).

To get a better understanding of cultural norms and values like these, here are some of the kinds of questions to ask.

- What, if any, cultural norms, values, or traditions influence the population?
- In what ways do they influence the population?
- What is the basis for these cultural norms?
- How might the cultural norms influence the communication objective?

Living Patterns

Think about a typical day in your own life. Where do you go? What do you do? Who do you see? Are there certain patterns that emerge? Maybe you drive to work the same way each morning or maybe you take the same bus. Maybe you stop for coffee at the same bagel shop. eat lunch at the same time every day, stay at home on Thursday nights and watch TV, shop for groceries and do laundry on Sunday nights. Whether you realize it or not, your day–to–day life probably follows certain patterns. These patterns can hold valuable information about you — information that can be used to make health education and health communication programs more effective. For example, in 1982, Don Morisky and colleagues observed that barber shops were a social gathering place for many African–American men, and thus began a hypertension education campaign based in these settings (Levine et al., 1982). By understanding how and where people spend their time, one is better able to reach them in a way and with messages that are in accord with their lifestyle.

Many health behaviors also follow patterns. Smokers, for example, will often have a cigarette soon after waking up in the morning, when they first get into their car, after a meal, or when drinking coffee or alcohol. When grocery shopping, many people start at one end of the store and walk back and forth down the aisles until they get to the other end of the store. Identifying these behavioral patterns provides a great opportunity to tailor health messages.

If one were developing a tailored communication program to promote healthier eating, it might be important to know who usually shops for the food in the participant's home. If it is the participant who does the shopping, our tailored message would likely focus on teaching shopping skills and strategies to encourage finding and trying healthier foods. But if the participant does not do the shopping, that message will be meaningless. Instead, the focus might be on communication between the participant and whomever does the shopping. It might, for example, encourage the participant to make a healthy grocery list for the shopper to take along. The message below is drawn from a tailored dietary intervention used in the Change of Heart cardiovascular disease risk–factor reduction study (Kreuter, 1997) and was designed for people who ate a high–fat diet and who usually did the grocery shopping and food preparation for their families. Note how the message addressed the shopping pattern described above.

> You told us you usually shop for and prepare most of the food you eat. That's good news—it means you're in control of your food choices! On your next trip to the grocery store, shop the corners and outside aisles first. That's where you'll find fresh produce, breads and baked goods, low–fat dairy products, and fish, chicken, and lean meats. Before leaving home, write out a grocery list that includes some low–fat foods. Planning ahead will help you make healthy choices.
>
> In your kitchen, you can avoid adding unwanted fat by preparing foods differently. Did you know that you double the fat content of some foods by frying instead of baking, or just by adding butter? The simple but effective low–fat cooking tips on the next page will help you get started.

To better understand the living patterns of an individual or group, here are some of the kinds of questions to ask:

- What is an average day in the life of someone in the target population?
- How do they spend their time?
- What do they do?
- Where do they go?
- What makes their lives easier?
- What makes their lives more difficult?

Social Networks

We are also interested in learning about the people who are important to, respected, and trusted by the participants. Who do they spend time with? Who influences their thoughts and actions? This information can help us understand the extent to which a person (a) has positive role models, (b) receives support and encouragement from others, (c) interacts with others who may be contributing to the person's problems, or (d) faces social pressures that could influence the person's motivation or ability to make changes.

Characteristics of a person's social network can be important determinants of change, and offer unique opportunities to tailor messages. As described previously in this chapter, "Doorway to Recovery®" is a tailored health communication program designed to help recovering alcoholics avoid relapse. As part of the program, tailored materials are generated for the recovering alcoholic to give to the person or persons who will be most supportive of their recovery efforts. These materials explain to the support person what he or she can do to be most helpful to the person in recovery. The tips provided must vary based on the nature of the relationship between the support person and the recovering alcoholic. Assume that the support person is the recovering alcoholic's spouse or partner. Might the kind of support provided by a spouse be different than that offered by a co–worker? Probably. Or what if the person was a sponsor from a support group? Might that person play a different role than a physician or clergy member? One such message from the "Doorway to Recovery®" (1995) program—tailored for a support person who is a sponsor from a support group like Alcoholics Anonymous— reads:

> As you may know, Bob recently made the decision to live alcohol free. He told us that he thought he could count on you to support his efforts. As Bob's support group sponsor, you can play an important role in his recovery. Listed below are some support tips that have worked for other people in your position. You may be in recovery yourself, and are already familiar with the suggestions listed below. We hope you will add to them your own experiences, to help Bob make this important change in his life.
>
> - Be patient. Bob may seem irritable or easily frustrated in the next few weeks. This is a natural reaction as his body adjusts to life without alcohol.
>
> - Be positive. Living alcohol–free won't be easy. Bob may be tempted to have a drink, and may even slip and have one. Whatever happens, be encouraging and supportive. Try to tell him about positive changes you've noticed since he stopped *drinking*.
>
> - Listen. Many people who are trying to stop drinking want or need to talk about life without alcohol. If he wants or needs to talk to someone, you can be helpful just by being a good listener.
>
> - Ask how you can help. Bob may want or need your support for some things, but not for others. The only way to find out is to ask him.
>
> - Let others help. You can encourage and be supportive of Bob attending meetings or groups that will help him live alcohol–free.
>
> - Don't blame yourself for Bob's drinking. Remember, you're not the one who made the decision to change, he is. You can be supportive and offer your help, but Bob is the one who has to live alcohol–free. You are not responsible for his success or failure.
>
> - Take care of yourself. There are support groups available to help you deal with Bob's drinking. To find them, look under the heading "Alcoholism" in the Yellow Pages, and call to ask about support groups.

Some of the questions you might want to ask about a person about their social contacts are:

- Who do they interact with on a regular basis?
- Who do they look to for support and advice?
- Who are the most trusted people in their lives?
- Whose advice and opinions do they respect?
- From whom do they get information about health?
- Which, if any, form of media do they regularly use?

Summary

When background research activities have been completed, you should have a clear sense of the factors that influence the health problem of interest, as well as a good understanding of the unique characteristics of the target population. This knowledge should be reflected in a distilled list of factors or variables that are to be addressed by the tailored health communication program. This list is used later in the development process to create questions for the tailoring assessment questionnaire (see chap. 6).

CHAPTER 5

Developing a Program Framework

Chapters 3 and 4 focus on developing a detailed understanding of the health and behavioral problems being addressed and the populations that are affected. Now we turn our attention to putting that information to work in building a tailored health communication program. This step in the planning process, *developing a program framework*, involvesthinking creatively about characteristics of the population and the nature of the health issues, identifying appropriate communication strategies to effectively address each, and translating these strategies into specific program activities.

Beginning with a big–picture view of the overall structure of the tailored health communication program, a narrowing approach is used to break down the program into its specific component parts, and then develop important details about each component.

The goal of these activities is to develop a program framework that provides both an overview of the whole program as well as details about each of its components. Such a framework allows program planners to carry out development tasks for a program's specific components without losing sight of how all the components ultimately fit together. A well thought out program framework can streamline the complex and sometimes disjointed process of developing and implementing a tailored health communication program.

In this chapter we discuss the purpose of developing a tailored health communication program framework and describe the four main considerations in this process:

1. Identifying program objectives;
2. Identifying program constraints;
3. Creating a general program framework; and,
4. Describing each of the framework components.

Understanding the Purpose and Nature of the Program Framework

Like a construction blueprint, a program framework for a tailored health communication program has two levels: a big–picture view of the overall program, and a detailed description of the each of the program components. In a construction blueprint, the big–picture view shows the main pieces of the structure—the landscape, buildings, and rooms. In a program framework for a tailored health communication program, the big picture view shows the major pieces of the program—the points at which data are collected from participants (*assessment modules*) and the points at which feedback is provided to the recipient (*feedback modules*). This big–picture view takes the form of a flow chart that includes each of the assessment and feedback modules, showing how each is related to the others, as well as the sequence in which each occurs within the overall program.

The detailed view in a construction blueprint describes the special characteristics of the different pieces of the structure—the size and shape of each room, the distance and relationship between rooms, and so forth. It also explains what each piece of the structure is made of (i.e., the building materials) and how it is put together (i.e., specifications for assembly). A program framework shares this detailed view in its description of each of the different assessment and feedback modules that appear in the big–picture view. The description of each module provides details about the functions that the module serves, its various subparts, and how it will be developed and implemented.

Developing the program framework is largely an idea–generating exercise in which program planners systematically consider possible intervention strategies to meet the program's communication objectives. Each participant in this exercise must have detailed knowledge of the health problem and the target population. The greater their understanding, the easier and more comprehensive the process will be. Begin by reviewing and presenting findings from background research that has been conducted to learn about the health problem and target population (see chaps. 3 and 4). Next, discuss any experience with, or knowledge of, other educational programs that have successfully addressed similar problems or similar populations. Even when there are no tailored health communication programs to draw from, we can look to certain aspects of nontailored health promotion and health communication programs for valuable insight. Pay particular attention to programs that:

- Used printed media as the means of intervention;
- focused on the individual as the point of understanding;

- collected complex quantitative data;
- intervened directly with individuals; or,
- involved complicated production and delivery activities.

When reviewing such programs, there are certain questions to be answered that are especially pertinent to tailoring. These include:

- Which characteristics of the target population were focused on in developing program activities or materials? Why were these characteristics selected?
- What methods were most effective for collecting data from members of the target population?
- How was health information effectively communicated to program participants?

Next, think creatively. There are numerous examples of health communication programs that have used the answers obtained from such questions to develop innovative approaches and appeals to address important public health problems. Three illustrative examples are described in this section.

First, in a program designed to promote breast–cancer screening among adult women, Rimer and colleagues (Rimer & Glassman, 1998) recognized that mammography messages could be added to birthday cards sent to women on their 50th birthday. This simple intervention cleverly links a characteristic of the health problem (i.e., annual screening is recommended beginning at age 50) with a characteristic of the target population (i.e., salience of the 50th birthday).

Second, in a child health program on the Navaho reservation, Tish Ramirez and colleagues (Ramirez, 1999) at the Indian Health Service were trying to find ways to encourage Navaho parents to use child safety seats with their infants. They came up with the idea of designing car seat covers to look like traditional Navaho cradle boards. Again, this approach simultaneously addressed a characteristic of the health problem (i.e., making the car seats more attractive) and the population (i.e., appealing to respect for cultural traditions).

Third, in St. Louis, Missouri, Teresa Parks–Thomas and colleagues (Hong, Kappel, Whitlock, Parks–Thomas & Freedman, 1994) sought to increase organ donation among African Americans by working through Black churches. Among other project activities, they produced a hand–held cardboard fan to distribute before church services. On one side of the fan there were full–color pictures of African Americans in the community who had recently received organ transplants. On the other side was a picture of leading pastors from St. Louis, captioned with a biblical scripture germane to the concept of organ donation. Like the previous examples, this intervention brought together values of the population (i.e., church scripture, respected leaders) with program objectives (i.e., dispelling the myth that African Americans do not benefit from organ donation and beliefs that organ donation is unholy). The ability to think creatively and turn creative ideas into concrete program activities and materials is an important skill for planners to bring to this process.

Experience with the nuts–and–bolts of developing and implementing a tailored health communication program is also a key skill for successful planning. In the absence of such experience, a review of the literature on tailored health communication programs, such as that provided by the remainder of this book, can help.

Identifying Program Objectives

Creating a program framework begins by answering the question "What does the program seek to achieve?" The program objectives that are identified will serve as the most basic guide to planners in making decisions about specific intervention activities. As such, objectives should be clear and specific.

The process of developing program objectives is well documented in health education literature (Green & Kreuter, 1991). Part of this process involves examining the health problem to determine what could ideally be achieved if individuals were helped to deal with each aspect of the health problem. If planners are uncertain what objectives would be realistic and what would not, resources such as Healthy People 2000 (1991) and the U.S. Preventive Services Task Force's Guide to Clinical Preventive Services (1996) can provide useful guidance. Once the level of change sought has been identified, it must be decided which aspects of the problem are most important to address and most changeable using a tailored communication approach (see chap. 4). Determining the relative importance of objectives involves ranking them such that, if achieved, those with the highest priority will have the greatest effect on the health problem. Importantly, these are not the ultimate program goals, such as reducing the rate of heart disease, but rather, on–the–way objectives, such as increasing the knowledge of causes of heart disease, or modifying a specific behavioral risk factor for heart disease.

Determining the relative achievability of objectives involves examining each one relative to the roadblocks that might get in the way of a person successfully completing that objective. At this point, careful consideration should be given to the unique abilities and limitations of tailored communication. Tailoring has special abilities to inform and motivate through very personal and highly relevant communication. At the same time, it has only limited ability as an information–based approach to effectively address societal or structural problems. There may also be other limitations due to characteristics of the target population, such as low literacy level, limited access to technology, hard–to–reach individuals, and time constraints that can limit the potential to achieve an objective. In the case of tailoring, easy access to individuals (to provide data and receive feedback) and participants' ability to use printed material (including such characteristics as literacy level) are especially important.

At the end of this process, program planners will have developed a set of objectives and organized them according to an importance–achievability matrix. Objectives that are both highly important and highly achievable are usually the primary focus of the program.

Identifying Program Constraints

Achievability of program objectives is affected not only by the abilities and limitations of tailoring and characteristics of the target population, but also by the resources available for developing and implementing the program. Thus, it is important to carefully examine program resources to determine whether there are limitations in the way objectives can be operationalized. In rare cases, resource constraints may require discarding certain objectives. More commonly, resource constraints simple require modifying the way that objectives can be addressed. Constraints include any factors related to the people or organizations carrying out program that may limit their ability to address one or more objective. These constraints include:

- Limited financial resources for developing or implementing the program;
- limited period of time before program implementation must begin;
- limited period of time during which the program must be carried out;
- limited skills, experience, or technology available to program developers; and
- social or political imperatives of the funding agencies and gatekeepers to the population.

For many tailored health communication programs, having a limited amount of time or money for building the program is the greatest constraining factor. Just as the majority of this book is devoted to describing activities involved in developing a tailored health communication program, so too are the majority of resources (i.e., time and expenses) spent on these tasks. It is important to give careful consideration to how much time and money can be spent developing the tailored communication program before these activities begin.

Creating a General Program Framework

When final objectives have been clearly identified and program constraints have been noted, the process of designing the overall intervention—drawing the big–picture view of our blueprint—can begin. From this birds–eye view, a tailored health communication program consists of a series of data collection and feedback delivery modules. Data collection usually occurs at least two times during a program—once at the beginning of the program (i.e., *baseline*) and once at the conclusion of the program (i.e., *follow–up*). In many programs, data are also collected at interim points. Each period of data collection is referred to in the program framework as an *assessment module*.

Production and delivery of tailored feedback also occurs at multiple times during the program. Each period of production and delivery is referred to as a *feedback module*. The framework begins by determining how many data collection and feedback modules are needed and when each should occur.

Considering the Health Problem and Population

Some health problems will demand multiple periods of data collection or feedback, whereas others may be effectively addressed by a single communication based on a single period of data collection. Some health problems require pinpoint timing of data collection and feedback modules, whereas in other cases, assessments can be administered and feedback delivered when it is most convenient for a participant or for program staff. When deciding how intensive a tailoring program must be, one should consider the unique characteristics of the health problem. For example:

- Can the health problem be effectively addressed with a one–time or short–term behavior change intervention, or is long–term behavioral change and maintenance needed?
  Changes that must be sustained over time may require more assessment and feedback modules.

- Is it important to monitor participants' progress during the course of the program?

If the program will be measuring or addressing changes over time in a participant's health or behavior, multiple assessment and feedback modules will be needed.

- Is there a strong need for reinforcing participants' efforts?
  If the program will be providing feedback based on the progress a person is making toward behavioral goals, multiple assessment and feedback modules will be necessary.

- How much information must be communicated to participants in order to meet program objectives?
  To avoid overwhelming participants with too much information in a single instance, multiple feedback modules may be needed.

As an example, if a tailored health communication program seeks to prevent relapse among those recovering from an addictive behavior, it may be important to provide feedback at times when relapse is most likely to occur. In the case of alcoholism and other substance abuse, the highest rates of relapse are during the first 4 to 6 weeks of recovery (Hunt, Barnett, & Branch, 1971). This suggests that a tailored health communication program might want to provide multiple feedback modules very early in the program (Doorway to Recovery, 1995). This multiple–contact "front–end loading" may provide the best chance to support recovery. On the other hand, if a tailored health communication program seeks to encourage a once–in–a–lifetime screening event, such as genetic testing, a single assessment and feedback module might suffice.

The capacity of the target population to provide data and attend to feedback are also important determinants of the number and frequency of modules to be included. Important questions to ask about population characteristics include:

- How motivated are participants to respond to assessments and read feedback?
  If motivation level is low, fewer modules may be better.

- How much time are participants willing or able to spend completing assessments for the program?
  If their time is limited, assessments should be few and brief.

- How accessible are potential program participants?
  If participants are hard to reach, it may be necessary to gather as much information as possible in a single module.

- In light of other demands on them, how likely will potential participants be to actively engage in program activities?
  If participants have excessive demands in everyday life, fewer modules that require less attention will be appropriate.

As an example, if a tailored health communication program seeks to enhance medication compliance among a population of patients dedicated to a clinical course of treatment, the motivation level of individuals to respond to requests for data and to integrate tailored feedback into their behavior change activities will likely be high enough to allow for multiple data collection and feedback modules. On the other hand, in a population that has unstable living conditions and does not have routine contact with the medical care system or a specific health care provider, fewer modules timed to occur during brief windows of contact may be more appropriate.

Considering Resource Constraints

The capacity of the sponsoring agency to carry out a tailored health communication program is often the ultimate determinant of the number and timing of modules. Ideally, the first step in dealing with resource constraints is to increase resources, but when full resource capacity has been reached, it becomes necessary to make the program fit the available resources. Two resource constraints that are especially important for tailoring are: having a short- versus long-term mandate and funding to carry out the program, and the existence or absence of structural support to carry out the program.

If the people or organizations carrying out the program have access to a network of support that they can draw on to complete development and implementation tasks—such as in a public health agency that has technical and human resources funded through other means besides the program at hand—more frequent modules may be used for a longer period of time. For example, if a program objective is to reduce the rate of relapse among recovering alcoholics, it would help greatly if the sponsoring agency already had extensive networks for collecting and delivering information, and/or a mandate that includes funding for ongoing recovery and treatment activities. Under such circumstances, more frequent periods of data collection and feedback with quick turn-around may be possible within the tailored health communication program. If, on the other hand, an agency has personnel and funding for only a discrete period of time, a single data collection and feedback module may be all that can be carried out.

Describing Framework Components

Once the number and timing of assessment and feedback modules has been determined, the next task is to create a detailed description of each module and specify its relation to other modules.

Feedback Modules

Describing feedback modules involves a top–down process that begins with a general question of purpose and ends with specific objectives that, if met, will achieve that purpose. Start by asking "what is the primary purpose or intended outcome of this module?" This question should be answered within the context of the overall program. For example, in a tailored health communication program that seeks to prevent relapse among recovering addicts and contains three feedback modules, the purpose of the initial module may be: To help the participant identify situations in which relapse may be most likely to occur, and to think about strategies to avoid or deal with those situations.

Once the primary purpose of a module has been identified, specific educational or behavioral strategies can be generated to meet that purpose. These strategies suggest the ideal content and approach of the module and will guide content developers as they create messages, algorithms, and design templates (see chaps. 7–10). If the primary purpose of a given module is to prepare participants to deal with relapse threats that they encounter during the initial period of recovery, specific educational and behavioral strategies might include understanding the process of lapse and relapse, developing self monitoring skills, and developing lapse containment strategies.

After educational and behavioral strategies have been identified, planners can turn their attention to the specific format and content of the module. Here, the main question is, "what format and content characteristics are appropriate for the strategies of this module, our intended audience, and logistic constraints?" Specifically, it is important to know:

- Through what mode of communication will the module be delivered?

Although this book focuses primarily on print media, any type of media conducive to tailoring may be used, including printed materials, telephone calls or counseling, tailored video, tailored web pages, or interactive kiosk.

- What form will the module take?

In the case of printed materials, this may include a newsletter, post card, professional letter, brochure, calendar, or many other formats.

- To what design characteristics will the module conform?

For example, format specifications for a printed newsletter will include the number and size of pages and the design style such as "serious" or "casual." The degree of detail developed for design characteristics at this stage depends on how important those characteristics are to the educational and behavioral strategies employed by the feedback module. If strategies beg for specific design characteristics, provide them now. Otherwise, they can wait until design template development (see chap. 7).

- What types of tailored messages will the module contain?

In the previous example (the initial module of a relapse prevention program), messages may include an introduction to the overall program, a description of the relapse process, a skill–building activity, a personal story from a similar other experiencing relapse, and a cover graphic that includes photographs of people similar to the participant. This content will, of course, be largely determined by the types of data collected by the tailoring assessment questionnaire.

- To what writing characteristics will each of the tailored messages conform?

Characteristics may include level of formality or authority, source of communication (e.g., peer or professional), level of literacy, and others. As with design characteristics, the degree of detail developed for writing characteristics at this point rather than when the messages are actually written (see chap. 9) depends on how important writing characteristics are to the educational and behavioral strategies employed by the feedback module and to the characteristics of the target population.

Assessment Modules

Once each feedback module has been described in detail, we turn to the assessment modules and describe how and when data will be collected in order to create tailored feedback. Each assessment will collect data that is used in at least one, but perhaps several, feedback modules. Therefore, the description of an assessment module begins by answering—for each feedback module to which it provides data—the following basic question: What do we need to know about an individual in order to provide him or her with the appropriate messages for this feedback module?

The answer takes the form of a list of topics for which data will be necessary in order to produce tailored messages about the issues to be addressed in that feedback module. Let's revisit the example of an initial feedback module from a tailored health communication program to prevent relapse among recovering addicts. To produce that feedback module, the participant's name, age, gender, past experience with recovery and relapse, and attributional style may need to be known. Importantly, this does not yet involve writing actual questions or even choosing actual types of questions, but simply stating the topic areas for which questions must be written when the assessment is developed (see chap. 6).

Once an assessment module's general content has been determined, the method of administering the assessment must be considered. As described in chapter 6, options include personal interviews, telephone interviews, self–administered surveys, web pages, and other electronic media–based approaches. The format selected should be based on the content of the survey, the characteristics and accessibility of the respondents at the time that data is needed, and, again, program constraints. For example, a self–administered, mailed survey may be most appropriate when collecting sensitive information, such an assessment that asks participants for information about addictive behaviors. A telephone or other interpersonal interview may be more appropriate if topics are complicated and likely to be misunderstood without interviewer explanation.

Conclusion

A well–conceived program framework is invaluable in guiding subsequent program development activities. At this early stage in the development process, the framework should be more broadly comprehensive than full of detail. Important details are added later, when those who write messages and algorithms, create design templates, and plan for implementation provide specific information about their "room" in the blueprint. Thus, as the program development process evolves, this program framework is refined.

CHAPTER 6

Developing a Tailoring Assessment Questionnaire: How to Measure Key Determinants

Tailored health communication is assessment–based. Therefore, once the background research process has been completed and key determinants of change have been identified, each individual's status on these determinants must be measured. Although some tailoring data may be obtained from existing databases such as a patient's computerized medical record (Rimer & Glassman, 1998), in most cases a tailoring assessment questionnaire must be developed to gather this information. This phase in the process of developing a tailored health communication program is primarily a questionnaire construction task. The objective is to create an assessment that is thorough in addressing all important determinants, yet relatively brief and simple for participants to complete, and easy to administer. Its questions should be conceptually clear and easily understood by participants, and should offer a wide enough range of response options to capture most of the variation among individuals on the key determinants. This chapter describes how to construct a tailoring assessment questionnaire that has these characteristics.

What Makes a Good Tailoring Assessment?

In many ways, a tailoring assessment questionnaire is no different than any other health survey or questionnaire. All the attributes of well–constructed questionnaires also apply to tailoring. As Aday (1996) has described, these attributes include:

- Having clear instructions for respondents;
- being well–organized, with questions on a similar topic grouped together;

- having smooth transitions between different sections of the questionnaire;
- ordering questions to avoid contextual and other biases;
- making skip patterns easy to follow;
- using balanced, even–handed questions and response scales;
- assuring clarity of questions, words, and phrases;
- using language that is familiar to the target population;
- providing appropriate response options;
- minimizing respondent burden;
- avoiding excessive length; and,
- using formative evaluation and pre–testing methods during development of the questionnaire.

Reviewing each of these principles is beyond the scope of this book. We refer interested readers to existing published resources on questionnaire construction and survey development (Aday, 1996; Converse & Presser, 1986).

What Makes a Tailoring Assessment Questionnaire Unique?

The distinguishing characteristic of a tailoring assessment questionnaire is the closed–ended nature of its questions. Closed–ended questions are those for which all possible response options are provided. For example:

What is the main reason you want to exercise more often?

(Check one answer.)

___ To improve my health

___ To look better

___ To get my body in better shape

___ To help control my weight

___ To give me more energy

___ To meet new people

___ To feel better about myself

Note that if the only reason a person wants to exercise more often is because they're trying to win a bet with a friend, that's not an option they can choose here. An open–ended question (i.e., "What is the main reason you want to exercise more often?" would provide this opportunity, but a closed ended question will not. Questions must either be closed–ended or open–ended and easily classified into predetermined categories. This makes it possible to create a comprehensive tailored message library ahead of time. In other words, to create all messages and combinations of messages that might be needed in a tailored health communication program, it must first be known, which possible answers a program participant could provide.

There are three important exceptions to the use of closed-ended questions and coding in a tailoring assessment questionnaire: Questions seeking personal identification information, questions requiring numeric responses, and questions gathering data that will be used in revising the current tailoring program.

Each of these is discussed briefly in the following.

Questions Seeking Personal Identification Information

Most tailored health communication programs gather some personal-identification information from participants. This may include the partici-pant's name, address, city, state, zip code, telephone number, and date of birth—information that will be totally different for each participant and thus can only be collected using open–ended questions. Such information is frequently used in tailored health communication programs to identify each participant's unique record in a computer database, provide a means of contacting the participant for delivery of tailored materials and completion of subsequent assessments, and allow for personalizing certain messages (e.g., addressing the participant by name within the tailored messages).

Questions Requiring Numeric Responses

For some questions about health and behavior, it is more efficient to let respondents enter a numeric answer than it is to provide a lengthy list of all possible responses. Common examples include:

- Age at the time of some event (e.g., initiation of smoking, first sexual intercourse, menarche);
- number of cigarettes smoked per day;
- height and weight;
- cholesterol level; and,
- blood pressure.

Note that information from some of the examples above could also be gathered from a close–ended question. For example, consider the following question that might be asked of smokers:

About how many cigarettes do you smoke in an average day?

(Check one answer.)

___ Less than 10 cigarettes

___ 10–19 cigarettes

___ 20–29 cigarettes

___ 30–39 cigarettes

___ 40 or more cigarettes

The information collected from this question will not be as precise as that collected from an open–ended question (i.e., About how many cigarettes do you smoke in an average day?), but it still allows one to distinguish between lighter and heavier smokers, pack–a–day smokers, and two–pack–a–day smokers. If this is all the information one wants or needs to tailor quit-smoking messages, this type of question might be acceptable. However, some important information is lost. For example, if it is decided to compute the amount of money each smoker would save by quitting, a much more precise figure can be obtained if you know exactly how many cigarettes a person smokes per day. As described previously, in many cases, numeric answers will end up being classified, or coded, into discrete categories anyway (e.g., *high, moderate,* or *low* for total cholesterol level). However, it is almost always simpler to let the computer program make these transformations than it is to demand that program participants do so in the assessment questionnaire (see chap. 10 on tailored message algorithms).

Questions Gathering Data that will be Used in Revising the Current Tailoring Program

Sometimes an open–ended "other" response choice is provided as part of an otherwise closed–ended question. For example:

What is the main reason you want to exercise more often?

(Check one answer.)

___ To improve my health

___ To look better

___ To get my body in better shape

___ To help control my weight

___ To give me more energy

___ To meet new people

___ To feel better about myself

___ Other (please specify) _____

Including this "other" can be a useful way to gather information that could be used to fine tune the tailored communication program in the future. If, for example, a majority of the people who choose this option report that they want to exercise more often to "help rehabilitate a health problem," it might be helpful to include this answer as a response option in future iterations of the program. For this same reason, inclusion of an open–ended "other" option is especially useful when pre–testing questions for a tailoring assessment. That said, in our experience, few respondents will choose this "other" option, and fewer still will actually write in a response in the space provided.

Narrowing the Focus of a Tailoring Questionnaire

It is a practical reality of tailoring that not all assessment questions or response choices will perfectly meet the needs of every participant. If we attempted to assess participants' status on a limitless number of determinants, each with an infinite number of possible responses, tailoring would be impractical. It would be impossible to anticipate every different response a participant might provide, thus, a comprehensive message library could never be completed. In theory, tailoring would still be possible under these circumstances by integrating artificial intelligence and inference programs into the tailoring engine (Abrams, Mills, & Bulger, in press). However, such technology is not presently available and has never been applied to tailored health communication programs. Yet this limitation of tailoring need not be a disabling one. Instead, it requires that planners of tailored health communication programs predetermine a limited set of questions and response options to be included in the tailoring assessment questionnaire. Much of this narrowing occurs during the completion of background research (described in chap. 4), but some also takes place during the construction of the tailoring assessment questionnaire.

To maximize the efficiency of tailored programs, we generally seek to identify those factors that have the greatest influence on the outcome of interest, along with the most common response choices for that factor.

Inevitably, this means that some questions or response choices that might be selected by only a few people are left out. However, in keeping with public health's population perspective, this is probably a worthwhile trade–off. The alternative—including a broader menu of questions and response choices—adds considerable complexity but yields only marginal benefits. Moreover, it can lead to an unwieldy, lengthy questionnaire that may discourage participation by some individuals who otherwise would have taken part in the program.

An important exception to this reductionist approach would be indicated if the persons whose options were not represented in the final assessment questionnaire shared particular traits or represented a disadvantaged or underserved population. For example, we could probably accept a given tailoring assessment that applied very well to all but 5% to 10% of a given population. From a population perspective, such as that espoused in public health, we would still be meeting the needs of a large population at risk. But what if the people who fell into that 5% to 10% were all the single working mothers in the population? If this were the case, the assessment almost certainly included systematic biases that excluded these women. The solution would include modifying the assessment and program, if feasible, to address the unique needs of this population subgroup, or developing a parallel track of the program to do this.

Limiting Response Options

A major task in developing the assessment tool is determining which response choices will accompany each assessment question. As described previously in this chapter, it is most efficient to select the fewest number of response choices that will capture the largest percentage of respondents' answers. To better understand why this is the case, consider the data presented in Tables 6.1 and 6.2 from a study of smokers invited to participate in a quit-smoking program (Brennan, Kreuter, Caburnay, & Wilshire, 1998). Table 6.1 shows the prevalence of selected beliefs about smoking and Table 6.2 shows smokers' perceptions of the biggest benefits of quitting smoking. Note that only 3% of smokers believe that "smoking less than 20 cigarettes per day is safe" (Table 6.1) and an equally small number perceive "pleasing their doctor" or "no longer feeling like a social outcast" as major benefits of quitting (Table 6.2).

If a tailored smoking cessation program for this population were planning to address beliefs about smoking and benefits of quitting, it might choose to exclude these low-frequency response options. Why?

Whenever there is little variability in individuals' responses to a given question on a tailoring questionnaire, the relative value of providing tailored messages addressing different responses to that question is minimized. For example, if only 3% of smokers erroneously believe it is safe to smoke less than 20 cigarettes per day—and thus need a tailored messages explaining why this is not the case—we might decide it is more efficient to save development cost and time and reduce participants' response burden by eliminating this choice. The converse is also true. If 97% of smokers erroneously believed it was safe to smoke less than 20 cigarettes per day, it might be more efficient to provide all smokers with an educational message setting the record straight than it would be to develop multiple tailored messages, of which only one message in particular was going to be sent to virtually all participants anyway. Importantly, reducing the scope of a tailoring assessment questionnaire is not driven by limitations in the process or capabilities of computer tailoring, but rather by the objective of keeping program development costs down, and developing concise surveys that will not be too burdensome for individuals to complete.

How will the Tailoring Assessment Questionnaire be Administered?

The tailoring assessment questionnaire may be self–administered, administered by an interviewer, or even by an interactive computer program.

Table 6.1

Prevalence of Selected Beliefs About Smoking (Thinking About Quitting, 1997).

Beliefs About Smoking	% agreeing with statement
Many people who quit smoking put on weight.	68%
Some people smoke all their lives and live to be a ripe old age, so smoking must not be all that bad for them.	29%
I started smoking when I was young, so the damage is already done.	25%
I'd have to smoke a lot more cigarettes than I do now to put my health at serious risk.	11%
If smoking was really harmful, the government would ban tobacco advertising.	10%
It's safe to smoke low–tar cigarettes.	6%
Smoking less than 20 cigarettes per day is safe.	3%

Table 6.2

Perceived "Most Important Benefits" of Becoming a Non–Smoker (Thinking About Quitting, 1997).

What Would you see as the Biggest Benefits of Becoming a Non-smoker?*	number of respondents agreeing
My health would improve.	73
I'd save a lot of money.	54
My risk of smoking–related diseases would decrease.	52
I would look and feel better.	41
I'd be taking more control of my life.	31
I'd be protecting the health of my family.	23
I'd be setting a good example for my family.	12
Family and friends would be proud of me.	6
I wouldn't feel like a social outcast for smoking.	4
I'd make my doctor happy.	1

* Respondents could select up to three benefits.

Each has its own advantages and disadvantages as presented in the brief descriptions that follow.

Self–Administered

Self–administered questionnaires are those that are completed with paper and pencil by the program participant. Most studies of tailored health communication published to date have used this approach. If a self–administered questionnaire is used, it must be simple to complete, with very clear instructions and skip patterns that are easy to follow. Its questions should be written at a reading level appropriate for members of the target population. There are several advantages to using a self–administered questionnaire in a tailored health communication program. First, most people are already familiar with answering survey questions in this type of format. Self–administered questionnaires also allow respondents to answer questions at their own pace, and may provide a sense of anonymity in answering questions of a personal or sensitive nature. In general, these questionnaires are also relatively inexpensive to produce and do not require staff time to administer. On the down side, they are less appropriate for populations with very low literacy and can require substantial data entry resources if questionnaires cannot be optically scanned and large numbers of questionnaires (e.g., thousands) must be hand–keyed instead (see chap. 12).

Figure 6.1 shows one page from a self–administered tailoring assessment questionnaire used in the *Partners in Women's Health* (1997–1998) program. This program sought to reduce the burden of heart disease and osteoporosis among menopausal women by increasing medication compliance. This particular page was one of three pages in the questionnaire focusing on hormone replacement therapy.

Administered by an Interviewer

Several tailored health communication programs have used interviewers to administer questionnaires by telephone (Shiffman, Gitchell, & Strecher, 1997; Skinner, Strecher, & Hospers, 1994). Using inbound calling, potential participants can dial a designated telephone number to reach an operator who administers the interview. Using outbound calling, interviewers place calls directly to potential participants to administer the questionnaire to those who are interested or willing to participate in the tailored health communication program. One of the main advantages of using an interviewer–administered questionnaire is that the participant can get immediate feedback from a live person. For example, the interviewer can welcome a new participant to the tailored communication program, answer questions he or she might have and even deliver some tailored counseling based on the participant's answers. Such interaction can help build rapport, trust, and goodwill that may enhance the credibility and effectiveness of the program. Using computer–assisted telephone interview (CATI) software, interviewers do not need to worry about complex skip patterns. Furthermore, participants' responses can be entered directly into a computer database, eliminating the need for an additional data entry step in operating the tailoring program.

The most significant drawback of this approach is its comparatively high cost relative to self–administered and computer–administered programs. Major costs include training interview and supervisory personnel, CATI programming, telephone and computer equipment and service, and promotional costs to generate awareness of the program phone number. These costs may exceed the budget of many tailoring projects, especially those that are of smaller scale. In some settings, such as a clinic where existing staff members already have regular contact with individuals who would be considered potential participants in a tailoring program, a tailoring assessment questionnaire might be administered in face–to–face interviews, instead of being administered over the telephone.

Figure 6.1

Self-Administered Tailoring Questionnaire (Partners in Women's Health, 1997-1998).

For each question, indicate your choice by placing a "✓" or "✗" in the circle beside that response, or write your response in the box beside the question.

Partners In Women's Health

Part 1

1. Are you presently taking oral hormone replacement therapy (HRT)?
   ○ yes   ○ no —————— If no, skip to Part 2 on page 4. ——→

2. How long have you been taking oral hormone replacement therapy (HRT)?
   ○ less than 3 months
   ○ 3-6 months
   ○ more than 6 months but less than 1 year
   ○ 1 year or longer

3. Does your current prescription require that you take HRT every day or on a cycle starting on a certain day each month?
   ○ every day
   ○ on a cycle

4. What type of HRT are you currently taking?
   ○ estrogen
   ○ progestin
   ○ estrogen plus progestin

5. Has your doctor ever changed the type of HRT or the dosage that you take?
   ○ yes   ○ no

6. What were the reasons you decided to start taking HRT in the first place?

	Check all that apply	
	YES	NO
My doctor recommended it.	○	○
I have friends taking HRT who recommended it.	○	○
I wanted to avoid hot flashes.	○	○
I was worried about my risk of heart disease.	○	○
I was worried about my risk of hip fracture or osteoporosis.	○	○
I wanted to reduce my mood swings.	○	○
I thought it would help my depression.	○	○
I was having trouble sleeping.	○	○
I had heard or read a lot about it in the media.	○	○
I wanted to relieve vaginal dryness.	○	○
I wanted to relieve painful intercourse.	○	○

PAGE 1

Administered by Computer

Just as a tailoring assessment questionnaire can be self–administered using a paper–and–pencil format, so too can individuals complete their own questionnaires using a computer. Such computer interfaces include the Internet, free–standing computer kiosks, or even computer–based telephone systems. Internet–based programs can allow individual users to answer questions and submit their data online. A major advantage of this approach is that individuals can receive tailored feedback immediately and in many formats (e.g., text, audio, video), and even print a hard copy if it is desired. Like a CATI system, an Internet–based questionnaire can be programmed to follow complex skip patterns in a way that is transparent to users, thus minimizing respondent burden. The main limitation of an Internet–based assessment is that not everyone who might benefit from a tailored health communication program has access to the Internet. A 1997 Business Week/Harris Poll found that 85% of Internet users are White, and 42% have annual incomes over $50,000 (Hof, 1997). Only 12% of Internet users have an annual income below $15,000, including students. Clearly this is not representative of the general population in the United States, and is especially unrepresentative of populations with the greatest health needs. Despite this present limitation, we believe universal Internet access is approaching, and will provide exciting opportunities for administering tailoring assessment questionnaires through this medium.

Interactive computer programs housed in a kiosk shell have all the advantages of Internet–based questionnaires for gathering data for tailoring purposes but are not as limited by restricted access. Once built, kiosks can be placed anywhere—doctors' office waiting rooms, pharmacies, community centers, inner–city clinics, shopping malls—to reach diverse populations (Strecher, 1998). Kiosks can even be moved around from one location to another. The primary disadvantage to using computer kiosks to administer a tailoring assessment is cost. Not only must an interactive assessment tool be developed, but each kiosk requires computer hardware, a shell, and regular maintenance.

Computers also guide many telephone–based assessment programs. When you place a phone call to a business today, a real person might answer, or you might get something like this:

> If you know the extension of the party you wish to reach, please dial the number now. If you wish to speak to someone in customer service, please press one. If you wish to speak with someone in accounts payable, please press two. If you with to speak with an operator, please press O, or stay on the line.

This is an example of voice–prompted telephone technology, a computer–based telephone program response. From the previous example, one can see how this technology might be applied in administering a tailoring assessment questionnaire: "If you're concerned about gaining weight after quitting smoking, please press one. If you're concerned that you won't be able to deal with stress without smoking, please press two ..." This approach overcomes many of the cost barriers associated with telephone–based tailoring interviews using live interviewers. However, it has several major limitations. First of all, it can take a long time to administer even a relatively brief assessment. Simple tasks like obtaining a person's name, address, city, and state become considerably time consuming for respondents:

> Please spell your first name. For each letter in your name, press the number that contains that letter, then press 1 if it is the first letter on that number, press 2 if it the second letter, press 3 if it is the third letter, and press 4 if it is the fourth letter. For example, for the letter 'A' press 2–1; for the letter 'B' press 2–2; for the letter 'C' press 2–3. When you are finished spelling your first name, please press the pound sign.

All that just to spell your first name! Second, many people have strong negative feelings about these systems, finding them excessively burdensome and associating them with long delays and being put on hold. Finally, there are also important methodological limitations. For example, a well–trained interviewer will always read every response option before asking for a respondent's answer. But using a poorly conceived execution of this technology, it is possible for an impatient respondent to select a particular answer and move immediately to the next question without hearing all the response options for the previous question. This would almost certainly limit the robustness of the tailoring program.

Table 6.3 summarizes the main advantages and disadvantages of each of these methods of administering a tailoring assessment questionnaire. In reading the table, recognize that the advantages and disadvantages are not weighted in terms of their importance, although this would need to happen if the table were used to make program decisions. For example, the difference in development costs between a kiosk–based assessment tool and a paper–and–pencil questionnaire could be $100,000 or more. If a tailored health communication program's budget cannot support development of a computer kiosk, then it really does not matter what other advantages the kiosk approach offers. In other words, the development costs in this case would be weighted much more heavily than other factors. Also, ratings for each method assume that best practices are being used. For example, a voice-prompted system could provide some tailored feedback to the respondent instantaneously after the assessment was completed. Not all voice-prompted systems do this, but because the technology supports this potential, voice prompted systems are rated more favorably on this characteristic.

Table 6.3

Summary of Advantages and Disadvantages of Different Methods of Administering a Tailoring Assessment Questionnaire.

	Method of Administering Tailoring Assessment Questionnaires				
Characteristics	Paper and Pencil	Tele-phone Interview	Internet-Based	Kiosk-Based	Voice Prompted
Data entry costs	Variable	Lower	Lower	Lower	Lower
Development costs	Lower	Variable	Higher	Higher	Higher
Personnel costs to administer	Lower	Higher	Lower	Lower	Lower
Respondent burden	Lower	Lower	Lower	Lower	Higher
Threat to respondent confidentiality	Lower	Higher	Lower	Lower	Lower
Time required to provide feedback	Longer	Shorter	Shorter	Shorter	Shorter
Suitability of complex skip patterns	Less	More	More	More	More
Suitability for low-literate groups	Less	More	Less	More	More
Suitability for populations with limited access to technology	More	More	Less	Variable	More

Abstracting Data from Existing Sources for Use in a Tailoring Program

As mentioned in the introduction to this chapter, not all data for tailoring must come from a tailoring assessment questionnaire. In some cases, data may be obtained from existing sources, such as medical records. For example, a very simple tailoring program to promote mammography might send customized reminder letters to women based on their age, date of their last mammogram, and whether or not their doctor had ever recommended they get a mammogram. Such data could easily be obtained by reviewing women's medical records. Tailoring based on existing data is often quite limited because one has little or no control over the types of data that are routinely collected and because these data are being collected for reasons other than application to a tailored health communication program. A second concern with such data is its currency and accuracy. If the information contained in these records is outdated or inaccurate, the specific tailored messages selected for a person may be inappropriate.

Conclusion

When this step in the development process is completed, you should have a complete set of questions and response choices to be used in the tailored health communication program. These questions should be worded and ordered in the same way they appear in the assessment and pretested among members of the target population (see chap. 13). The resulting questionnaire can then be laid out for printing, or programmed into a computer application to be administered to participants via telephone, Internet, or kiosk. Once the tailoring assessment questionnaire is finalized, the process of developing message concepts and a tailored message library can begin. Chapters 8 and 9 describe these next steps.

CHAPTER 7

Developing Design Templates

A tailored page is similar to the front page of a standard newspaper. The front page contains set spots for the placement of stories, advertisements, and graphics. Day after day, its layout and many of its graphic elements remain the same; only the story text, story–specific graphics, and advertisements change. A tailored page is the same, except that rather than content changing from day to day, it changes from person to person. In both cases, the design and layout information needed to assemble each version of the page, from day to day or from person to person, is determined by a design template. For a tailored feedback unit, the design template is an empty copy of the tailored feedback unit, containing all fixed elements (generic text and graphics that remain the same from person to person), and indicating the location and characteristics of tailored message blocks (text and graphics that change from copy to copy). Each tailored feedback unit in a tailored health communication program has a single design template. This template serves as a guide to the creation of actual message content (see chaps. 8 and 9) and the development of the tailoring software (see chap. 11).

In this chapter we discuss the development of this design template (see Fig. 7.1). First, let's clarify its purpose and show how it fits in the overall tailored health communication program. The design template functions primarily as a guide to development of other parts to the tailored health communication program. A complete design template will:

- Provide a visual framework in which the message developers can visualize their messages. To this end, it should accurately convey what a final tailored page produced for a single individual will look like.

- Provide an organizational framework for message developers to see how each message block relates to the entire tailored feedback unit and to each of the other message blocks. To do so, the design

Figure 7.1

Empty and Full Pages.

template must show where each message block appears on each page of the tailored feedback unit and provides general information about the topic of each message block.

- Guide tailoring software developers in the layout of pages that the software prints. The template must indicate the exact location and boundaries for each message block and how the text and graphic content of each message block should be formatted.

- Contain completely designed and rendered pages for printing stationery—the preprinted paper stock on which the tailored messages will be printed. The final design template should indicate colors and other printing specifications and be ready for output to press.

To accomplish these objectives, we develop a comprehensive design template that contains three main elements. These include: (a) A visual design that describes the overall feel and look of the final printed piece and provides details about the format of the graphic elements and typesetting on the pages; (b) An organizational framework that delimits the location of the individual message blocks on each page; and (c) Stationery page files containing the preprinted elements—background graphics and text that will be preprinted before tailored messages are printed—ready to be output and reproduce.

Let's take a closer look at each item (see Fig. 7.2).

Developing the Visual Design

Good visual design can be as important to the success of a tailored communication piece as the message content itself. A good design draws readers into the communication. This is a constant challenge in public health, where messages often focus on topics that are initially uninteresting or even off–putting to the reader. Once the intended reader becomes an actual reader, good visual design makes the information more understandable and helps the reader retain the content (Wileman, 1993). To accomplish this, we must design each tailored feedback unit to interest the reader, help the reader navigate content and focus on key information, reinforce and reiterate the content of the messages, and present the most important information in a memorable and useful format. The final product of this part of the design template is a verbal description that captures and conveys the nature of the visual design, along with sketches showing how elements are arranged on each page and highlighting specific visual elements (typesetting, graphic style, etc.).

Making It Interesting

Developing a design that is interesting begins with getting to know the audience. Doing so requires resisting the usual tendency to develop a design that is interesting to us, or, when we recognize that the target audience is different from us, to turn to popular culture and advertising for inspiration.

Figure 7.2

The Three Pieces of a Design Template.

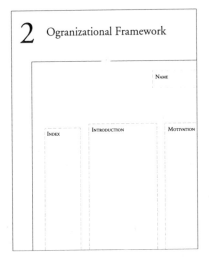

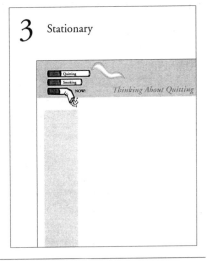

Each population served has distinct interests in its own right. One of the best ways to capture these interests is to research existing communication materials designed for the audience. This begins by developing loose profiles of likely readers —their demographic, educational, and cultural characteristics—reading what they read, and copying the best elements in these materials.

For example, in developing a visual design for a tailored feedback unit about smoking cessation, our first question is, "Who is the reader?" If we determine that she is likely to be an African–American women in her 50s, living in rural North Carolina, we will then want to know what types of communication women like this are most likely to read, watch, or otherwise use. Local newspapers and church newsletters may stand out. We will also want to know how each of these items is received by this population. Otherwise, we run the risk of simply recreating poorly received materials. Gathering together church bulletins and small–town newspapers and assessing the reaction to these materials (by discussing them with individuals from the target population) may lead us to develop a design that is simple, not fancy or trendy in style (not a glossy Madison Avenue product), and that uses highly recognizable iconographic visuals, such as highly characterized people or symbols like question marks or light bulbs. Such a design may not be interesting to many people, but if we did our homework correctly, the visual selected is likely to be received as familiar and legitimate educational material by readers from our target population. We've accomplished the first objective: gaining interest.

Making It Easy to Navigate and Focus

Getting lost in a novel may be a good thing, but getting lost in health communication materials probably is not. A good novel has a story that is compelling enough to make the reader turn the page simply to learn more and to remember the story simply because of its profundity or artistry. In contrast, most health communication relies on the reader's existing (or provoked) interest in learning specific information, and subsequently his or her satisfaction that the information is indeed there. To this end, it is critical to create a visual design that makes it easy to navigate the various messages and to hone in on the important elements in each message.

The first step in making a tailored feedback unit easy to follow is to develop a simple grid for the pages—an invisible pattern of guides that indicates the vertical and horizontal boundaries of elements on a page. The grid is used to determine the placement of each text column, heading, graphic, or other element. Once a grid that suits the content has been developed, it should be reused on most or all other pages in the tailored feedback unit. Doing so lets the reader know that stories will always start here and flow to there, graphics in this spot relate to stories in that spot, and so forth. The goal is to allow the reader to browse naturally and comfortably without having to learn a new layout with each turn of the page. Creating a standard grid can be challenging for tailored pages.

Because each final printed (and tailored) piece is an assemblage of a few messages chosen from hundreds or thousands of messages, the final page should vary considerably from copy to copy. The grid developed has to be flexible enough to accommodate all possible message choices and combinations for a single page. A very simple grid works best (see Fig. 7.3).

Within the macrolevel organization defined by the page grid, we can develop visual cues to help the reader select the messages they are most interested in reading first. Iconographic elements are especially useful for this. For example, using a checkbox icon to represent a list of things to do will make the purpose of this to–do message obvious with little or no reading. Linking different colors to different topical areas—green for messages about positive alternatives to smoking, red for messages about situations to avoid—provides further cues. Photos of a doctor can indicate a message from an authority on the topic. Dropping a giant question mark behind a list of question–and–answer messages draws attention to this familiar format.

Finally, for each message block, we can create visual cues to highlight the most important information. A text pullout—an emphasized phrase or sentence from a message that has been reproduced in larger type next to or on top of the message—can summarize the gist of the message before it is read, or reinforce it afterwards. Likewise, a bulleted list may be used to summarize the most important content, such as a set of action steps. These techniques make it easier to follow and focus during initial reading and help reiterate the most important content during subsequent rereading or reference to the communication piece.

Reinforcing the Content

Once the reader has zeroed in on a message, our objective is to reinforce its textual content with nontextual elements. To this end, the visual design should match the messages, employing techniques and using graphic elements that say what the message says. To do so, we develop a design that mimics the feel of the messages, reinforcing the messages from the background rather than taking center stage, and containing graphic elements that clearly supplement individual concepts and key points of a given message or set of messages.

Mimicking the feel of the messages starts with determining the level of formality, seriousness, authoritativeness, and modernity of the messages. The choice of type style, colors, and page structure (e.g., square and weighty, or light and airy) should reinforce this feel. For example, a serious

Figure 7.3

Sample Page Grids.

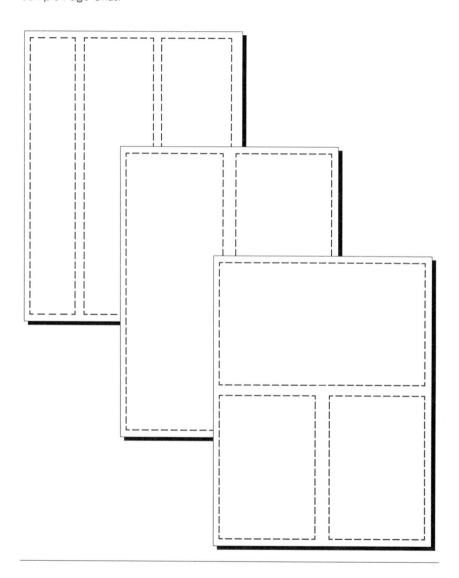

message about the risks of smoking will demand a serious design with a formal, rigid, layout of elements, a schoolbook–like type style, and limited use of color. An upbeat message about the positive effects of living smoke–free can be backed up by a fun design with vibrant colors and whimsical layout. One of the most important and often overlooked tools for conveying the feeling of a message is type style. There are thousands of typefaces available, each one originally developed out of a need to convey a specific feeling. Experimenting with typefaces is an inexpensive and relatively safe way to reinforce content with visual design. However, be cautious not to overdo it by mixing too many different typefaces in the same communication. This can be distracting to readers and ultimately compromise the effectiveness of messages.

Keeping the visual design in the background and letting the messages take center stage sounds contrary to the way we normally think of visual design—as an artistic endeavor. In advertising, design may be a separate element distinct from the content and sometimes even intended to obscure or confuse the message. Health communication, on the other hand, relies on design simply to reinforce and reiterate the content. Because most health communications are content–intensive (even those that are primarily intended to motivate), the visual design often needs to be understated to avoid adding work to the process of reading and understanding. The best visual designs for tailored communication seems secondary to the content, and often goes unnoticed. Perhaps the most useful way of accomplishing this ideal is to develop the initial layout of a tailored feedback unit with only the initial versions of each message on the page (i.e., with no color or other graphic elements). Then, add in the design elements, paying attention to how each new element adds to or detracts from the message. Use colors that are complementary and subtle. Limit typefaces to a few well–matched ones. Develop a single style of illustration or graphic and use it throughout.

Finally, ensuring that illustrations and photographs supplement rather than detract from the messages begins with becoming thoroughly familiar with the messages themselves. The objective is to choose and develop graphics that illustrate the concepts in each message or message concept. For example, a message about the cost of smoking may contain a giant dollar sign in a light color behind the text. At a minimum, the graphics should not clash with the message content. A message focusing on the special issues of African–American women trying to quit smoking should not be backed up by a photograph that prominently features a Euro–American man. Whenever a graphic element is needed and no good matching candidate can be developed, a good middle–ground alternative is to use a purely decorative graphic (containing no identifiable message in itself). For example, a flower border can lend visual appeal while reinforcing the calm feeling intended to be conveyed by the overall tailored feedback unit. That said, keep purely decorative graphics to a minimum. Too many of them will make the final printed piece look busy and amateurish.

Making It Memorable and Usable

In health communication, the ultimate goal is often a change in personal behavior. Accomplishing this not only requires providing information to an individual, but also conveying it in a memorable and usable way. A good visual design can go a long way toward accomplishing this goal. Making a message memorable means making it stand out in a bold way. Some useful techniques for this include the following:

- Developing a bold layout that contains a message within generously empty space (also called *white space*);
- using typeface combinations that make key points, headlines, or pullouts stand out dramatically;
- creating pullouts that can literally be pulled out of the printed page, such as a perforated card;
- using humor;
- using vivid and attention–catching graphics; and,
- using bright, contrasting colors to differentiate contrasting message topics.

For example, a boldly presented message about the financial costs of smoking may include a dollar amount (tailored to the number of cigarettes the reader smokes each day) printed in heavy type in the middle of a seemingly blank page with a list of items that could be purchased for that amount of money printed in small type at the bottom of the page. This design would not only make the dollar amount memorable, but through the process of revealing the list of items, it could also make the material benefits of quitting memorable.

A note of caution: The temptation to become memorable by being bold must always be balanced by the previous imperative—the need to reinforce rather than overpower the message. Boldness for the sake of boldness may leave the reader with something to remember, but unless it is a remembrance of the intended health message, we have failed to accomplish our objective and may have hindered it. Be bold, but make sure it truly reinforces the content.

Principles of Visual Design

Though most program planners do not have the experience or intuitive design talent of a professional graphic artist, there are a few key design principles that can demystify the design process. By having a good understanding of the target population and being familiar with the message content, one can apply these principles to ensure good visual design for a tailored feedback unit.   The principles include:

- Know your audience. Ideally, this would be an individual for whom the design would be tailored along with the message content. In reality, however, a design is usually developed based on a profile of a likely reader.

- Know the purpose and specific objectives of the tailored feedback unit. Try to have a single, overriding purpose. If there are multiple objectives, separate them into multiple pages or other distinct units within the tailored feedback unit.

- Choose a single feel for the tailored feedback unit and stick with it. If it is authoritative, be authoritative, not whimsical.

- Don't fill the page. Empty space is as important as occupied space. It makes the page more approachable and lends emphasis to the message contained there.

- Be consistent with illustration or photographic style. Settle on a single level of visualization (from realistic to iconographic) and a single graphic style (e.g., realist or abstract, color or black and white, line art or filled, avant garde or traditional).

- Be consistent with type styles. Limit the design to a few well–chosen type styles in each tailored feedback unit.

- Use bold special effects sparingly. Reverse type, shadows, and other effects made easy by computer–based design can be great, but too much of this makes the page difficult to read.

- Use color purposefully, if not sparingly. Aside from the cost savings, doing so can lend cohesiveness and looks professional.

The End Product

The end product of this piece of the design template is a verbal description of the visual design of the tailored feedback unit, along with sketches that demonstrate specific visual elements. The final verbal description should include information about:

- The overall feel of the piece—whether it is authoritative, fun, lively, fast–paced, stoic, or other adjectives that convey the feeling that the reader should have upon initial reading.

- The grid or other pattern being employed to tie together elements on each page—that is, the margins, the number of columns on each page and the position of headlines, messages, and graphics.

- The type styles to be used—specific typeface, sizes, and styles of the various headline and body–text segments.

- The graphic style to be used—whether it will include illustrations or photos; the level of realism in illustrations, whether they will be iconographic, illustrative, or decorative; and any stylistics applied to graphics.

- Colors to be used—which colors and their purpose and location throughout the document.

- Characteristics of the paper to be used, such as size, weight, color, and so forth.

For example, the visual design of our smoking cessation newsletter (see Fig. 7.4) is described as follows:

The newsletter is designed to be authoritative and teacherly. Important health issues related to the reader's smoking are stated boldly and distinctly on each page and are followed by messages that explain and help the reader absorb the health issue and consider behavioral changes related to it.

Messages are laid out in a five–column grid with one–inch margins on each side of the page, one inch at the top of the page, and one–and–a–half inches at the bottom of the page. Each message block spans two columns on either side of the page. The unused column in the center of the page is reserved for graphics that link the messages on either side of it. A single graphic spans all five columns along the bottom of the page (below the messages). Headlines begin at the top margin as well as half way down the page. Pullouts are used once on each page, with pullout text spanning a single column and associated white space around each pullout spanning three columns.

Headline text is a sans–serif typeface with rounded edges, sized 16– to 20–point, with very tight leading. Body text is set in a serif typeface with rounded edges, sized 12 point, with moderate leading. Pullouts are set in a heavy black serif typeface, sized 26– to 30 point, with very loose leading.

Graphics are limited to original illustrations. They are located in the center column and the bottom of the page only and do not overlap or merge with text. All graphics are illustrative and clearly relate to an adjoining message. Style is bold ink lines with flat, shaded fills.

Three colors are used — burgundy red, royal blue, and black. Illustrations use blue and red. Lines separating pullouts and messages are red. Message text is black (laser printed).

The newsletter will be printed on bright white, matte finish, coated 100–pound text stock. This will make colors and text appear extra crisp but not glossy, and the overall piece will be weighty and seem important.

Developing the Organizational Framework

Once we have developed a visual design that suits the tailored feedback unit's topic and the reader's characteristics, we turn our attention to organizing the placement of the messages on each page. Each tailored feedback unit contains one or more distinct message blocks. For example, our smoking cessation newsletter contains separate message blocks for an introductory message, a testimonial, and a feature story, among others. The task at hand here is to determine the location to be occupied by those message blocks on the printed page. We do this by creating an organizational framework, which consists of each page of the tailored feedback unit with the location and boundaries of each message block delimited. Once complete, the framework functions as an invisible guide to the placement of each message on each page. The organizational framework should be designed in response to three imperatives: locating the message blocks according to their topics, fitting the visual design just completed (or, more likely, in progress), and fitting the differing lengths of the different message blocks.

Locating the Message Blocks Topically

As with other aspects of the design template, the nature and content of the messages often suggests the location and layout of message blocks. Messages that are related topically should be related spatially. Those that are distinct may be separated, and those that depend on others should follow those others. For example, a combination of self–assessment and goal–setting messages may suggest beginning with a self–assessment message block, following it with motivational and educational message blocks, and concluding with goal–setting message blocks. To make the distinction even more clear, these three topics may be placed on separate pages. A health problem with a clear step–by–step remedy demands a logical, controlled ordering of message blocks that build on each other, whereas a health problem with multiple distinct remedies may be presented in unrelated distinct message blocks, allowing the user to choose the remedy that is right for him or her.

Figure 7.4

Visual Design Sketches.

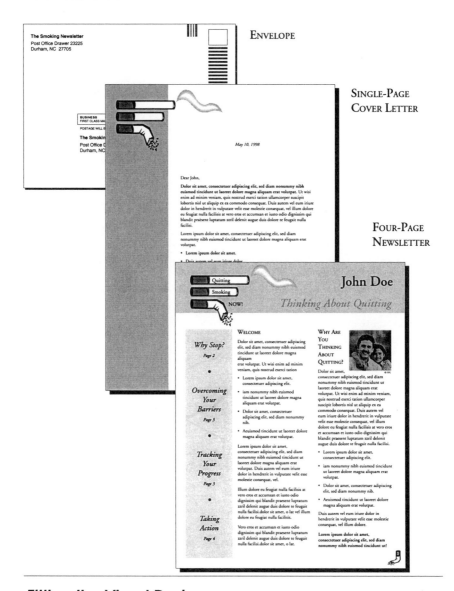

Fitting the Visual Design

The visual design contains organizational elements, such as the grid layout, number of columns per page, horizontal or vertical flow of stories, and amount of white space. These dictate where message blocks can be placed on any given page. Look back at the visual design sketches developed thus far, and choose message blocks that fit each page. In all likelihood, several combinations of message blocks fit the visual design.

Fitting the Message Sizes

Each message block has defined boundaries, usually expressed in number of words of text (or, for a graphic, in actual height and width). When placing message blocks on a page, enough space must be reserved to accommodate the largest possible version of each message block. At the same time, to accommodate the chance of a reader receiving the shortest message in a message block, they must be placed in such a way as to minimize the appearance of unexpected empty space—space reserved for the message but left empty because a smaller version of the message was selected. To deal with this situation, start by organizing the blocks on the pages to fit the longest anticipated message for each message block. Once a reasonable layout has been developed, try out the shortest possible version of each message block. Chances are, message blocks need to be shuffled around to avoid major gaps in the event of multiple short messages. If the messages simply can not be assembled in any reasonable way to fit the pages, it may be necessary to put new limits—larger minimum sizes or smaller maximum sizes—on the messages. Developing the design template concurrently with message concepts makes this easier.

The End Product

The final product of this part of the template is a set of pages—each page of the tailored feedback unit—with message blocks delimited and labeled (see Fig. 7.5).

Creating Stationery Pages

Ideally, everything that is printed on a page, including the messages, page colors, and graphic elements, would be tailored. Photographs that vary from copy to copy (tailored photographs) would be full color. Key text in a message would be printed in a separate color from the rest of the text. Background and illustration colors would vary from copy to copy, reflecting the most appropriate color scheme for characteristics of the reader. If we printed the page using a high–quality color printer, we could have a colorful, fully tailored, professional communication piece.

Figure 7.5

Organizational Framework.

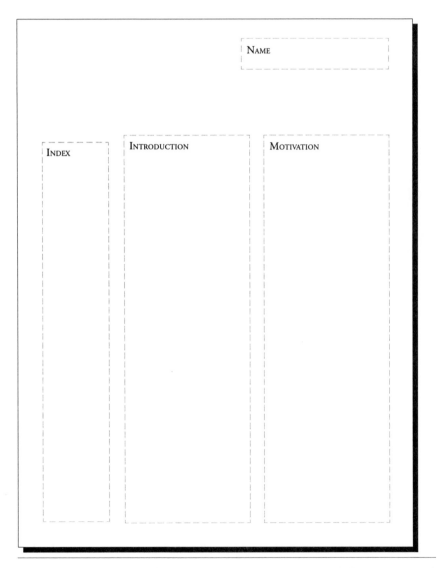

The recent emergence of high–speed digital presses and their associated software is slowly making this vision a reality. However, the cost of single–copy color printing is still prohibitive for all but the most well–funded programs and those reaching only a very small population.

The printing of tailored messages is usually performed on a standard monochrome laser printer. Unfortunately, this can leave us with final tailored documents that are colorless and bland. The cost–effective and professional–looking alternative is to use the monochrome laser printer to print black tailored content on *stationery*—paper that contains elements preprinted in color. The goal is to design stationery that, with tailored content printed on top of it, becomes a single cohesive piece that appears as if all elements—tailored and stationery—were printed in a single step, just like a generic communication piece would be.

In this piece of the design template we determine which stationery elements are to be preprinted on the paper before assembling those preprinted color pages (see Fig. 7.6).

Determining Fixed Elements of the Stationery

By looking back at the organizational framework, we can identify places on each stationery page where fixed elements may be preprinted. As a general rule, the following situations present the best opportunities to create fixed elements:

- If a spot on the page has no tailored content printed there (i.e., no message blocks appear in that spot), a nontailored color element may be preprinted there. For example, a masthead, page number graphic, or decorative graphic may be preprinted in color at that location.

- If all messages of a message block share a common piece of content, such as a title or an associated graphic, and the space to be occupied by the messages is reserved for that message block alone (i.e., it will never be occupied by another message block or item), a graphic associated with the topic of the message block or a colorful headline can be included to make the message appear less like laser–printed text. For example, a color photograph of a doctor may be preprinted in a message in which a doctor answers the reader's questions. In this case, text of the message block would change from copy to copy and the same photo appears no matter which message version was printed.

- If a section of the page is designated to accommodate many different message blocks, but all the message blocks will conform to the same boundaries, then shading or border lines that lie beside, behind, or around the message blocks can be created to separate and highlight the message. For example, this would apply to a page section in

Figure 7.6

Printing Tailored Content onto Preprinted Color Stationery.

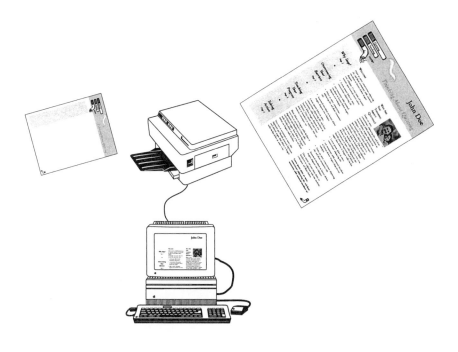

which an individual would receive an introduction or a testimonial—never both—and both would be located in the same place on the page. A page also could be divided into three columns with each column preprinted in a different, very light color. If the message blocks were all laid out in a three–column format, the message blocks will always be printed on top of colored blocks that fall directly behind the final printed messages no matter which specific message blocks appear on the page or which order they appear in.

Some of the more common fixed elements of stationery include mastheads, headlines, graphics that accompany a message (e.g., the advisor's photograph in an advice column), page numbers, tables of contents, decorative graphics (e.g., question marks on a question–and–answer page), lines and boxes that function as borders to messages, and colored shading behind messages.

The End Product

The final product of this piece of the design template is a set of stationery pages with fixed elements laid out and with the prepress characteristics (color, screen values, paper stock, etc.) described. This layout is used to reproduce the preprinted stationery (see Fig. 7.7).

Pretesting

As with all aspects of a tailored health communication program, the design template should be pretested. Indeed, at this point, we have our first opportunity to pretest the tailored feedback in a form similar to the final printed piece that readers will receive. To create a version of the communication piece for pretesting, simply lay out a copy of the stationery developed, place an initial version of each message in the spots designated by the organizational framework, and format the messages according to the characteristics of the visual design. Print the pages in color and assemble them as necessary.

During the pretest of the design template, look for elements of the design that are misunderstood, offensive, incomplete, or that otherwise negatively affect the degree to which the feedback module meets the objectives we have set for it. A comprehensive pretest of the template will seek to answer the following questions:

- Is the piece appealing enough to motivate the recipient to begin to read? Is it attractive? Is it attention–getting?
- Does it keep the reader's attention? Does he or she like it?
- Is the layout easy to follow and use?
- Does the design convey the general feeling intended?
- Does the reader identify with the piece as personally relevant and "for me?" Is it credible?

For further information on pretesting see chapter 13.

Conclusion

The process of designing and assembling a comprehensive design template draws equally on creative talents and an understanding of the messages and the health problem and population being addressed. The end result is a template that gives message developers a structure in which to imagine

Figure 7.7

Preprinted Stationery.

their content, gives programmers a description of where messages are printed and how messages are laid–out, and gives program project staff members a set of laid–out pages from which preprinted stationery can be reproduced. Getting there requires a careful and deliberate process of understanding the messages and building appropriate designs that improve them. A healthy dose of creativity and experimentation will help, too.

CHAPTER **8**

Message Concepts

What Do You Want Each Message to Say?

Message concepts are the detailed ideas about what you want to say in each message and how you want to say it. Once a program blueprint and assessment tool have been developed, one can begin writing message concepts. To illustrate the purpose of message concepts, imagine being asked to create an outline for a persuasive speech to be delivered by a local community leader. Because the speech itself will actually be written by someone else, the outline must detail all the important points to be included. When the outline is completed and given to the speech writer, she should have all the information needed to create a persuasive presentation. Ask: "Was everything clearly explained? Were any key points missed? Were the main points emphasized? Were they given the attention intended? Were minor points overlooked? Was the length, format and tone for the speech specified?" These are exactly the kinds of details that must be considered when developing message concepts for tailored health communication programs.

Specific concepts are created for the entire message library—that is, for all possible messages. As is the case in developing any health communication program, the information that has been gathered about the intended audience and the decisions made about which communication strategy to use form the basis for designing tailored messages.

Message concepts are not unique to tailored health communication. They are also used in developing generic and targeted health messages in order to determine the most appropriate message ideas for the intended audience. A fundamental difference, however, is that the concepts for tailored health communication are data driven. No assumptions need to be made about what message ideas are most appropriate for an individual. Message recipients have already revealed what they want or need to hear by completing the assessment tool.

Why Not Just Begin Writing?

Literally hundreds of distinct messages are developed for any one tailored health communication program, and these can be combined in countless permutations. Because the message development task is often quite large, clear direction and organization are necessary. Before writing can begin, the source of data driving each message must be clearly identified. In most cases, the data source or origin is either a response option to a particular question in the assessment tool, a combination of different responses (e.g., a woman who indicates that she is pregnant and is a smoker), or a manipulation or calculation derived from a particular response option (e.g., the amount of money a smoker would save by quitting, depending on how many and what kind of cigarettes they usually smoke). Message writers must consider how one response option differs from another and, consequently, how much the content of one message should differ from the content of another. Equally important, they must always be aware of where a particular message fits in the overall program. Is it presented early or late in the program? How does it relate to surrounding messages? Will the message be reinforced or referred to at a later point? Does it build on earlier messages already delivered?

Consider the case of a tailored weight management program consisting of nine different newsletters distributed to overweight adults over a 6–month period. Included in the program are two different sets of tailored messages, both focusing on a person's motives for losing weight. This topic is addressed in the first tailored newsletter, then again in the sixth. The first tailored messages on motives may be encouraging and supportive. They may be surrounded by, and complement, messages designed to help participants overcome barriers to starting a weight–loss program, and adjust unrealistic expectations about weight loss. In contrast, the second set might reinforce the person's commitment to behavior change. This set may be surrounded by messages addressing triggers to overeating. So even tailored messages on the same topic, in the same program, may be quite different.

Messages in a single communication should be complementary and hold a common theme. In other words, no messages are acontextual. Each has a defined place in a broader set of messages designed to meet a specific health improvement objective. Detailing the what, when, where, how, and why for each message prior to actual writing results in messages that are strong, poignant, and better integrated.

As previously described, tailored health communication requires developing large volumes of intervention materials. Because a tailored message library may consist of hundreds or even thousands of health messages, the writing task is often accelerated by using a writing team. As is true of any successful team endeavor, clear communication is a key. By organizing message concepts ahead of time, the left hand knows what the right is doing, and duplication of effort is avoided. When writing message concepts, remember that another team member may write the actual message itself. Thus, all details of the ideas for a particular message should come across clearly in the message concepts.

Generating Ideas

Generating ideas for messages should be a group process. Brainstorming about messages and ways to present them (including format and tone) can stimulate creativity. Team members, including message writers and template designers, should come to the group with a firm understanding of the program objectives and of results from the background research. For each separate tailored feedback unit in the overall tailored communication program, the group should thoroughly discuss the details of each message block. (Recall that a *message block* is a set of messages with a common communication objective but varying main points and concepts. An individual participant is matched to receive only one message from each message block.)

Topics for discussion include the content or communication objective for each message block and the appropriate length, format, and tone for each message. Redundancy between messages can only be eliminated with well–coordinated planning. The data source for each message must also be identified. This is usually accomplished by matching messages to questions in the assessment tool. As discussed in chapter 7, it is also advantageous to consider the page–design layout of the overall communication (i.e., what messages go where) as a team. Discussing the rationale for where specific messages fit in the overall program gives team members a better idea of how to present each message. Carefully evaluating the pros and cons of different message ideas results in a more highly polished health communication program with messages that are useful and interesting.

Message Concept Booklets

One method of organizing message concepts for a tailored health communication program is to create message concept booklets. Using this approach, every message block in a tailored communication will have its own message concept booklet. The first page of the message concept booklet provides organizational direction for the message block, including the project title, the location of these messages in the overall program (e.g., newsletter 2, page 3), the message topic, the overall communication objective for the entire message block, message parameters, and message characteristics (see Fig. 8.1). Page two of the message concept booklet consists of the program framework so that writers will be aware of surrounding messages, including where and how this particular set of messages fits into the overall program (see Fig. 8.2).

Page three of the message concept booklet lists all possible messages in the message block (see Fig. 8.3) and the conditions under which each would be received. For any given message, missing data are always a possibility because respondents may not answer every question in tailoring

---

Figure 8.1

Message Concept Booklet, Page 1.

Project: Project title

Material: Intervention medium (i.e. newsletter, web page, etc.)

Location: Where message falls in program (i.e. nltr. 2, page 3)

Message: Message topic

I.   **Communication objective**

What is the intended effect of this message?

II.   **Message parameters**

Type: Type of tailoring employed (i.e. tailored text, tailored graphic, micro-tailoring, etc.)

Length: Approximate number of words per message.

Origin: The source(s) of data driving this particular tailored message. Which specific questions in the assessment tool provide the basis for these messages?

Other: Any special conditions related to the presentation of the messages that the author(s) need to know about before writing begins.

III.   **Message characteristics and content**

Format: How will the information or skills be presented?

Theory: What behavioral theory or empirical evidence provides rationale for use or presentation of these messages?

Tone: What are the emotional or cognitive characteristics of the messages? What response is the message expected to elicit?

Figure 8.2

Message Concept Booklet, Page 2 (Template).

Newsletter One

Introduction

Word count: 230

Format: straight text

Tone: informative

Beliefs	Self efficacy
Word count: 150	*Word count: 150*
Format: poll results	*Format: bullet points*
Tone: reinforcing	*Tone: empowering*

Figure 8.3

Message Concept Booklet, Page 3.

Feedback variables (all possible messages within the message set)

- Response to question X = 1 THEN message 1 provided
- Response to question X = 2 THEN message 2 provided
- Response to question X = 3 THEN message 3 provided
- Continue until all response options are exhausted
- If participant did not respond to question X, THEN message 4 (a default) provided

assessment questionnaires. Thus, consideration should be given to developing or assigning a default message that program participants would receive in the event that they did not answer a particular question in the tailoring assessment. In some cases, more than one default message is warranted.

Figure 8.4

Message Concept Booklet, Subsequent Pages.

Message Title:

Message number or feedback variable number:

Main issue: What problem or issue is indicated by this particular response?

Message concepts: What are the main points, strategies, or skills to be communicated in this message?

••

Message:

The actual tailored message goes here.

A major advantage to identifying all possible messages at this early stage is that this allows more detailed planning for the volume of messages that will need to be developed. Furthermore, it should help eliminate surprises when testing the accuracy of the algorithms (see chap. 5), because all messages will be accounted for from the start.

Subsequent pages in the message concept booklet pertain to the distinct messages within the message block. For each individual message, the main issue is defined and multiple message concepts are identified. On completion, the framework is set for message writing (see Fig. 8.4).

Defining Message Parameters: How Do You Want to Say It?

Types of Tailored Messages

Types of messages found within a tailored health communication program include tailored message blocks (text or graphic), standard message blocks with microtailoring, and tailored message blocks with microtailoring. These different types of messages are presented here in order of increasing complexity and specificity.

A *tailored message block* is a set of messages with a common communication objective but differing main issues and message concepts. The format, length and tone of the messages in a single message block may be the same, but the content is distinctly different. This is sometimes referred to as macrotailoring because an entire chunk of text or graphic is written to address a particular response. Individuals will receive the one message block that is most appropriate for them based on their response to one or more questions in the tailoring assessment tool.

Figure 8.5 is an example of a tailored message block. The communication objective in this case is to encourage the participant to take steps toward reducing dietary fat intake. Messages are tailored based on the most prominent source of fat in the person's diet. Message one is for a person

---

Figure 8.5

Macrotailoring: Three Tailored Messages within a Single Message Block.

Message 1: *(for person whose primary source of dietary fat is meats)*
Trimming the fat...
You don't have to give up meat to eat less fat, just be smart about the kinds of meat you choose, and the way you prepare it. Here are a few tips to help you get started:

- Choose cuts of meat such as "loin" and "round"—they are the leanest.
- Trim any visible fat off meat before cooking.
- When cooking meat, bake, broil, grill or microwave it. Avoid frying.
- Eat smaller portions. A 3 ounce serving is best—that's about the size of a deck of cards or the palm of a woman's hand.
- Remove the skin from chicken or turkey, and choose white meat over dark—it's lower in fat.

Message 2: *(for person whose primary source of dietary fat is dairy products)*
Trimming the fat...
You don't have to give up dairy products to eat less fat, just be smart about the kinds of dairy products you eat and cook with. Here are a few tips to help you get started:

- Eat 3 or fewer eggs per week, or use egg substitutes.
- If a recipe calls for cream or whole milk, use skim or 1% milk instead.
- Use fat free sour cream and cream cheese in cooking and in baking.
- When cooking vegetables, use a vegetable spray like Pam instead of butter.
- Use freshly grated Parmesan cheese instead of cheddar or Swiss—you'll use less, but still get the flavor of cheese.

Message 3: *(for person whose primary source of dietary fat is fried foods)*
Trimming the fat...
You don't have to give up all the foods you enjoy in order to eat less fat, just start eating more low fat foods that aren't fried. Here are a few tips to help you get started:

- Like the taste of fried chicken but want less fat? Try baking a breaded skinless chicken breast—it's tasty and low in fat!
- Instead of chips and french fries, try low fat snacks like pretzels, air popped popcorn, or light potato chips.
- Want some cookies? Reach for vanilla wafers, ginger snaps, or fig bars—all 3 are low in fat.
- Cut the fat in desserts you make yourself by using 2 egg whites when your recipe calls for 1 egg. Also, use margarine instead of butter.

Figure 8.6

Microtailoring.

Micro-Tailored message with all possible response options:

This newsletter has been prepared especially for you, based on the information you provided in the HealthQuest enrollment survey. It contains advice and ideas *specific to your needs*, designed by national medical experts, health researchers, and other Questran users like yourself.

Over the next three months, your HealthQuest newsletters will **{IF I_PA.leisure=1 AND I_PA.PADL=0 THEN** show you ways to keep up the good work you're already doing with exercise, **ELSE IF I_PA.leisure=0 AND I_PA.PADL=1 THEN** show you ways to maintain the physical activity you've already built into your daily routine, **ELSE IF I_PA.leisure=1 AND I_PA.PADL=1 THEN** show you ways to keep up the good work you're already doing with exercise, **ELSE IF I_PA.leisure=0 AND I_PA.PADL=0 AND IF I_PA.total≥1 THEN** show you ways to build more physical activity into your daily routine, **ELSE IF I_PA.leisure=0 AND I_PA.PADL=0 AND I_PA.total=0 THEN** show you ways to get started building physical activity into your daily routine, **END IF} {IF I_fatLevel=1 AND I_fatMainProb=1 THEN** cut down on high fat meats, the leading source of fat in your diet, **ELSE IF I_fatLevel=1 AND I_fatMainProb=2 THEN** cut down on high fat dairy products, the leading source of fat in your diet, **ELSE IF I_fatLevel=1 AND I_fatMainProb=3 THEN** cut down on fatty seasonings, the leading source of fat in your diet, **ELSE IF I_fatLevel=2 THEN** continue with the low-fat diet you're eating, **ELSE IF I_fatLevel=1 AND I_fatMainProb=0 THEN** cut down on the high fat foods in your diet, **END IF} {IF I_FVlevel=1 THEN** and add more fresh fruits and vegetables to your food choices. **ELSE IF I_FVlevel=2 THEN** and make sure you keep choosing plenty of fresh fruits and vegetables. **END IF}** Interested? Read on!

Actual Message: (for person: currently exercising, high fat diet, primary fat source meats, usual intake of fruits and vegetables less than adequate)

This newsletter has been prepared especially for you, based on the information you provided in the HealthQuest enrollment survey. It contains advice and ideas *specific to your needs*, designed by national medical experts, health researchers, and other Questran users like yourself.

Over the next three months, your HealthQuest newsletters will show you ways to keep up the good work you're already doing with exercise, cut down on high fat meats, the leading source of fat in your diet, and add more fresh fruits and vegetables to your food choices. Interested? Read on!

whose primary source of fat is meat products. Message two is intended for those whose primary source of dietary fat is dairy products, and message three is intended for those whose primary fat source is fried foods. The data source in all three cases is an individual's responses to a dietary assessment tool. By tailoring on this variable, we are able to provide feedback that specifically addresses the source of fat most problematic for that person. Further, the information provided is not clouded by messages that are

Figure 8.7

Tailored Graphics.

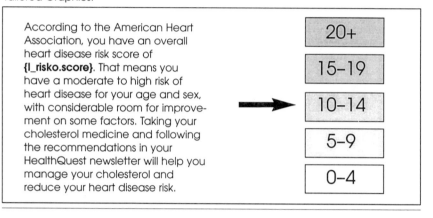

Figure 8.8

A Straight Narrative Tailored Message (for someone who has identified health as a motive to quit smoking).

Here's to your health! As soon as you quit smoking, your body begins the process of healing itself. Within 12 hours of having your last cigarette, your body is working hard to clean the carbon monoxide and nicotine out of your system. Then your heart and lungs will begin the process of healing themselves. Every day that you don't smoke gives your body the chance it needs to heal itself. By quitting, you're improving your chances for a longer life, and those extra months and years will be healthier and more productive ones for you. Most people realize that quitting smoking will reduce their risk for lung cancer. But did you know that by quitting, you will also reduce your risk of death from heart disease, stroke, chronic bronchitis, emphysema, and other cancers, too? Your whole body is affected by nicotine, and your whole body will be glad you quit!

irrelevant to the person. For example, a woman who is lactose intolerant and cannot eat or drink dairy products would never receive information encouraging her to reduce dietary fat by cutting back on dairy products.

Graphics such as pictures, symbols, tables, or graphs may be tailored in much the same way as text. Often, tailored graphics may accompany tailored text. For example, in a health communication program promoting physical activity, one may choose to focus on barriers to physical activity and tailor on the person's preferred activity. One participant may receive tailored text about walking, whereas another may receive a message about aerobic exercise, and yet another may receive a message about swimming. Accompanying the text may be a picture or graphic of that

Figure 8.9

Interactive Exercise (self-scoring diet quiz tailored on stage of readiness to make diet changes).

HOW AM I DOING?

In the last newsletter, we gave you some ideas about ways you could continue to eat healthier. Since you were already thinking about making those changes, let's check your progress!

In the last month...

I checked my snacks and convenience foods for hidden fat.	YES	NO
I got vitamin A through yellow–orange and dark green fruits and vegetables.	YES	NO
I changed one of my regular dinners to a lower fat meal.	YES	NO
I read a new food label.	YES	NO
I stuck with my healthy eating changes for more than two weeks.	YES	NO

SCORING. How many "yes" answers did you circle?:

0   Think about making just one change and sticking to it. Even a small change can help.

1   You've taken the first step! Now turn one of your "no" answers into a "yes."

2   You've got a good thing going now, so keep it up!

3   You're over the halfway mark! Stick with these changes and add some more.

4   A near-perfect score! That's a great sign of how well you do in the future.

5   Great work! You've made changes and stuck with them. Keep it up!

particular activity, better yet, of a person overcoming a specific barrier to carry out that activity. Some tailored communication programs have even tailored graphics and photographs to a person's age, sex, and race (Skinner, 1994).

A *microtailored message* is essentially one message with small but important variations. Microtailoring is generally used when only a few words or short phrases differentiate one message from another in a given message block. Computer–programming language is inserted into the text of the message in order to indicate the linkage between the tailored phrase and the participant's response to a particular question on the tailoring assessment. This allows for multiple variations of a single message without the need for writing out the dozens or hundreds of different versions of a single tailored message. Figure 8.6 is an example of a microtailored message taken from a cholesterol management newsletter. The main objective for this message is to introduce the tailored newsletter and explain what the newsletter has to offer the participant. In this single message, there are

Figure 8.10

A Tailored Graphic (for someone who doesn't read labels regularly and whose primary source of dietary fat is dairy products).

LET'S MAKE A DEAL

The new nutrition label, "Nutrition Facts," is loaded with helpful information! Did you know the "saturated fat" information helps you eat healthier? Look beyond the "light" or "low fat" advertising claims and check the nutrition label.

If you don't read nutrition labels very often, you might not know that looking at two labels side-by-side tells you which food to buy. Like checking the price, check the label for a good health "deal."

What's a good health deal? Dairy foods tend to be high in saturated fat, which can raise your cholesterol. Make sure the saturated fat number is no more than 1/3 of the total fat per serving. Hint: If the fat in a food (like cheese) stays "hard" at room temperature, that food is probably high in saturated fat.

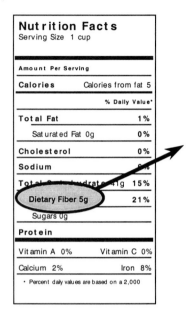

three different instances where microtailoring is employed. First, there are four microtailored phrases on a preferred type of physical activity. These are highlighted in green. The four microtailored dietary fat intake phrases are highlighted in red, and the three microtailored fruit and vegetable intake phrases are highlighted in blue. In combination, this single message has a total of 60 possible variations.

Microtailoring also allows for easier interpretation of continuous variables or open–ended questions (e.g., a person's name) or of numbers (e.g., age, height, weight or cigarettes smoked in an average day). Figure 8.7 shows a microtailored graphic, which provides feedback on heart disease risk. The tailoring is programmed such that the individual's risk score for heart disease is plotted on a continuum. The accompanying message is tailored as well.

Any combination of tailored, microtailored, and, on occasion, non-tailored messages may be employed in a tailored health communication program. Further, macrotailoring and microtailoring may be combined. In other words, microtailoring may be used in a macrotailored message.

Figure 8.11

A Bullet Point Message to Reduce Risk of Falls (for someone who has already experienced a bone break or fracture as a result of osteoporosis).

You've experienced first hand what it is like to break or fracture a bone, so no one needs to tell you how important healthy bones can be! You know that even a minor fall or one wrong step off a curb can result in a serious injury like a broken hip.

There are plenty of things you can do right around your home to reduce your risk of falls and injuries. Here are just a few:

When you're at home:

- Wear sturdy, low-heeled, soft-soled shoes; avoid wearing floppy slippers and sandals.

- Secure your rugs to the floor; avoid using small throw rugs that can slip and slide.

- Remove or secure any loose wires and electrical cords you could trip over.

- Keep halls, stairs, and entry ways well lighted.

- In the bathroom, use grab bars and nonskid rubber mats near the sink and shower.

- In the kitchen, avoid using slippery waxes; watch out for wet floors; clean up spills immediately.

When you're going outside:

- In winter, carry a small bag of rock salt, kosher salt, or kitty litter in your pocket or car. Sprinkle it on sidewalks or streets that are slippery.

- Wear warm boots with rubber soles for added traction.

- If sidewalks look slippery, walk on the grass for better traction.

Once the general logic of providing tailored feedback is understood, the possibilities are limitless.

Length

The length for each set of messages must be coordinated with the development of the design templates (see chap. 7). Each message in a message block should be approximately the same length and follow a consistent format. As a general rule, the word count for each message should vary no more than 10%. This minimizes the complexity of page layout and simplifies the task of writing message concepts and messages. As technology for tailoring evolves, these constraints will become much less important.

Format

Message format refers to the specific tactic or communication approach used to present the tailored information. For example, information on the

Figure 8.12

An Action Plan Tailored Message (for someone who has indicated that they are not currently physically active).

Making a personal activity plan that works!

Here are some simple steps you can take to develop a personal plan for increasing physical activity in your life.

Step 1—Start with a goal. Ask yourself how much activity you'd like to be doing within the next two months— how many minutes, on how many days. Let's call that your "goal."

Step 2—Think about your current level of physical activity. What kinds of exercise are you doing? How many days per week are you doing it? How many minutes per day are you spending doing it? Let's call that your "starting point." If your starting point is no exercise, don't worry. That gives you more room for improvement!

Step 3—Make sure your goal is reasonable. If the gap between your starting point and goal is too big, lower the goal. It's better to set a realistic goal and meet it than to set a goal so high you can't ever get there!

Step 4—Choose a physical activity that you like to do. Some of the best forms of exercise are the activities that are part of daily life. For example, did you know that raking leaves for 30 minutes, shoveling snow for 15 minutes, or pushing a stroller for 1-1/2 miles in 30 minutes gives you the same health benefit as bicycling 4 miles in 15 minutes, or swimming laps for 20 minutes?

The key to making your plan work is to record what you do. The sample 4-week activity chart below shows how your progress can be recorded. The activities are marked by the numbers 1, 2, and 3. If you engage in Activity 1 for 25 minutes, you simply "stack" the number 1 up to the 25 minute level for that day. This will give you a picture of your progress each week. Put the chart in a place you're sure to see every morning—like your bathroom mirror. Fill it out every day. Steady, gradual progress toward life-long changes is what you're after. Small, consistent increases— not big jumps—will get you there!

---

health risks of smokeless tobacco use could be presented as a list of medical facts but could also be presented as a dialogue between a doctor and patient, a testimonial from a victim of mouth cancer, or as an advice column from a teenage girl to the recipient. Variation in format from one message block to another is important in order to maintain reader interest and acceptability. Format in a single message block is usually consistent for the sake of simplified page layout but could in fact be tailored.

The most common and least creative format is *straight narrative* text. Figure 8.8 shows an example of this format. The communication objective here is to reinforce a person's stated motives to quit smoking. Notice that this message is positive, yet serious. Additionally, it is filled with facts about the health benefits of quitting. Straight narrative is most appropriate for messages that are serious and direct or for messages that explain something to the reader.

Figure 8.13

A Resource Referral Message (provides list of resources on stress management for someone who has selected audio tapes as their preferred medium).

Stress Solutions

Are you looking for even more ways to manage your stress? Look no more! The audiotapes listed below can provide you with additional stress management tips. Listen to them in the car on the way to work or at home while you do chores. You can find them at your local library or bookstore.

- How to Relax by Patricia Carrington
- The 10 Natural Laws of Successful Time and Life Management and Proven Strategies for Increased Productivity by Hyrum W. Smith
- Conquer Stress by Bob and Deirdre Griswold
- Best Organizing Tips: Quick, simple ways to get organized and get on with your life by Stephanie Winston
- First Things First by Stephen Covey

On the other end of the spectrum, *interactive exercises* call on the reader to participate, and may be more engaging. Examples of interactive exercises include self–scoring quizzes and checklists. Figure 8.9 provides an example of a self–scoring quiz. Although it can't be illustrated with a single example, the actual questions on the quiz can vary from one person to the next. In other words, they can be tailored to assess specific needs identified by the participant. In this example, simply asking the participant whether he or she has read a new food label or switched to lower fat meals implicitly recommends that they do so. Interactive exercises are particularly useful when skill building is needed and when behavioral rehearsal may be important.

Graphics and illustrations are great for visual emphasis. They are especially useful in presenting quantitative or numeric information, in illustrating a technique or approach, or when asking a participant to model a desired behavior. Figure 8.10 offers an example of a tailored graphic. Text encouraging nutrition label reading and a reduction in saturated fat intake is reinforced by the nutrition facts graphic. A cheese food label was chosen because dairy products were identified as the primary source of dietary fat for the recipient of this message. Saturated fat grams is highlighted for clarity. Tailored illustrations have also been used to demonstrate specific stretching exercises to prevent injury during physical activity and to demonstrate proper techniques for self–breast exams.

Bullet points are often used to highlight key points or to provide specific action steps. They can also be used to provide a quick summary. Figure

Figure 8.14

A Testimonial Tailored Message (for female, less than 35 years old, in complation stage to begin a weight loss program and who has failed at several previous weight loss attempts).

(FOR FEMALE AGE 35)

Hi, I'm Nora. My doctor asked if I would be willing to share my story with others— she thought it might be helpful for me and for other people going through the same thing. So, here I am. I'm 29 years old and I've been heavy for as long as I can remember. Even as a kid. It's not that I haven't tried to lose weight, because I have. Lots of times. I'd like to weigh less, but I guess lately I've just gotten used to being this size. I know that sounds pathetic, but it's the truth. Then, at my annual checkup, Dr. Sheppard asked if I wanted to make a serious commitment to lose some weight and keep it off. She offered to help, and asked me to think about it. Her interest took me by surprise, but it was kind of inspiring, too! Even though my life's a little crazy right now, I decided I'd give it another shot.

8.11 is an example of a bullet point message taken from an osteoporosis risk reduction program. This message is for a person who has already suffered a broken bone or fracture due to osteoporosis. It is designed to help them reduce their risk of falls in the home. Notice that the bullet points are short, direct action statements. Much like bullet points, step–wise approaches and action plans are also a useful format when the participant is called on to take some action. Figure 8.12 provides an action plan message promoting physical activity. Each step in the process builds on the previous steps.

Tailored messages that provide additional resources are particularly desirable when space is limited and the participant is being encouraged to seek further relevant information. This message format may include titles of books, newsletters, web page addresses, phone numbers, and other resources relevant to the outcome of interest. In a web–based health communication project, other resources may include links to additional recommended web sites. Figure 8.13 provides a resource list of stress management audio tapes. By providing further resources, independent research and education on the part of the participant may be supported and encouraged.

Testimonial messages are desirable for issues that may be emotional, sensitive, or personal. Figure 8.14 provides a testimonial message tailored on readiness to begin a weight–management program. The message is personal. Those intended to receive this message are obese women, age 35 and younger who have tried to lose weight before and are thinking about it again. If testimonial messages are successful, participants may identify with the character and thus be more likely to attend to the health

Figure 8.15

A Tailored Advice Column (for someone who has identified time as a barrier to eating less fat).

Dear Marci,	Dear Rushed,
I've been thinking about switching to a low-calorie, low-fat diet. But with my busy lifestyle, it's not always convenient for me to eat healthy foods. How can I make the change when it's so much easier to fit fast food into my schedule? Rushed in Rockford	Choosing pre-packaged foods and fast food restaurants can be very tempting with your hectic lifestyle. But, if it's convenience you're looking for, you don't have to give up your low-calorie and low-fat plans. Today, even fast food restaurants are offering healthier choices like salads, baked potatoes, and grilled meats. For convenient snacks while you're on the go, try pretzels, raisins, or fat-free crackers. Fresh fruits like apples, bananas, pears, and oranges also make easy, portable snacks. For a quick meal when you're at home, try pasta with tomato sauce or steamed vegetables and a broiled chicken breast!

message being provided. Advice columns and question–and–answer interviews also work well for sensitive issues and are also well suited to messages where expert opinion may be important. Figure 8.15 is an advice column message tailored on barriers to eating less dietary fat. In the message, Marci is a registered dietitian and provides expert opinion on nutrition. Additional format ideas that have been used previously in tailored communication programs include recipes, menus, greeting cards, and clip–out coupons. Message formats are limited only by the creativity of the writing team.

Tone

Tone refers to the emotional or cognitive characteristics of a message. Tone is determined by considering the response one hopes to elicit from the reader. For example, a message may be informative, hopeful, encouraging, empowering, reinforcing, understanding, sympathetic, empathetic, challenging, persuasive, serious, warning, or fear arousing. Notice the difference in tone in each of the following messages aimed to reduce childhood lead poisoning. Consider how a person might respond differently to each message.

The first message is informative (see Fig. 8.16). It is not intended to elicit much emotion, but provides facts related to the risk of lead poisoning and what to do to prevent it. The second is a self–efficacy (Bandura, 1977) message (see Fig. 8.17). It is intended to be empowering. The underlying message is, "You're a great parent. You can do this!" It's positive and

Figure 8.16

An Informative Message (for a parent who has reported that his or her child spends a lot of time in the kitchen).

The kitchen can be one of the busiest rooms in your home. Think about all those trips to the fridge for a snack! But, what does the kitchen have to do with lead poisoning? A lot. Has Billy ever dropped a toy on the kitchen floor and then later put the same toy in his mouth? Do family members ever wear shoes inside the house and into the kitchen? If you answered 'yes' to either question, Billy could be at higher risk for picking up lead dust from your kitchen floor. Here's what to do:

• Wash floors with powdered Cascade® or Trisodium Phosphate (TSP);

• Use a separate mop head just for cleaning lead dust, and;

• Don't forget to rinse the floor with water so lead dust won't stick.

encouraging. The third message is persuasive (see Fig. 8.18). Our intent here is to convince the reader of the benefits of doing something that he or she really doesn't enjoy. Finally, the last message is intended to elicit a strong emotional reaction from the reader (see Fig. 8.19). In this case, the tone is serious and may even be fear arousing. Message tone can be applied to the message block as a whole, or, like content and format, can be tailored, differing from version to version.

Overt Versus Covert Tailoring

Participants in tailored health communication programs receive messages based on the information they've disclosed in the assessment questionnaire. Simply by informing them of this fact, messages may appear to be more personally relevant. For example, a message might start out by saying, "You told us 'this' about yourself . . ., so here's what you need to do." This overt tailoring may cue readers to pay attention to the message they're receiving. Conversely, if it is not clear to the participant that the information they provided in the assessment is driving the feedback, the messages may appear to border on invasive. Participants may question: "How do they know so much about me?" Certain issues may be too sensitive for overt tailoring. Messages such as "You told us you're bulimic . . . ," "So you're an alcoholic . . ." or "You told us you're constipated . . .", may be too personal, and may not be well received by the reader. In such cases, covert tailoring may be more appropriate. Testimonial and advice–column formats or posing hypothetical questions are probably better approaches under these circumstances. Importantly, these messages are still tailored, but the tailoring itself is less overt. Even a straight narrative format that is informative but not identifying may be quite effective in these cir-

---

Figure 8.17

An Empowering Message (for a parent who is somewhat confident he or she can clean the house regularly to remove lead dust).

Dust Busters!

You'd do anything to keep Billy healthy. For example, you said you're somewhat confident you can clean the surfaces in your home at least twice a week. That's important, because your efforts to keep your home free of lead dust really can make a difference. When you clean, remember these four tips:

1. Separate: keep a pail, mop and sponge just for cleaning, and a different set for rinsing.

2. Mix 1/8 cup Cascade® or Trisodium Phosphate (TSP), powder form, with 1 gallon of warm water.

3. Change the cleaning solution and the rinse water frequently to avoid using dirty water.

Protect your hands from the detergent by wearing gloves.

---

cumstances. More research is needed to determine the relative effectiveness of overt versus covert approaches to tailoring.

Defining What You Want to Say in Each Message

The "what" in what you want to say refers to the content of the message itself. The content of each message must relate directly back to the program objectives and to the communication objective for the message block. Message content is directed by these objectives, which have been derived from the background research. Thus, each step in the process builds on prior steps. In the end, a final message library is created that is both comprehensive and cohesive. Each message is distinct, not redundant, but fits in the program like a puzzle piece. Without each individual piece, the puzzle is incomplete.

Communication Objective

In deciding on the communication objective for any given set of messages, the program planner defines what he or she expects to accomplish by sending these particular messages and what information or skills will be provided to participants. The communication objective for each message set should directly relate back to the overall program objective. An example of a communication objective might be: to increase the reader's self–efficacy for reducing dietary fat intake or to increase participants' ability to effectively communicate with their doctors.

Figure 8.18

A Persuasive Message (for a parent who reports "dislike" as a barrier to house-cleaning).

But I don't enjoy cleaning!

You aren't so different from most other people! You can probably think of lots of things you'd rather be doing than cleaning your home. Maybe you've put off cleaning so long that the job has become too big. You feel overwhelmed by it. Don't be. It may help if you think of cleaning as several small tasks instead of one big job. Having smaller tasks you can complete quickly and easily will make cleaning less of a burden. You still may not enjoy cleaning, but think of how much its going to help Billy stay healthy. Here are some tips to get you started.

- Reward yourself by fitting in activities you like to do between each task.
- Rotate the chores so you don't get bored as easily.
- Ask others in your family to help out with the household chores.

Figure 8.19

A Fear Arousing Message (for a parent who's child is crawling, but not yet old enough to wash his or her own hands).

Billy depends on you to feed him, bathe him, and protect him from dangers such as lead poisoning. You said he's crawling now. That's great, but it also means he's more likely to come in contact with lead dust that has settled on the floor. If he gets lead dust on his hands, then puts his fingers in his mouth, that's trouble. That's why he needs you to properly wash his hands as often as you can. He's still too young to do it himself. Washing after he plays in dirt and before eating are especially important to prevent lead from getting into his mouth. You can start teaching good washing habits early on by having Billy watch you do them. Frequent hand washing will reduce his risk of lead poisoning.

The Main Issue

The main issue or primary point to be expressed should be stated for each message in a message block. The main issue should always be closely related to the communication objective for the message set. In determining the main issue, consideration must be given to how each message differs from the others. An example of differentiation in main issues can be seen in messages addressing motives to quit smoking. The communication objective for this message set may be to reinforce a smoker's motives for quitting. In the message block, there are several different messages derived from a question about motives for quitting. The main issue for each message addresses a specific motive. Those who have identified improved health as a motive for quitting smoking receive a message about the health benefits of quitting. Those who have said they would

Figure 8.20

Message Concepts and Corresponding Message.

Communication objective: To promote initiation of or compliance with cholesterol lowering medication by presenting realistic expectations of medication effects and recommended follow-up.

Main issue: Participant has not started taking cholesterol lowering medication yet. Can expect drug to lower blood cholesterol by 15 -30 percent. Must continue other lifestyle changes as well.

Message concepts:

- You're planning to start taking a cholesterol lowering medication. Here's what you can expect.
- This drug has been shown to lower blood cholesterol by 15 - 30 percent.
- It may take up to one month before effect can be seen
- Constipation is a possible side effect.
- Should have cholesterol checked 6 weeks after medication is initiated.
- Must continue cholesterol lowering diet.
- Must continue increased physical activity.

****

Message:

If you've not yet started taking your cholesterol lowering medication, but are planning to in the next few weeks, you may be asking yourself: What can I realistically expect it to do for me? All cholesterol lowering drugs are prescribed in conjunction with important life style changes. You must continue your attempts at increasing your physical activity and following a cholesterol lowering diet. Your cholesterol lowering medication is not a replacement for all your hard work. Sometimes diet and exercise alone cannot lower your cholesterol far enough. That is when a cholesterol lowering drug is employed. These medications have been shown to reduce blood cholesterol by 15 to 30 percent. This translates into a 30 to 60 percent reduction of your risk for heart attack!

After you have begun taking your cholesterol lowering medication, you may experience a few temporary side effects. Constipation is the most common. Be sure to sit down with your doctor to discuss side effects you may experience, and concerns that you may have.

Your cholesterol level should be checked again, six weeks after the medication is initiated. It may take up to one month before a cholesterol lowering effect can be seen.

So, be patient. Continue your efforts with lifestyle changes, begin your medication therapy, and watch for progress to evolve.

like to quit smoking in order to look and feel better receive a message reinforcing these benefits. Those who have identified saving money as a motive for quitting receive a message on the financial gains associated with quitting. Although the communication objective is common to all messages in the message block, the main issue and what is said in each distinct message are quite different.

Defining the Details for Each Message

Just as the main issue for each message is different, the message concepts or the details supporting the main issue for each message should also be distinct. One may have several concepts for each message that are consistent with the communication objective for the message set. Each concept must be pertinent to the message. Message concepts should include all information needed to accomplish the main issue—no more, no less. These message concepts give direction to the writer about the exact content of each message. If microtailoring is to be used in a message, this is also where one would communicate that fact (e.g., "Microtailor on current weight and on stated weight–loss goals."). Figure 8.20 provides an example of a set of message concepts for a single message on medication compliance and realistic expectations of medication effects. Read the message concepts first, and then look at the actual message. Note that the message is polished and creative, but the content is the same as that of the message concepts.

Next Steps

As message concepts are completed, message writing can begin. The directions in comprehensive message concept booklets should be clear to any message writer, even those with little knowledge of the project. In the next chapter, we discuss how to write tailored messages.

CHAPTER 9

Writing Tailored Messages: Creating the Feedback

Why is it that most people don't know how to program their VCRs? It came with an instruction manual, didn't it? And what is it about tax forms and legal documents that drive people away? We know the information they contain is important, and we want to understand it but just can't make sense of it. Why? It probably has a lot to do with the way the information is presented. Documents like these are usually dry, using big words and long sentences. They are boring and hard to follow. There is little creativity, use of interesting adjectives, or use of examples—just a lot of technical jargon and legalese. Let's face it, if self–help quit-smoking guides were written like VCR instruction manuals, there would be no takers. Because the skills required to change health–related behaviors are considerably more complex than programming a VCR, it's that much more important to present health information in a clear and engaging fashion.

This chapter is about writing effective health messages for tailored communication programs. It demonstrates the way in which all preparation for writing—from determining program objectives and target audience to writing message concepts—applies to the final product. It addresses special concerns that are unique to tailoring and reviews basic principles that hold true for all print–based health communication.

Pulling it All Together

Writing is the final step in developing tailored health messages. If the team has prepared properly, this task should be very straightforward. Program objectives have been identified, so team members understand the intended purpose of the messages and for whom they are being written. A specific communication objective has also been defined for each topic set. The team knows, for example, which messages are addressing a person's barriers to behavior change, perceptions of health risk, and readiness to change behavior. Team members also know where each message fits on the page and when it is used. Message parameters like length, format, and tone have all been clearly defined, as have the number of words that make up each message, and the way each message is formatted. By writing message concepts, the main ideas addressed in each message have also been defined. Figure 9.1 shows a summary of such background information gathered prior to message writing for a tailored stress management program used in health care and worksite settings.

Given extensive detail like that in Fig. 9.1, the actual task of writing is relatively simple. It's remaining focused that can sometimes be difficult. When writing tailored messages, it is important to closely follow information generated in the developmental steps. Remember, the writer is not writing messages based on what he or she feels like saying but rather based on what the recipient has indicated that he or she wants or needs to hear. Closely adhering to the message concepts that have been developed helps keep the message writer from straying too far from predetermined communication objectives. Fig. 9.2 shows a tailored message that might be developed based on the information contained in Fig. 9.1.

Message Writing 101

When writing tailored health messages—just as when writing any written health communication program—some general principles apply. These include: clearly conveying the purpose of the message, writing to the intended audience, maintaining a consistent writing style, and following standard rules of grammar. When writing or evaluating any message in a program, consider the following:

- What are you writing about?
  The purpose of your message should be clearly conveyed upon first reading.

- Who are you writing to?
  The needs of your intended audience should be understood and addressed.

- How is the information presented?
  All materials must be well organized and must make sense.

What Are You Writing About?

With any printed health communication, the main purpose of the material should be easy to identify. How often have you received written materials that you had to read two or three times before understanding it? It happens

Figure 9.1

An Example Tailored Message with Preliminary Directions.

Project: Stress management in a worksite setting

Material: Tailored newsletter

Location: Newsletter 1, page 2

Message / Topic Set: Skills training

Communication objective:: Reinforce and validate the importance of the training method chosen to help the participant manage stress, and provide resources for obtaining the training

Message Parameters:

Type:	Tailored message block
Length:	@ 180 – 190 words
Origin:	Based on assessment 1, question 5: " Some people feel that skills development training can help them deal with work-related stress. Which, if any, of the following types of training would be of interest to you?"
	response choice 3: "time management skills training"

Message Characteristics:

Format:	Text intro with bullet points
Theory:	People pay more attention to information they're interested in
Tone:	Validating, informational
Main issue:	Participant feels that time management skills training would be helpful in dealing with work-related stress

Message Concepts:

• Time management training will help you learn to prioritize your work

• Doing this can reduce work-related stress

• Ask your employer to send you to a time management workshop

• Try a community college or workplace seminar

• Ask co-workers to help support your efforts

• Start now by setting deadlines and making "to do" lists

all the time when messages are not clear. Sometimes the main purpose of a communication is difficult to discern. This may be because it contains extraneous information, or perhaps because the writer is attempting to convey more than one main point in a single message. It's easy to go off on a tangent and include all kinds of information that seems important but doesn't truly reflect the purpose of that particular message. When preparing to write, ideas may be categorized as information the reader

---

Figure 9.2

Corresponding Message to Figure 9.1.

What would time management skills training do for me?

A lot! Even with minimal training, you can start to make better use of your time. You'll learn to plan ahead for deadlines, prioritize tasks, and find the resources you need to get the job done. Would that help relieve some of the stress you've been feeling at work? To get started, try one or more of these ideas:

- Ask your employer if you can attend a time management workshop. Your workplace may even offer training programs on site.

- Set some rules for yourself. Set weekly deadlines to mark your progress on big projects. Write out a simple "to do" list every morning and work to get through it. Don't take phone calls after 2:00 p.m. A little self-discipline can really save time in the long run!

- Enlist the help of co-workers. Ask them to respect your "work time" by keeping interruptions to a minimum and by scheduling an appointment when they need to talk with you.

- Call your local community center. Self-improvement classes that help to develop time management skills are frequently offered.

(187 words)

---

needs to know, information that would be nice for the reader to know, and information that the writer simply wants to tell. Stick with information that the reader needs to know. Then make the point clear.

Take a look at the health message in Fig. 9.3 addressing the role of salt in high blood pressure. It was taken from a national health promotion program. The communication objective here isn't clear, but assume the objective is to heighten the reader's awareness of the connection between intake of dietary sodium and health risk.

There's a lot of information here—some important, some not so important. The main point of this message is obscured by its level of detail. In striving for comprehensiveness, many health communicators and health educators opt to provide all the details—not just information that the reader needs to know. This frequently occurs at the cost of effective communication. For example, the message in Fig. 9.3 could and should be condensed considerably. Fig. 9.4 provides a reasonable alternative message.

In this second example, a lot of the details are eliminated, but the main point comes across clearly: "Talk to your doctor about salt and your blood pressure." The message is a lot shorter now, but the essential information is still there. Information on other factors that might cause

Figure 9.3

Health Message on Salt and High Blood Pressure.

You might be aware of dietary advice to consume a moderate amount of sodium. Some people mistakenly try to eliminate foods that contain sodium from their diets. But sodium is an essential nutrient, and your diet must supply a small amount of sodium to meet the body's requirements. A common sodium recommendation that you might see is to consume "less than 2,400 milligrams of sodium per day." Other guidelines for sodium exist, however, because it is difficult to identify a single value that is right for everyone. As scientists work to understand more about the role of sodium in health, including how different individuals respond to this nutrient in their diets, the current guidelines for sodium may change.

Most people have heard that excess dietary sodium can be associated with high blood pressure or hypertension. Hypertension is one factor that increases the chances of heart disease and stroke, but the exact causes of high blood pressure and how to prevent it are not fully understood. For certain people who have hypertension, high intakes of salt are linked to their condition. Imbalances in the body of other nutrients like calcium, potassium and magnesium may also play a role in the development of hypertension. Excess intake of calories is a cause of overweight or obesity. Obesity is another factor that can increase your chances of developing hypertension. Researchers are also studying genetic factors linked to high blood pressure. Since high blood pressure can involve different factors for different people, it is best to speak to your physician regarding personal concerns about high blood pressure.

Figure 9.4

Alternative Message on Salt and Blood Pressure.

Talk to your doctor about how salt in your diet could affect your blood pressure. We all need some salt in our diets, but too much salt has been linked to high blood pressure or hypertension (hi-per–TEN–shun). High blood pressure is a serious condition that could lead to heart disease or stroke. The exact cause of high blood pressure isn't fully understood. Your diet plays a role, but other things like your weight and whether or not your parents, brothers, or sisters have had high blood pressure are also important. Talk to your doctor—find out if cutting back on salt is a good idea for you.

high blood pressure such as obesity, other nutrient imbalances, and genetics have been dropped, and for good reason. Although the statements are valid, they are not directly relevant to the issue of sodium and high blood pressure. By providing all these additional facts, the audience may miss the message's main point.

Sometimes the purpose of a message is not clear because the writer has not stated it explicitly enough. Tailored health messages should

---

Figure 9.5

Two Example Messages on Social Support.

Message 1

Studies show that people who have support do better losing weight and keeping it off. Family and friends can provide emotional support. They can boost your self-confidence by listening and giving you words of encouragement. Or they can help with information, like ideas on places where you can exercise or stores where you can find the best selection of low-fat cheeses. Close friends and family members are also great for getting down in the trenches with you, exercising and counting calories.

Message 2

If you haven't done it already, now's the time to start looking around for people who will support your efforts to lose weight. Think about how others' support has helped you in the past. You know support feels valuable and scientific research has proven it works. Studies show that people who have support do better at losing weight and keeping it off. How do you ask for support? Here are a few examples:

- "I've started a walking program. How about walking with me this weekend?"
- "I'm trying to eat healthier foods and exercise. It's hard for me. Can I call you to talk about it if I need to?"

Consider what you need and want from family and friends. Then, ask for it. Let people

---

explain to readers what they need to do, not just what they need to know. Using the active voice (e.g. "take your medication three times per day") rather than the passive voice (e.g. "medication should be taken three times per day") more directly commands the reader to act. It's seldom enough to simply tell people why they should take action without also stating specific actions they should take and how to carry out those actions.

When health communication materials are attempting to influence behavior, its recommendations should be specific and direct. Each step necessary to enact the behavioral change should be addressed. For example, a dental assistant might tell patients, "You need to floss your teeth regularly." Although this advice sounds simple enough to follow, a closer look reveals that there are some important steps that have not been addressed. In breaking down the health behavior of flossing into its smallest component parts, we might identify steps such as knowing what kind of floss to buy, knowing where to buy it, knowing where to find it in the store, buying it, understanding how to use it correctly, making time to floss, trying flossing, flossing regularly, and making it a part of one's daily routine. Flossing is a relatively simple behavior and the steps may seem fairly obvious, but for many health-related behaviors, this is not the case. Few people floss regularly, despite how easy it is. Consider the two messages on social support shown in Fig. 9.5. The first describes social support for behavior change in very general terms. Its informational approach makes the point that social support can be helpful, but it doesn't say much about how to get social support. The second message is more direct and specific. The purpose of its message is clearer. It commands the reader to seek social support and recommends specific ways to ask for it.

Table 9.1 summarizes the recommendations from this section for assuring that messages address the intended topic. If you lose focus when writing tailored health messages, go back and re–read the message concepts. Look at the program objectives as well as the communication objective, and identify the main issue for each message. Each message should have a clear take-home message. From the message title to the summary statement, every paragraph and every sentence chosen should lead the reader toward the main purpose of the message.

To Whom Are You Writing?

Address Your Audience Directly

The most distinguishing characteristic of tailored health communication is its highly individualized feedback. In other words, the target audience for any single communication is really a specific individual. Aside from one–on–one counseling, no other form of health communication can make this claim. At the same time, however, tailored communication should also be sensitive to more general characteristics of the target population. When writing tailored messages, everything we know about the target population, such as cultural variables, age, gender, and reading

---

Table 9.1

Summary: What Are You Writing About?

- The main purpose of a message should be easy to identify.
- Stay focused on the main point of each message.
- Information alone may not be enough; provide specific action steps.
- Be explicit in describing main points and action steps.
- Identify and address all steps necessary to complete the behavioral action.
- Use the active voice in writing.

---

level, should be considered (see chap. 4). We can then apply what we know about both the population and the individual to create the most pertinent messages. The more individualized or tailored the feedback, the more likely the reader will be to pay attention to the information presented. For example, something as simple as addressing the reader by name or using second person (i.e., "you") rather than third person (e.g., "some people," "he," "she," or "they") draws the reader's attention. Consider the message tailored for a person who identified the high cost of low–fat foods as a barrier to healthy eating in Fig. 9.6. At first glance, it's not clear to whom this message is directed. It's not until the sixth sentence that the individual recipient is addressed specifically ("It's good that you've tried . . ."). Instead, much of the message is written in third person ("People have trouble making . . .").

Now, read through the revised message in Fig. 9.7. Consider the differences between the two. In this revision, the reader is engaged in the very first sentence by the question posed. We know this question is personally relevant to the reader because he or she has told us when answering the assessment questionnaire that cost is a barrier to following a low–fat diet. This revised message does a better job than the previous one of addressing the individual reader directly.

No Jargon

Estrogen is defined as a substance that induces estrus, but this straight-forward definition does not reflect the diversity of physiologic effects produced by the estrogens.

Figure 9.6

Tailored Message (on cost as a barrier to following a low-fat diet).

People have trouble making changes in their diets for many reasons. Many find that making changes can be hard at first, but they soon find that they enjoy eating healthier. The cost of healthy foods may be stopping them from making changes. It's true that some low-fat and low-calorie foods can be expensive. This may be especially true for fruits and vegetables when they are not in season. But even then, canned or frozen fruits and vegetables can be a low–cost, healthy choice. It's good that you've tried to find healthy food choices where you shop. But you don't have to let the cost of low–calorie and low–fat foods stop you from improving the way you eat. There are plenty of foods that are healthy and affordable, too. Try these less expensive healthy options:

- buy pasta, rice, and other grains—they're both inexpensive and naturally low in fat.

- shop at local farmers' markets or produce stands—they often have the freshest foods and lower prices than grocery stores.

Figure 9.7

Revised Tailored Message (on cost as a barrier to following a low-fat diet).

Are the high costs of healthier foods keeping you from making changes in your eating habits? It's true—some low-fat and low-calorie foods can be expensive. For example, even fruits and vegetables are costly when they're not in season, but many healthy foods aren't expensive at all. Take pretzels. There're one of the healthiest and cheapest choices in the snack food jungle. And if you need fruits and vegetables in the off season, canned or frozen ones are always available, and usually cost much less! Don't let the cost of low-calorie and low-fat foods stop you from improving the way you eat, and controlling your weight. There are plenty of foods that are both healthy and affordable. Here are a few ideas to help you get started.

- buy pasta, rice and other grains—they're both inexpensive and naturally low in fat.
- shop at local farmers' markets or produce stands—they often have the freshest foods and lower prices than grocery stores.

What exactly did that sentence say? This definition may be precise, but it's not at all straightforward or helpful. In fact, it's confusing. It's medical jargon.—the only ones who understand it are those who work in the field. In most cases, those aren't the people who are the recipients of tailored health messages seeking to explain such concepts. For a tailored message to be effective, it's got to be read and understood. Messages must be written in such a way that the intended audience understands the point one is making. Keep the information simple. Ideally, this means avoiding the use of jargon such as scientific or biomedical terms; technical names for health conditions, symptoms, or procedures; and, names of theories or constructs.

In many cases, scientific or technical terms can be replaced by more familiar language. For example, Table 9.2 presents some frequently used terms from breast cancer diagnosis and treatment, and offers alternatives that are likely to be more understandable to nonmedical professionals (Developing Breast Health Materials That Make a Difference, 1999).

In other cases, however, medical terms may be unavoidable. If so, they should at least be explained in more common language. Look back to the sodium and high blood pressure examples in Fig. 9.3 and Fig. 9.4. To a physician or dietitian, the first message (Fig. 9.3) might make sense, but to the lay person, the main point of the message is confused with a lot of technical, medical jargon, such as nutrient, imbalances, potassium, magnesium, and genetic factors. By focusing on the communication objective and minimizing the medical jargon, the revised message is able to convey the purpose in less than half the text. The term "hypertension"

Table 9.2

Alternatives for Medical Jargon.

Medical terms	Alternatives for the general public
Chemotherapy	Treatment using anti-cancer drugs
Lymphedema	Swelling of the underarm
Mammogram	X-ray picture of the breast
Mastectomy	Surgical breast removal
Prosthesis	Artificial breast form

was used, but only once. It was defined, and a pronunciation guide was even provided so that readers would know how to say the word correctly when talking with their doctor. Carefully evaluate the words used. If it's possible to simplify a message by using terms common to the target population, do so.

Testing for Readability

Reading level refers to the number of years of education a reader must have to understand a particular health communication. Readability formulas typically measure the difficulty of the vocabulary in a communication by counting the number of polysyllabic words in a given passage selected from the communication. The SMOG test (McLaughlin, 1969) and the FRY formula (Fry, 1997) are two useful tools for assessing the reading level of tailored materials. Both are simple to use, with clear instructions available in print (U.S. Department of Health and Human Services, 1992). Applying the SMOG test to the message in Fig. 9.3 reveals a reading level of grade 16! That's a pretty clear indicator that the message needs to be simplified. Note, however, that these formulas measure the complexity of words used but cannot measure the reader's level of comprehension. Thus, readability formulas are most useful when their results are considered along with pretest findings obtained from other methods for assessing understandability of the materials. (See chapter 13 for details on program evaluation.)

Importantly, it is also possible to tailor health messages based on a person's reading level. For example, in a tailored health communication program, to promote compliance with hypertension medication, we might present the same idea in four different ways based on whether individual patients have eight or fewer years of education, 9 to 12 years

Table 9.3

Summary: To Whom Are You Writing?

• Directly address the individual reader.

• Use personalization or second-person voice.

• Avoid using technical or scientific jargon.

• Assure reading level is appropriate for the target audience.

---

of education, some college education, or an undergraduate or graduate degree.

Because such tailoring greatly expands the scope of program development (increasing the message library by fourfold in this example), it has not yet become commonplace. Chapter 14, discusses the potential of this approach in greater detail. Table 9.3 summarizes the recommendations from this section for recognizing and addressing characteristics of the target population in message writing.

How is the Information Presented?

Remember the old adage in speech writing: Tell people what you're going to tell them; tell them; then tell them what you've told them. The same holds true for the structure of tailored health messages. Each message should have an introduction, a body, and a conclusion. The introduction allows the reader to anticipate what's to come and what to look for in the message. The conclusion reinforces the take-home message. And in between the introduction and conclusion, messages should be pithy, yet succinct. For example, principles of proper grammar and good writing such as those listed in the following should be followed:

• Limit each sentence to one idea.

• Limit each sentence to 15 words or less.

• Present information in short sentences and in short paragraphs.

• Make instructions easy to follow.

• Adhere to rules of grammar.

• Spell words correctly.

• Avoid using abbreviations and acronyms.

What's more, make the materials interesting to read. This is where creativity comes in. Use well-suited examples to illustrate and reinforce important points. Use descriptive adjectives and action-oriented verbs to enliven a message. For example, "a greasy pork steak" creates a more vivid image than "a high–fat pork steak." Figure 9.8 further illustrates this point with additional examples.

Of utmost importance, ensure that any claims are supported by sound scientific evidence and are not misleading. Sacrificing this integrity for the sake of more colorful or entertaining messages is irresponsible, and ultimately undermines the efforts of health educators and health communicators. That said, consider which of the phrases in Fig. 9.8 catch your attention. Which are most interesting? Convincing? The message format and the words used will certainly affect whether or not a message is read, let alone understood.

Table 9.4. Summarizes the recommendations from this section for presenting information in tailored messages.

Missing Data and Making Assumptions

Tailoring is data–based communication. At its best, it provides individuals with health messages and information that address their exact concerns,

---

Figure 9.8

Example Use of Vivid Adjectives and Action-Oriented Verbs.

1. "Slash blood cholesterol levels with vegetables, beans, and whole grains."

   vs.

   "Vegetables, beans, and whole grains could lower your blood cholesterol level."

2. "A Mediterranean diet could start unclogging arteries."

   vs.

   "A Mediterranean diet could reverse heart disease."

3. "Osteoporosis leads to broken bones."

   vs.

   "Osteoporosis can cause bone fractures."

4. "Cut your risk of breast cancer by cutting back on beer, wine, and hard liquor."

   vs.

   "There is evidence that breast cancer risk increases with alcohol consumption.

Table 9.4

Summary: How is Information Presented?

• Each message should have a clear organizational structure.

• Express ideas concisely.

• Avoid using acronyms and abbreviations.

• Follow rules of grammar and spelling.

• Use descriptive adjectives.

• Use action–oriented verbs.

• Use clear examples to illustrate or reinforce important points.

• Messages should not exaggerate health benefits, or in any way mislead readers

needs, or interests. Good tailored messages are highly differentiated and very specific. In other words, it's not just a word or sentence that differs from one message to the next, but rather each message uses whatever content and approach is best suited to the communication objective. But what happens when you don't have access to the data needed to generate a given message or set of messages? For example, what if a person doesn't answer every question on the tailoring assessment questionnaire? You may still want to address the topic that was missed by the participant, but you don't have the assessment data needed to direct tailored feedback. In such cases, there are three basic options.

First, one might decide not to provide any message at all. Although this is the simplest solution, it has several major drawbacks. For one, it means that potentially important topics may be left unaddressed in the tailored health communication program. Many times, providing high-quality generic messages may be better than providing no message at all. In addition, if the feedback template has designated a space on the page for a given message, providing no message leaves a big empty space on the final printed product. This is also highly undesirable.

A second option is to use an existing tailored message that was written for another purpose. In some cases, this approach can work adequately. For example, review the tailored messages on nutrition label reading in Fig. 9.9.

Message 1 in Fig. 9.9 is intended for a participant who has indicated that he or she does not read nutrition labels. However, it may also be

---

Figure 9.9

Topic Set of Three Messages on Reading Nutrition Labels.

Message 1

It's important to know what you're eating. Would you buy a car without knowing what features it had? Probably not. So, if you're serious about trying to lose weight, you'll need to learn the nutritional features of the foods you're eating. A quick glance at food labels can help. Food labels contain important information about the nutritional content of foods. By reading labels, you're making an informed decision about what you're buying and eating.

Message 2

It's clear that you recognize the importance of knowing what you're eating. Because you regularly read nutrition labels, you've got a great chance to help control your weight by eating healthier. As you may have found out already, understanding food labels can sometimes feel like trying to learn a new language. Use the tips in this newsletter to learn even more about understanding food labels and making the best food choices.

Message 3

It's clear you're making an effort to learn what's in the foods you eat. Even if you don't always read the nutrition labels on foods, at least you read them some of the time. If you're buying the same foods over and over again, you may already know the label information about these foods and not need to read it every time. But remember to look at the nutrition label for any new or unfamiliar products you're buying. And from time to time, watch for changes on the labels of your regular food purchases.

---

acceptable for someone who didn't answer this question on the tailoring assessment questionnaire. Note that the other two messages would not be appropriate as default messages because they assume certain characteristics of the reader that would not be known.

Now consider the assessment question and the corresponding messages reinforcing motives for weight loss in Fig. 9.10. Each of these messages is very specific. To assume that any one of these messages would be appropriate for someone who did not answer the assessment question on weight loss motives would be unwise. Even a single inappropriate message or "tailoring misfire" could compromise the credibility of the entire program.

The third option for dealing with messages that lack the data required to generate them is to develop default messages. A default message is one in which the content addresses a specific topic but does so in a generic way such that it should not be inappropriate for any given recipient. In the aforementioned weight-loss example, a fourth message that is generic and nonassuming should be developed as the default message. The message in Fig. 9.11 might serve as one such default.

Figure 9.10

Topic Set of Messages Reinforcing Motives for Weight Loss.

Assessment question:

What is the main reason you want to lose weight?

• to look and feel better

• for your family

• to reduce current health problems

Message 1—to look and feel better

When you filled out your survey you said you wanted to lose weight so you would look and feel better. Are you starting to notice any improvements? Are your clothes beginning to fit a little better? Remember, this is what you've been working for!

Message 2—for your family

When you filled out your survey you said you wanted to lose weight to set a good example for your family. Is it working? Have family members commented on your efforts? Do they see you differently? See you as an achiever? Are they following your lead and making healthy lifestyle changes themselves? Remember, this is what you've been working for!

Message 3—to reduce current health problems

When you filled out your survey you said you wanted to lose weight to help manage current health problems. Have you seen your doctor lately? Has your doctor noticed any positive changes? Fewer symptoms? Improved health? Remember, this is what you've been working for!

A tailored health communication program might gather information from participants at only one point in time. Although this is sufficient for providing an initial set of messages, it won't yield any information about how a person is progressing in the program. Consider the following example. In a tailored weight management program consisting of one assessment and three tailored feedback units, tailored feedback is provided on each person's individual weight-loss goals. In the first set of tailored feedback, one topic set of messages acknowledges and comments on the person's weight-loss goals. In a subsequent set of tailored feedback, a different topic set of messages teaches relapse prevention skills to help the person keep from slipping back to old behavioral patterns. Can these latter relapse prevention messages assume that participants have met their stated weight-loss goals from the first set of tailored messages? No. In fact, they can't assume the person has lost any weight at all. Thus, without follow–up data, the message set on relapse prevention must be written in such a way that allows for the possibility that participants may have lost a lot of weight, a little weight, or no weight at all.

Figure 9.11

Default Message: Reinforcing Weight Loss Motives.

Think back to when you filled out your survey. What was motivating you to lose weight? Why did you want to do it? Was it to look and feel better? For your family? For your health? For all these reasons? Ask yourself, are you beginning to see the benefits you'd hoped for? Remember, this is what you've been working for!

Figure 9.12

A *Posing Questions* Default Message.

Consider what kinds of support would be most important to you. Do you need help in choosing foods? Counting calories? Planning exercise? Maybe you'd like help in finding information, like places where you can exercise. Perhaps you just want to hear, "I know this is hard; you're doing a good job." Think about it. When you know what kind of support you need, you can find people who can provide it.

When writing default messages for a tailored health communication program there are three basic strategies available: (1) posing questions, (2) presenting "if–then" type contingencies and, (3) covering all possible bases.

Posing Questions

Using this strategy, the default message poses the same kind of questions that were asked originally in the tailoring assessment questionnaire but that were left unanswered by the participant. Raising the questions again serves to orient the individual to the issue being addressed, and may stimulate self–assessment thoughts that were relevant to the communication objective. A default message using this strategy for seeking support for weight management is shown in Fig. 9.12.

Presenting "If – Then" Contingencies

This approach uses a kind of self–selecting tailoring as the basis for the default message. For example, "If A was a problem for you, you might try this; if B was a problem for you, try that." This strategy allows the individual to answer the missing question in his or her own mind, and self–select the best action step from a brief listing of all possible options. An application of this type of default message for weight management is shown in Fig. 9.13. Here we present two options for gaining social support for weight loss.

Figure 9.13

An *"If–Then" Contingency* Default Message

You can get support for your weight loss efforts and do it in a way that's consistent with your personality and makes you feel comfortable. If you enjoy talking to others about what's on your mind, you may want to join a weight loss support group. On the other hand, if you're not comfortable in a group setting, consider gaining support through existing relationships. Call a friend to go to a park for a walk, or find someone who'll go to the movies with you without sampling the heavy snacks. It's tough enough losing weight; don't make it harder by trying to do it all alone.

Figure 9.14

A *Cover All the Bases* Default Message

Improving your diet will help you lose weight and improve your health. But keep in mind that the safest way to lose weight is through lasting change. Be patient and persistent. Think about how losing weight will help you avoid future health problems. Even a small weight loss can have health benefits. There are other benefits to weight loss too, like giving you more energy to do the things you want to, and the way it makes you look and feel. You can make the healthy changes needed to control your weight. Making wise food choices is one of them.

Covering All Possible Bases

In this case, the default message incorporates concepts from each of the tailored messages in the topic set. This truly generic default provides all the potentially important points relating to that message. The reader may then choose to pay attention to what is pertinent to him or her. Fig. 9.14 provides an example of this kind of default message. Here the reader is asked to consider all the possible reasons for wanting to lose weight as a means of reinforcing their motives to continue dietary changes for weight loss. Other messages in this set may specifically emphasize an identified motive for weight loss such as to look and feel better or to have more energy. Here, however, we include several possible motives because we don't know what is most important to the reader.

Clearly, it is desirable to avoid missing data when at all possible. Thus, it's important to carefully think through the entire program from the start, particularly when developing tailoring assessment tools. It's always possible to go back and revise your assessment if needed. But even then, it's difficult to control for everything. Missing data occurs, and should be anticipated. And when information is not available, ask, "what's the most appropriate message for someone who hasn't given us this data?"

Figure 9.15

Message Checklist.

Content Review
Purpose
1. Is the main purpose of the material easy to identify?
2. Is the main purpose clearly stated in the title?
3. Does the material include all information needed to accomplish the main purpose?
4. Does the material include too much or extraneous information?
Audience
1. Is it difficult to determine who the material is intended to reach?
2. Is the content of the material appropriate given the age, sex, race, education and income of the target population?
Organization
1. Is the content of the material presented in a logical order?
2. Are headings used to create an outline?
3. Do the headings help the reader find a specific topic or piece of information?
4. Do visual markers like bullets, indentation, or bold-face separate important points and clarify the organization of the materials?
Summary
1. Is there a clear "take home message"?
2. Is there a summary of the main points or messages?
Interactivity
1. Are simple interactive techniques like checklists or self-scoring tests included?
2. Are more complex interactive techniques used?
Behavior Change
1. Do materials explain what readers should do, not just what they should know?
2. When a behavior is described, are any necessary steps omitted?
3. When a behavior is described, are the instructions easy to follow?
4. Are the resources needed to enact the behavior available to the target audience?
5. Are any of the recommended behaviors inappropriate for the target audience?
6. Are recommendations specific and content concrete rather than vague and abstract?
7. Are instructions stated in the positive ("choose low fat alternatives") rather than the negative ("don't eat fatty foods")?

Writing and Literacy Review
Reading level
1. Is the reading level appropriate for the target audience?
2. What is the reading level based on the SMOG test?_____
Vocabulary
1. Are familiar, everyday words used rather than jargon or technical language?
2. Does the material explain technical terms when they are used?

Message review

Before they are finalized, messages should be subject to review to ensure that all major aspects of effective print communication are addressed. This includes checking the content, writing, and literacy, and elements of

Writing style and grammar
1. Do most sentences contain only one idea?
2. Is writing succinct?
3. Are most sentences 15 words or less?
4. Are there sentences you did not understand the first time you read them?
5. Are there grammatical errors?
6. Do instructions use the active voice rather than the passive voice?
7. Is text written in second person rather than third?
8. Are vivid and descriptive terms used?
9. Is the tone of the material appropriate for the content and objectives?
10. Is the tone consistent throughout the material?

Visual Communication Review
Text
1. Are the type faces easy to read?
2. Are too many type faces used?
3. Are too many different styles (e.g., bold, italic, underline) used?
4. Does the size of the text make the materials difficult to read?
5. Do the text and headings use a mix of upper and lower case letters?
6. Does the color of the text make it difficult to read?
7. Is each line generally 8–12 words across?
Images
1. Does each image explain, illustrate, or reinforce the text?
2. Are any images inappropriate or offensive to the target audience?
3. Are there places where images are needed to help clarify the text?
4. Do people in the images represent all segments of the intended audience?
5. Are any images outdated?
6. Are words used when an image would express the same idea more simply or clearly?
7. Are images used when words would express the same idea more simply or clearly?
Layout
1. Is the layout cluttered?
2. Does the layout effectively integrate text and images?
3. Are the images close in proximity to the text they support?
Physical attributes
1. Are colors used effectively to emphasize important points?
2. Does the size and shape of the material make it easy to use?
3. Is the printing quality clean and crisp?
4. Does the quality of the paper interfere with use or readability of the materials?

visual communication. The checklist in Fig. 9.15 was originally developed by Strecher and colleagues (Strecher, 1994) and adapted for use elsewhere. Content is reviewed for focus, clarity, organization, audience–appropriateness, interactivity, and use of behavioral approaches. Writing is reviewed for length and complexity of sentences, reading level, grammar, vocabulary, tone, and voice. Visual elements are reviewed for selection of type styles, use of color and images, integration of text and images, and layout. Previewing messages with this type of checklist helps ensure that a tailored health communication program is conveying its intended purpose, addressing its intended audience, and presenting its messages in a well organized and interesting manner.

Two publications by the National Cancer Institute also provide important general guidelines for writing health messages:

- Clear and Simple: Developing Effective Print Materials for Low Literate (National Cancer Institute, 1994); and,

- Making Health Communication Programs that Work: A Planner's Guide (U.S. Dept. of Health and Human Services, 1992).

Testing Messages

Once you've finished writing and reviewing messages, the next step is testing them. Pretesting messages with the intended audience is the best way to find out whether or not the messages are accomplishing what was intended. Even if messages have passed readability formulas and were developed following basic communication principles, it is still important to pretest them. One of the difficulties in pretesting tailored health messages is the fact that there are literally hundreds of messages for a single program. It would be difficult, if not impossible, to pretest every possible combination of these messages. An alternative is to choose a representative selection of messages from the whole for pretesting. Even then, messages must be matched to specific individuals. For example, have pretest subjects complete the tailoring assessment questionnaire, then prepare the right combination of messages for each person based on their responses to the assessment questions. This does not eliminate the difficulty of having all messages reviewed and pretested, but at least those messages selected are received and reviewed by the individuals for whom they were intended.

Next Steps

Before implementing a tailored health communication program, there must be a system in place that connects the messages that have been written to individuals' response choices in the tailoring assessment questionnaire and to a space on the feedback template. This organizational system or instruction is based on tailoring algorithms. Chapter 11 explains tailoring algorithms, the next step in preparing to implement a tailored health communication project.

CHAPTER 10

Creating Tailored Communication Programs: Linking Messages and Algorithms

Writing Tailoring Algorithms: Linking Questions, Answers and Messages

Think about some of the decisions you make every day. What time do you need to wake up to get to work on time? What clothes will you wear? What tasks do you need to complete? Where will you have lunch? Although you may spend little or no time consciously thinking about some of these decisions, there are usually a number of factors that must be taken into account before making even the simplest of decisions. Consider the decision about what to wear to work. If you could super-impose a linear and logical train of thought on human decision making, it might look something like this:

> IF it will be cold outside today and it will be cold at my office, THEN I need to wear something warm and bring a coat.
>
> ELSE IF it will be cold outside today and it will be warm at my office, THEN I need to wear something light and bring a coat.
>
> ELSE IF it will be warm outside today and cold at my office, THEN I need to wear something light and bring a jacket or sweater.
>
> ELSE IF it will be warm outside today and warm at my office, THEN I need to wear something light.

If none of these choices can be met, then you have to go with a default or back–up plan (e.g., most of my clothes are at the dry cleaners or they are dirty, so I will have to wear whatever is clean).

Obviously, human decision making is a multifaceted, dynamic process and not always this logical. But the example illustrates how any given decision might be traced from its origin (i.e., specific factors that we've considered in the decision making process) to its final outcome. In tailored health communication, every judgment about which person will get which messages is based on a similar set of decision rules. These rules are called tailoring algorithms.

What is the Purpose of Algorithms in Tailoring?

Tailoring algorithms serve three basic functions: They identify all available options or choices, establish priorities among these choices, and indicate a back–up plan in the event that none of the choices is selected.

An algorithm also has two important characteristics. First, it is *progressive* (if the first set of conditions is not met, move to the second, and continue until a set of conditions that is met). Second, algorithms are dependent on one another (if you arrive at a decision of low priority, you know that none of the higher priorities are true for this individual).

A closer look at the progressive steps of an algorithm reveals its *linear structure*—a series of ordered conditional statements. Returning to the opening example in this chapter, consider the first "IF" statement (IF it will be cold outside today and it will be cold at my office, THEN I need to wear something warm and bring a coat). This statement defines a set of conditions: (a) the temperature being cold outside and (b) the temperature being cold at the office. If it is not cold in both places, then this set of conditions is not met, and we would move on to the next statement. The linear relation between the conditions also signifies the interdependence of all of the conditions. If the final "IF" statement is reached (ELSE IF it will be warm outside today and warm at my office, THEN I need to wear something light), then we know that it's not cold outside and cold at the office, it's not cold outside and warm at the office, and it's not warm outside and cold at the office. Tailoring algorithms integrate the different modules of a tailored health communication program into one interdependent system. The tailoring assessment measures all of the factors considered in the logic statements (e.g., temperature outside, temperature at the office) and the message library contains all of the possible outcomes (e.g., wear something light, wear something warm).

Most tailored health communication programs operate using a computer–based system. These algorithms, or logic sequences, provide instructions that inform the computer programs of two basic operations: (1) how to connect the assessment responses for specific questions to the corresponding topic sets; and, (2) how to place the messages of those topic sets in the appropriate message blocks on the feedback template.

The instruction code embedded in the algorithms is the foundation for the computer program. It is sometimes referred to as *pseudo–code*, an intermediate step to the final system code.

This chapter is designed to provide a detailed synopsis of the process of creating algorithms for a tailored health communication program. It begins with the creation of an *Algorithm Table*, a document that links all of the components of the tailoring program, and describes the three different types of variables that are used to create the Algorithm Table: Raw Variables, Intermediate Variables, and Feedback Variables. Later in the chapter, the process of *Microtailoring*, or creating algorithms in the actual text of individual messages, is described, and we will introduce the *System Test*, a tool designed to measure the accuracy of the Algorithm Table and Microtailoring. Finally, the end product is shown followed by a summary of special considerations when writing algorithms.

The Algorithm Table and Variable Formulas

When writing a tailoring algorithm, the data gathered in the tailoring assessment (chap. 6), the design template for the messages (chap. 7), and the messages themselves (chap. 9) are linked together. Algorithms simplify the relation among these different elements by creating one set of variables to represent information gathered from the assessment, a second set of variables transforming the first into a more usable form, and a third set of variables that denote message blocks in the feedback. These are called *raw variables*, *intermediate variables* and *feedback variables*, respectively. Figure 10.1 illustrates the sequence of steps used to develop tailoring algorithms:

Raw Variables

Raw variables are created from the questions and response options contained in the tailoring assessment. Raw variables, as suggested by their name, supply us with the raw data collected directly from the participants. The raw variables represent participant responses from the assessment in a predominantly numeric system. Consider the following question taken from the assessment questionnaire in a tailored communication program designed to increase physical activity:

> What, if anything, would make it most difficult for you to increase your level of physical activity?
>
> (Check one answer only.)
>
> ___ I don't have time.

Figure 10.1

The Sequence of Steps Used to Develop Tailoring Algorithms.

Step 1: Creating the Raw Variables   representations of the data
                                       collected in the assessment

Step 2: Creating the Intermediate Variables   transformations or
                                                calculations of raw variables

Step 3: Creating the Feedback Variables   representations of message
                                            blocks and algorithms
                                            indicating a specific message
                                            of a topic set

Step 4: Developing Microtailoring   a variable representation of
                                      an algorithm indicating
                                      specific text to be inserted
                                      within a message

Step 5: Performing a System Test   a tool used to evaluate
                                     accuracy of the Algorithm
                                     Table and consistency
                                     of all modules with the
                                     Algorithm Table

___ I don't have the right equipment.

___ I don't have anyone to exercise with.

___ My family is not supportive of my efforts.

___ Exercise equipment and gym memberships cost too much.

___I don't have any place to exercise.

___ I can't exercise when the weather is bad.

___ I don't have the willpower to exercise regularly.

___ Nothing would make it difficult for me to do this.

There are eight different response choices for this question measuring barriers to increasing physical activity (i.e., no time, not having the right equipment, no one to exercise with, no family support, cost of exercise equipment and gym memberships, no place to exercise, bad weather, and no willpower). If a participant does not select one of these eight choices, he or she can indicate there are no barriers to increasing physical activity by selecting the ninth or final response option. From this question, a raw variable representing "barriers to physical activity" can be created. We will call this variable R_PA.Barriers. The "R" in this variable name indicates that it is a raw variable and the "PA.Barriers" is simply an abbreviation for physical activity barriers. This variable has a range of possible values of 1, 2, 3, 4, 5, 6, 7, 8, and 9. A value of 1 indicates that a participant selected "I don't have time" as a main barrier, a value of 2 indicates "I don't have the right equipment," and so forth. The possible values for the variable also include an "empty" option for those participants who did not respond to that question (see Table 10.1).

These variable names and values are summarized in table format. The raw variable table has three columns: one for the variable name, another for the variable description, and the third for possible values of the variable. Table 10.1 demonstrates a raw variable table for physical activity barriers. The raw variable table includes not one, but all raw variables derived from the tailoring assessment, including personal identification information such as name and address.

Creating the raw variable table is the first and easiest step in writing algorithms for a tailored health communication program. Everything

Table 10.1

Raw Variables.

Variable Name	Description	Possible Values
R_PA.Barriers	What, if anything, would make it most difficult for you to increase your level of physical activity?	Empty = not entered 1 = I don't have time. 2 = I don't have the right equipment. 3 = I don't have anyone to exercise with. 4 = My family is not supportive of my efforts. 5 = Exercise equipment and gym memberships cost too much. 6 = I don't have any place to exercise. 7 = I can't exercise when the weather is bad. 8 = I don't have the willpower to exercise regularly. 9 = Nothing would make it difficult for me to do this.

required for developing this part of the algorithms comes from the tailoring assessment (see chap. 6). Begin with a blank table in the following format:

Variable Name	Description	Possible Values

In the first column, labeled Variable Name, use the questions from the assessment to name each of the raw variables. Raw variable names should be closely related to the topic of the question they represent. For example, a question on marital status such as:

Are you:

___ married

___ widowed

___ divorced

___ single

could be given the variable name R_Marital. Consistently using a common prefix like "R" to denote the type of variable it is (i.e., R = raw will help keep algorithms simple and organized as the tailored health communication program grows more complex).

In column 2, labeled Description, provide a brief description of the variable. It is easiest to simply copy the question verbatim into the column, but one could also describe what information the question is asking for in sentence form (i.e., participant's marital status).

The last column, labeled Possible Values, identifies the range of possible values the variable can take. This is simply a reflection of the response choices given in the assessment. There must also be an "empty" value for all variables in the Possible Values column to indicate when data have not been provided by the participants.

One exception to the rule of having an empty value for all variables is a question that requires a response for a participant to be included in the program. In this case, the participant would have to respond in order to be included in the program. Therefore, this variable always has a value, or is nonempty. In tailoring algorithms, all of the variables must be identified at all times with some value, even if it is an empty value.

Some participant responses contain information that remains in numeric or character form as originally indicated by the participant. These questions have an open–ended response option, as follows:

First Name: _____

Last Name: _____

What is your date of birth?_____

For these variables, values are indicated as a string of numerals or characters. For numerals there may be an acceptable range of values (e.g., the date of birth may be indicated as MM/DD/YY and therefore can be represented as a string of six digits), but for character variables there may be an infinite number of acceptable values (e.g., participants' names can vary dramatically in number and arrangement of characters). For character variables, we can impose a maximum number of characters, if necessary. For example, the participant's name may be split into two variables: one indicating a first name with a maximum of 20 characters and one indicating a last name with a maximum of 30 characters.

The Possible Values portion of the raw variable table may take three different forms: a maximum number of characters that could have been identified for that variable (used when open–ended questions require a text response); a maximum number of digits (used when open–ended questions require a numeric response); or, a list of numbers that represent response choice options given in the assessment. Examples of variables with different Possible Values are shown in Table 10.2. Additional examples of each type of variable are shown in Table 10.3.

Table 10.2

Examples of Variables With Different Possible Values.

Variable Name	Description	Possible Values
R_First.Name	Participant's first name.	20 characters
R_Last.Name	Participant's last name.	30 characters
R_DOB	Date of birth.	Empty = not entered 6 digits (MMDDYY)
R_Marital	Participant's marital status.	Empty = not entered 1 = married 2 = widowed 3 = divorced 4 = single

Table 10.3

Additional Examples of Variables.

Example A: Open-ended question with text response.

Variable Name	Description	Possible Values
R_State	The abbreviation for the state the participant lives in.	Empty = not entered 2 characters

Example B. Open-ended question with numeric response.

Variable Name	Description	Possible Values
R_Cigs.Day	About how many cigarettes do you smoke in an average day?	Empty = not entered 3 digits

Example C. Closed-ended question.

Variable Name	Description	Possible Values
R_First.Cig	How soon after waking up do you usually smoke your first cigarette of the day?	Empty = not entered 1 = within 5 minutes of waking up 2 = between 6 and 30 minutes of waking up 3 = between 31 and 60 minutes of waking up 4 = more than 60 minutes after waking up

Multi–Part Questions. Some questions, like the one following, have multiple parts.

In the last 6 months, has your doctor told you to do any of the following things:

	Yes	No
Get more physical activity?...	____	____
Eat less fat in your diet?...	____	____
Quit smoking?...	____	____

In this example, we want to know if the respondent's doctor told her to get more physical activity, and/or eat less fat and/or quit smoking. To capture all this information in a single variable would be too complex, so instead we make each of the parts of the question its own raw variable. We might call these variables R_Recommend.PA (1 = *yes*, 2 = *no*), R_Recommend.Diet (1 = *yes*, 2 = *no*), and R_Recommend.Smoke (1 = *yes*, 2 = *no*).

Open–Ended Data. Some questions require participants to provide their answers in numeric or character form (e.g., address, name). In these

Table 10.4

Open-Ended Data.

Variable Name	Description	Possible Values
R_FirstName	What is your first name?	Empty = not entered 15 characters
R_LastName	What is your last name?	Empty = not entered 20 characters
R_StreetAddress	What is your street address?	Empty = not entered 20 characters
R_ApartmentNumber	What is your apartment number?	Empty = not entered 5 characters
R_City	What city do you live in?	Empty = not entered 15 characters
R_State	What state do you live in?	Empty = not entered 2 characters
R_ZipCode	What is your zip code?	Empty = not entered 5 digits

cases, the answer provided becomes the actual value of that variable. In the raw variable table, a range of acceptable values for each such variable is usually defined. For example, we may allow 15 characters for first name, 20 characters for last name, 20 characters—not including apartment number—for street address, 5 characters for apartment number, 15 characters for city, 2 characters for state, and 5 digits for zip code. An example of these variables is shown in Table 10.4.

Intermediate Variables

An intermediate variable is any one that transforms, categorizes, or summarizes data from one or more raw variables in a meaningful way. It is called intermediate because its transforming function is the middle step between defining raw variables and creating feedback variables. To begin creating intermediate variables, set up a table similar to the one used to organize raw variables (see the following).

Variable Name	Description	Formulas

Notice that the first two columns in this table are the same as the raw variable table, but the third column here indicates a formula as opposed to a range of possible values. Starting with the first column, intermediate variables are named in the same way as raw variables, although these names are not derived from the assessment. Instead, their names should reflect the outcome of the variable transformation. For example, in a tailored weight management program, it may be necessary to calculate an individual's body mass index based on the raw variables of "R_Height" and "R_Weight." This new intermediate variable could be named "I_BodyMassIndex," or "I_BMI." Here, the "I" denotes that this is an intermediate variable, and "BMI" defines the content of the variable.

In the second column, the actual transformation to be completed is described. For example, a description of the variable I_BMI could be "calculation of participant's body mass index (BMI)."

In the third column, the transformation formula is defined. For body mass index, this formula would be weight in kilograms divided by height in meters squared (Thomas, 1995). To derive weight in kilograms and height in meters, the participant's weight (in pounds) is divided by 2.2 and the participant's height (in inches) is multiplied by 0.0254, respectively. This particular transformation of a raw variable uses a mathematical calculation, one of four different types of transformations possible. The others are condensing data into fewer categories, changing data to text, and combining multiple raw variables into a single new variable. Each transformation is described in detail in the following.

Performing Mathematical Calculations. Mathematical calculations involve transforming a participant's numeric raw data into a new desired value via some computation (e.g., adding a constant, changing the metric of a response such as feet to inches, or dividing by another numeric raw variable). Table 10.5 is taken from a tailored health communication program designed to help smokers quit. One of the topic sets for this program discusses a participant's motives for quitting smoking, and one of the messages in this set addresses the benefit of saving money by not purchasing cigarettes. Intermediate variables in this program use the number of cigarettes the participant smokes daily to estimate the amount of money

Table 10.5

Mathmatical Calculation.

Variable Name	Description	Formulas
I_Cost.Month	Cost of cigarettes per month.	(R_Cigs.Day * 30) * 0.125

the person spends on cigarettes in one week, month, or year. This intermediate variable calculates the cost per month (I_Cost.Month) by multiplying the number of cigarettes smoked per day (R_Cigs.Day) by 30 (days in a month) and again by $0.125 (the cost per cigarette in a $2.50 pack). The resulting value, $75 for a pack–a–day smoker, becomes the value of this intermediate variable. Consider the difference in impact between a message telling a smoker exactly how much money he or she spends on cigarettes each month as opposed to a message generically describing the high cost of smoking.

Condensing Data. Condensing a participant's data involves recoding the responses, or categories in a raw variable, to better fit the context of a specific message. This transformation is especially beneficial when continuous numeric data must be stratified into a smaller number of groups to match the appropriate message. Consider a tailored health communication program created to increase rates of mammography screening. A topic set in this program describes the recommendations for mammography screening. Because the participants' risk increases with age, the messages in the topic set are different for women in different age groups. Looking at Table 10.6, an intermediate variable categorizes each participant into the relevant age group (i.e., 18 to 39, 40 to 49, and 50 or more years of age). This method of condensing participants' data is desirable for reducing the number of messages that need to be written (in this case, 3 vs. 60+ messages).

Changing the Content to Match the Context. In some cases, variables in a tailoring algorithm need to capture words or phrases as opposed to numbers. Most raw variables recode participant responses from words or phrases to numbers. Sometimes, an intermediate variable is used to reverse this process by taking numeric raw variables and assigning specific text values. The example in Table 10.7 is also drawn from the tailored quit–smoking program. It creates a support card that is directed toward someone the smoker has identified, a person who will be supportive of their efforts to quit. Use of the appropriate personal pronoun to identify

---

Table 10.6

Condensing Data.

Variable Name	Description	Formulas
I_Age.Strata	Polychotomous variable indicating which age group the participant falls into: 18-39, 40-49, and 50+.	INITIALIZED 0 IF 18 $\leq$ R_Age $\leq$ 39 THEN 1 ELSE IF 40 $\leq$ R_Age $\leq$ 49 THEN 2 ELSE IF R_Age $\geq$ 50 THEN 3

Table 10.7

Changing Content to Match Context.

Variable Name	Description	Formulas
I_Gender.Pronoun	Participants' gender converted into the appropriate personal pronoun.	IF R_Gender = 1 THEN "her" ELSE IF R_Gender = 2 THEN "him"

the smoker in the support card is a small change but adds a greater degree of personalization to the support message.

Combining Multiple Raw Variables into a Single Variable. This transformation creates a single variable that summarizes the content of multiple raw variables. Because many health risks and health behaviors are multifaceted, it is often necessary to consider multiple factors in order to accurately determine an individual's needs. The smoking cessation program discussed here provides many good examples of this type of transformation. For example, to get a better indication of the smoker's level of addiction to nicotine, we should consider the number of cigarettes he or she smokes per day and how soon after waking up their first cigarette of the day is smoked (Fagerstrom, 1978). We may also want to know whether the smoker is pregnant (to warn of the risks to an unborn baby) or whether they have a working smoke detector in their home (cigarettes are a leading cause of house fires; U.S. Department of Health and Human Services, 1989). Table 10.8 illustrates how each of these intermediate variables would be created by combining multiple raw variables.

Feedback Variables

Feedback variables determine which message from a topic set will be placed in the corresponding message block on the feedback template. Feedback variables are based on raw and intermediate variables and define a specific set of conditions under which a respondent would receive a particular message. In creating the feedback variables, again we start with a three–column table.

Variable Name	Description	Algorithm

Table 10.8

Combining Variables.

Variable Name	Description	Formulas
I_Addiction	Participant's level of addiction to cigarettes: very high (1), high (2), low (3) or very low (4).	INITIALIZED 0 IF R_Cigs.Day ≥20 AND R_First.Cig = 1 THEN 1 ELSE IF R_Cigs.Day ≥20 AND R_First.Cig = 2 THEN 1 ELSE IF R_Cigs.Day ≥20 OR R_First.Cig = 1 OR R_First.Cig = 2 THEN 2 ELSE IF R_Cigs.Day < 20 AND R_First.Cig = 3 THEN 4 ELSE IF R_Cigs.Day < 20 AND R_First.Cig = 4 THEN 4 ELSE IF R_Cigs.Day < 20 OR R_First.Cig = 3 OR R_First.Cig = 4 THEN 3
I_Pregnant. Smoker	Indication of whether the participant is a pregnant smoker.	INITIALIZED 0 IF R_Smoke = 1 AND R_Pregnant = 1 THEN 1 ELSE IF R_Smoke = 2 OR R_Pregnant = 2 THEN 2
I_Smoke. Dectector	Indication of whether the participant is a smoker and has a working smoke detector.	INITIALIZED 0 IF R_Smoke = 1 AND R_Detector = 1 THEN 1 ELSE IF R_Smoke = 2 OR R_Detector = 2 THEN 2

As with raw and intermediate variables, feedback variable names are chosen in a way that identifies what type of variables they are (the prefix "F_") and what they represent. For example, a topic set that contains different low–fat recipes from a variety of international cuisines might be labeled F_Recipes. Importantly, feedback variable names should be derived from the message concept booklets, messages, or the message blocks in the design templates, not from the assessment.

The next step in creating a feedback variable is to describe it. These descriptions can be very detailed or very simple; the level of detail should reflect the complexity of the program. For example, a tailored weight management program might include three different assessment modules and 12 different tailored feedback units. The feedback variable descriptions would then address which assessment questions are used (e.g., is the message responding to a person's weight change since the baseline assessment or since the second assessment?) and the specific content of each message (e.g., if the message is focusing on reinforcing the person's reasons for wanting to lose weight, how will this message be unique from those before it that may have addressed the same topic?).

The third column of the table includes the algorithm, or decision rules, for each of the feedback variables. In writing an algorithm for a feedback variable, always refer back to the message concept booklet developed for that message block. This shows which assessment questions and corresponding response choices have been used to write these messages. With this information, determine which raw and/or intermediate variables are needed to assign each participant to the appropriate tailored message in that topic set. Use these variables to construct a series of "IF . . ., THEN . . ." logic statements similar to the ones shown in the example at the beginning of this chapter. Each logic statement begins with an initialized statement. This is the default statement and tells the computer programmer to refer the participant to the default message when no other choices are met in the algorithm. To illustrate how these logic statements work, consider the following example.

A 60–year–old male, Philip, completes an assessment that shows he may be at higher risk for having a heart attack because: (a) he has a family history of heart disease; (b) he is a smoker; and, (c) he eats a diet very high in fat. Using decision rules like the ones in the opening example, an algorithm can be created to determine what type of feedback Philip should receive.

INITIALIZED (default message applicable to all participants)

IF the participant is male, 40 years or older, has a family history of heart disease, smokes, eats a high–fat diet and has a sedentary lifestyle, THEN he will receive tailored communication explaining why his risk is high, and designed to help him make the following behavioral changes to reduce that risk: quit smoking, reduce the fat in his diet, and increase his physical activity.

ELSE IF the participant is male, 40 years or older, has a family history of heart disease, smokes and eats a high–fat diet, THEN he will receive tailored communication explaining why his risk is high, and designed to help him make the following behavioral changes to reduce that risk: quit smoking and reduce the fat in his diet.

ELSE IF the participant is male, 40 years or older, has a family history of heart disease and smokes, THEN he will receive tailored communication explaining why his risk is high, and designed to help him make the following behavioral changes to reduce that risk: quit smoking.

This example illustrates the logic involved in creating feedback variable algorithms. However, when creating an actual algorithm, raw and intermediate variables replace the short phrases aforementioned. For example, R_Gender = 1 indicates the participant is male; R_Age ≥40 indicates the participant is 40 years or older.

Importantly, the decision rules in this example are only a small part of the full set of algorithms that would also include women, people younger than 40 years, and people with different health status and behavioral profiles. However, it should be clear that based on these decision rules, Philip would meet the second set of conditions because his risk factors do not include sedentary lifestyle (as in the first decision rule), but he does eat a high–fat diet (not represented in the third decision rule).

The link between the assessment, or raw variables, and the messages occurs through a series of decision rules that depend on a numeric encoding of the messages, as illustrated in the following examples:

Feedback Variables for Standard Text Feedback. Table 10.9 illustrates the standard (or untailored) text option. As described in greater detail in chapters 8 and 9, standard text messages are used when messages do not need to be tailored. For such messages, the feedback variable descriptions need only include as much detail as necessary to identify the function of this algorithm. Standard text messages will always have only one untailored message to choose from, so they will be INITIALIZED to 1, as indicated in the example.

Feedback Variables for Tailored Feedback. The example in Table 10.10 depicts the algorithm for a simple tailored feedback message from a smoking cessation program. It is dependent on the participants' response to two assessment questions: average daily cigarette consumption and length of time from waking in the morning to smoking the first cigarette of the day. These two raw variables have been combined in an intermediate variable (I_Addiction, see Table 10.8) to indicate very high, high, low, or very low levels of addiction. In this algorithm, the variable has been initialized to 5. This means that if the participant did not provide the necessary information to be classified as very high, high, low, or very low (i.e., 1, 2,

---

Table 10.9

A Standard or Untailored Text Option.

Variable Name	Description	Algorithm
F1_Introduction	Which introduction message is received in newsletter 1.	INITIALIZED 1

Table 10.10

The Algorithm for a Simple Tailored Feedback Message From a Smoking Cessation Program.

Variable Name	Description	Algorithm
F1_Addiction	Which addiction to cigarettes message is received in newsletter 1.	INITIALIZED 5 IF I_Addiction = 1 THEN 1 ELSE IF I_Addiction = 2 THEN 2 ELSE IF I_Addiction = 3 THEN 3 ELSE IF I_Addiction = 4 THEN 4

3, or 4), the participant would receive message number 5 (the default message). Feedback variables for graphic message blocks are treated identically to text message blocks.

Feedback Variable for Barriers to Physical Activity. In a topic set of five messages addressing different barriers to physical activity, a feedback variable, denoted F_PA.Barriers, would have a range of possible values 1 to 5, with 1, 2, 3, and 4 representing different barrier messages (i.e., lack of time, bad weather, no social support, and no place to exercise) and 5 indicating a default message for participants who did not respond to the question assessing barriers. In Table 10.11 the messages addressing barriers to physical activity are arranged such that message one addresses lack of time as a barrier; two, three, and four incorporate bad weather, no social support and no place to exercise, respectively; and five is the default message. Lack of time would be the number one priority because it is the most common barrier and one that is very difficult to overcome. In a similar manner, the other response options would be prioritized based on these criteria (i.e., how common the barrier is and how difficult it is to overcome).

Feedback Variable for Barriers to Physical Activity Including Physical Activity Preference. Let's say the barrier messages were to include recommendations specific to each participant's preferred type of physical activity. If so, one would also need to use the values from the preferred type of physical activity raw variable (R_PA.pref, 1 = sports, 2 = aerobics, 3 = child care, and 4 = work in the home) to create the algorithm. As shown in Table 10.12, there would be 17 messages that include all possible relations between the responses for barriers to exercise and the responses for exercise preferences. Therefore, if a participant checks "bad weather" as a barrier to getting regular exercise and "sports" for preferred type of exercise, then the participant will have a value of "2" indicated in the raw variable for barriers to physical activity and a value of "1" for

Table 10.11

Algorithm for a Topic Set of Five Messages Addressing Different Barriers to Physical Activity.

Variable Name	Description	Algorithm
F_PA.Barriers	Which barriers to physical activity message is received.	INITIALIZED 5 IF R_PA.Barriers = 1 THEN 1 ELSE IF R_PA.Barriers = 2 THEN 2 ELSE IF R_PA.Barriers = 3 THEN 3 ELSE IF R_PA.Barriers = 4 THEN 4

physical activity preference. This leads to a value of 5 for the feedback variable for barriers to physical activity. On the feedback template, there is a message block labeled "barriers to physical activity" that holds a place for one of the barrier messages. This example algorithm will choose message 5 from the "barriers to physical activity" topic set to be placed in the barriers message block for this individual's feedback (see chap. 11 for the computer programming to place messages in feedback templates). Importantly, the message library would have to have been created with this combination in mind. In other words, simply writing four barrier and four exercise preference messages would not be sufficient, you've got to write 16 barrier and preference messages.

There are three essential rules to follow when creating feedback variables. First, there must be an INITIALIZED value for all variables to indicate when a default message is necessary. Second, some tailored health communication programs may provide feedback to an individual on multiple occasions. In such cases, the feedback units may be treated as isolated units with their own set of intermediate and feedback variables, or they may be treated as one unit including all of the intermediate and feedback variables. In the case of including several distinct feedback units, the feedback variable names should reflect the unit they refer to (e.g., F1_Introduction is the introduction message for the first tailored feedback unit, F2_Introduction is the introduction message for the second tailored feedback unit, etc.). Third, decision rules should always be listed in priority order. A prioritization strategy is based on the theoretical or empirical evidence showing that the content of one message is more important than that of another in cases that allow multiple responses to be indicated. Because computer programs process these algorithms in the order they are presented (see chap. 11), this prioritization strategy ensures that the first set of conditions to be met by the participant will be the highest priority message for that participant.

Table 10.12

All Possible Relationships Between Barriers and Preferences.

Variable Name	Description	Algorithm
F_PA.Barriers	Which barriers to physical activity message is received.	INITIALIZED 17 IF R_PA.Barriers = 1 AND R_PA.pref = 1 THEN 1 ELSE IF R_PA.Barriers = 1 AND R_PA.pref = 2 THEN 2 ELSE IF R_PA.Barriers = 1 AND R_PA.pref = 3 THEN 3 ELSE IF R_PA.Barriers = 1 AND R_PA.pref = 4 THEN 4 ELSE IF R_PA.Barriers = 2 AND R_PA.pref = 1 THEN 5 ELSE IF R_PA.Barriers = 2 AND R_PA.pref = 2 THEN 6 ELSE IF R_PA.Barriers = 2 AND R_PA.pref = 3 THEN 7 ELSE IF R_PA.Barriers = 2 AND R_PA.pref = 4 THEN 8 ELSE IF R_PA.Barriers = 3 AND R_PA.pref = 1 THEN 9 ELSE IF R_PA.Barriers = 3 AND R_PA.pref = 2 THEN 10 ELSE IF R_PA.Barriers = 3 AND R_PA.pref = 3 THEN 11 ELSE IF R_PA.Barriers = 3 AND R_PA.pref = 4 THEN 12 ELSE IF R_PA.Barriers = 4 AND R_PA.pref = 1 THEN 13 ELSE IF R_PA.Barriers = 4 AND R_PA.pref = 2 THEN 14 ELSE IF R_PA.Barriers = 4 AND R_PA.pref = 3 THEN 15 ELSE IF R_PA.Barriers = 4 AND R_PA.pref = 4 THEN 16

A More Complex Example of Writing a Feedback Variable Algorithm.
The message block is for recipes (F_Recipes) and the message concept booklet shows an intermediate variable is needed to indicate whether the participant has a high– or low–fat diet as well as a raw variable that signifies the type of cuisine the participant prefers. The intermediate variable (I_Diet.Risk) has three possible values: 1 = high–fat diet, 2 = low–fat diet, and empty = unknown diet (treated as neither high– nor low–fat diet). The raw variable (R_Cuisine) has possible values: 1 = American, 2 = Mexican, 3 = Soul food, 4 = Chinese, 5 = Vegetarian, 6 = Italian, and empty = unknown cuisine (treated as *none of the above*). The message concepts also indicate that each recipe has an introduction that either informs the participant that they have a high–fat diet and need to think of ways to reduce the fat, or that they have a low–fat diet and should continue choosing low–fat foods. With this information, it is now possible to outline the algorithm. There AREthree general sets of messages: one for participants with high–fat diets, one for participants with low–fat diets, and one for participants with unknown dietary fat consumption. The algorithm would look like this:

IF I_Diet.Risk = 1 (high) THEN (first set of messages)

ELSE IF I_Diet.Risk = 2 (low) THEN (second set of messages)

ELSE IF I_Diet.Risk = 3 (unknown) THEN (third set of messages)

Notice that the high–fat diet messages have been placed first, the low–fat diet messages second and the unknown third. Although these values are mutually exclusive, it is consistent with other feedback variables in the program to place the decision rules in priority order (i.e., high–fat diet messages are the highest priority). In addition, placing the conditions in order by priority provides greater consistency for later addition of variables to the decision rules and for creating more complex algorithms.

The next step is to look at the cuisine variable. In this case, the participant may select more than one type of cuisine, so a priority ranking needs to be established for these messages. Generally, the strategy for setting priorities should include placing higher risk individuals, higher risk behaviors, and more unique or rare responses at higher priorities. Priorities may have been set at the message concept or message writing steps, but if they have not, they must be set now. In this example, the criteria for setting a priority is which recipe has the highest nutritional value. The algorithm would look like this:

IF R_Cuisine = 4 THEN (Chinese recipe)

ELSE IF R_Cuisine = 5 THEN (Vegetarian recipe)

ELSE IF R_Cuisine = 2 THEN (Mexican recipe)

ELSE IF R_Cuisine = 6 THEN (Italian recipe)

ELSE IF R_Cuisine = 3 THEN (Soul food recipe)

ELSE IF R_Cuisine = 1 THEN (American recipe)

The final step is to put these two algorithms together and to make sure that there is a default:

INITIALIZED 18

IF I_Diet.Risk = 1 AND R_Cuisine = 4 THEN 1

ELSE IF I_Diet.Risk = 1 AND R_Cuisine = 5 THEN 2

ELSE IF I_Diet.Risk = 1 AND R_Cuisine = 2 THEN 3

ELSE IF I_Diet.Risk = 1 AND R_Cuisine = 6 THEN 4

ELSE IF I_Diet.Risk = 1 AND R_Cuisine = 3 THEN 5

ELSE IF I_Diet.Risk = 1 AND R_Cuisine = 1 THEN 6

ELSE IF I_Diet.Risk = 2 AND R_Cuisine = 4 THEN 7

ELSE IF I_Diet.Risk = 2 AND R_Cuisine = 5 THEN 8

ELSE IF I_Diet.Risk = 2 AND R_Cuisine = 2 THEN 9

ELSE IF I_Diet.Risk = 2 AND R_Cuisine = 6 THEN 10

ELSE IF I_Diet.Risk = 2 AND R_Cuisine = 3 THEN 11

ELSE IF I_Diet.Risk = 2 AND R_Cuisine = 1 THEN 12

ELSE IF R_Cuisine = 4 THEN 13

ELSE IF R_Cuisine = 5 THEN 14

ELSE IF R_Cuisine = 2 THEN 15

ELSE IF R_Cuisine = 6 THEN 16

ELSE IF R_Cuisine = 3 THEN 17

This algorithm illustrates the combined use of variables to choose a specific message from a topic set, how to deal with missing data, and how to select a default message. Look at the first "IF" statement that produces message 1. The decision rule indicates that message 1 is for someone who has a high–fat diet (I_Diet.Risk = 1) and prefers to eat Chinese food (R_Cuisine = 4). Now look at the "IF" statement that chooses message 13. It is not clear from this decision rule whether the participant has a high– or low–fat diet. However, by reading through the entire algorithm it is apparent that anyone who has indicated a response choice for both the diet risk and cuisine variables has already fallen in one of the previous message categories (1–12). Therefore, messages 13 to 17 are for those participants who did not fit to the high– or low–fat values. The algorithm is initialized to message 18. This means that message 18 is the default message. If a participant does not signify values for the diet risk and cuisine variables, then they will receive message 18.

Microtailoring

Microtailoring is considered part of algorithm writing. However, micro-tailoring actually occurs in the messages themselves using raw, intermediate, and feedback variables from the algorithm tables. *Microtailoring*, as its name suggests, is the process of creating simple, efficient algorithms in the text of a message. It is used for cases in which it would be inefficient to develop multiple messages to change only a small part of the message. The purpose of microtailoring is to enhance the individualization of messages by allowing an even greater amount of tailoring to occur in the messages themselves. This is done by writing algorithms (or decision rules) within the message to manipulate small amounts of text (i.e., words, phrases, or sentences). Microtailoring may be included in tailored messages, standardized (or untailored) messages, tables, or graphics.

To microtailor messages, the first step is to identify the variables to be used and all of their possible values. Raw, intermediate, or feedback variables may be used in microtailoring. For example, imagine that in a support message algorithm, the response choices were assigned values of 1 through 5, plus a default. To set up the microtailored text that goes in the support message, state:

"IF [the variable] = [1st value] THEN [message that corresponds to 1st value] ELSE IF [variable] = [2nd value] THEN [message that corresponds to 2nd value], and so on . . . ELSE [the default response] ENDIF".

In microtailoring, as in the creation of other algorithms, all possible responses have to be accounted for. That's why after the first "IF . . .

THEN . . .," there is "ELSE IF . . . THEN . . ." for other response choices, ending with a default response for instances in which none of the assessment response choices were chosen. Most of the time, the last ELSE statement is just ELSE (not ELSE IF). See the example message text below.

Example of a Microtailored Message

By now you've probably got the message: Support is important to your success! Well, here's one way to get some. We've attached a card for «IF R1_Most.Support = 1 THEN your spouse, partner, or the family member you said would be most supportive ELSE IF R1_Most.Support = 2 THEN the friend or coworker you said would be most supportive ELSE IF R1_Most.Support = 3 THEN the doctor or other health care professional you said would be most supportive ELSE IF R1_Most.Support = 4 THEN the member of your weight–loss support group who is most supportive ELSE IF R1_Most.Support = 5 THEN the person you said would be most supportive ELSE the person you think would be most supportive END IF» of your weight–loss efforts. The card includes specific ways your support person can encourage you and understand how you're feeling. Please read it yourself first, then give it to your support person and talk about it.

How a Message Would Actually Appear in Feedback Form: (when support person is a friend/co-worker):

By now you've probably got the message: Support is important to your success! Well, here's one way to get some. We've attached a card for the friend or coworker you said would be most supportive of your weight loss efforts. The card includes specific ways your support person can encourage you and understand how you're feeling. Please read it yourself first, then give it to your support person and talk about it.

A word of caution: Microtailoring can make the computer programming considerably more complex. Thus, the decision about how much micro-tailoring to use should be based on the programming capability of the team working on the tailored health communication program. Table 10.13 is useful in discussing the amount of microtailoring to include in the message library with the computer programmer.

Performing a System Test

As should be obvious by now, there are many details involved in writing algorithm tables. Furthermore, the dependency of each of the variables on other variables means that an error at one level may result in an error that ripples through the entire system. Therefore, it is always necessary to perform a system test on the algorithm table to eliminate any problems before all of the pieces of the tailored communication program are sent to the computer programmer. Essentially the system test checks that:

Table 10.13

The Amount of Microtailoring to Include in the Message Library.

Programmer Capability	Time Available for Programming	Use of Microtailoring
High	Sufficient	Use anywhere applicable
High	Insufficient	Use sparingly
Medium	Sufficient	Use with reservation
Medium	Insufficient	Use sparingly
Low	Sufficient	Use sparingly
Low	Insufficient	Do not use

1. Each topic set, and corresponding message block, is represented by a feedback variable, with an appropriate name, in the Algorithm Table (e.g., F1_Intro is on the front page of the appropriate message booklet).

2. Final message versions match the size of the message blocks on the feedback templates.

3. The correct numbers and topics of messages exist.

4. Default message(s) are accounted for and appropriate in content.

5. The content of all the messages matches their corresponding algorithm.

6. Microtailoring in messages is accounted for in the algorithms and proofread for logical flow.

7. The priority systems, if present, are checked for accuracy.

Before beginning the system test, make sure the final versions of the assessment(s), messages, and algorithms are readily accessible. Conducting the system test requires at least two people (however, three may be preferable) who are very familiar with the entire tailored health communication program. The ideal system test team would include someone involved in creating the assessment, someone who developed messages, and someone who wrote the algorithms. The system test works backward from the messages through the algorithms to the assessment. There are six basic steps that have to be repeated for each topic set or feedback variable. The steps are presented in Fig. 10.2.

Although this process can be time consuming, it is critical to ensuring a high–quality, smooth–running program.

Figure 10.2

Six Basic Steps in the System Test.

Step 1:   **Begin with the messages**

The message development person holds all of the messages. This person selects the first message from the first topic set (corresponding to the first message block in the feedback template) and examines the message for content (i.e., what decision rule it fits with) and microtailoring.

Step 2:   **Align with algorithms**

The algorithm person proceeds to identify the decision rule for message one by referring to the algorithm for the corresponding feedback variable and verifies with the message person that the decision rule is appropriate for the content.

Step 3:   **Check consistency with assessment**

At this point, any raw and intermediate variables included in the decision rule for message one should be checked for accuracy as well. The assessment person checks the assessment questions and response choices against the algorithm table.

Step 4:   **Evaluate microtailoring**

If there is any microtailoring within this message, it should be shown to the algorithm person so that it may be checked for accuracy in the logic of the decision rules used as well as for consistency with the raw, intermediate, or feedback variables used.

Step 5:   **Identify errors immediately**

If any errors are discovered, they should be marked right away so that changes can be made at the end of the system test.

Step 6:   **Repeat the process and check default messages**

The remaining messages within this topic set should be checked in exactly the same way (following steps 1-5). When all of the messages have been reviewed for a topic set, then the algorithm person needs to make sure that default messages exist and are reflected in the algorithms.

Return to Step 1 for next topic set until all topic sets are checked.

Special Considerations

Multiple Assessments

Some tailored health communication programs may include multiple assessments given periodically over time. In these cases, the assessments may be treated as isolated units with their own set of intermediate and feedback variables, or they may be treated as one unit that forms the foundation for all of the intermediate and feedback variables. The decision regarding whether to treat multiple assessments independently or as a whole is based on the content of the message concepts and messages.

If the messages require data from all of the assessments (e.g., a weight management program that has multiple assessments to track how much weight the participant loses over time), then the assessments must be treated as an aggregate of all the raw variables. In this case, the raw variables should have labels to indicate the assessment they reflect (e.g., R1_Name and R1_Weight to reflect the first assessment; R2_Height and R2_Weight to reflect the second).

In addition, if the program being created is very comprehensive, with multiple assessments and tailored feedback units, more detailed descriptions of all the variables are desirable. Recall the weight management program for which an intermediate variable for body mass index (BMI) was created. If this program contains multiple assessments and feedback, an intermediate variable for BMI (I_BMI) may be defined as a calculation variable based on participant's given height (R1_Height) and weight (R1_Weight) to indicate their baseline body mass index (BMI). In this case, another BMI variable (I_BMI.2) can be created later in the weight management program to indicate progress, stability, or relapse in the individual's performance in the program.

Accuracy and Application

Be practical when deciding how many variables to include in the algorithm for a feedback variable. Always make sure all of the variables in the algorithm are important to the content of the message so that messages with little application to the participants in your program are not created. It is always beneficial to the tailored program if the algorithm developer double checks the logic of the message writers in creating specific messages, the prioritization of the messages, and the content of the default to make sure it accurately represents the participants who can receive it.

End Product

The final set of algorithms appears in a booklet form with a cover page and each of the tables: raw, intermediate, and feedback (see Fig. 10.3). Now, the algorithm booklet, all of the messages in their final form, and the feedback templates are given to the computer programmer to put the

Figure 10.3

An Example of What a Complete Algorithm Table Would Look Like Using Several Variables as Examples.

Raw Variables		
Variable Name	Description	Values
R_CigDay	About how many cigarettes do you smoke in a day?	empty = no response 3 digits
R_Marital	What is your marital status?	1 = married 2 = never married 3 = divorced or separated

Intermediate Variables		
Variable Name	Description	Formula
I_Addiction	Whether addicted to cigarettes.	IF R_CigsDay > 20 OR R_FirstCig = 2 THEN 1 ELSE 2
I_Stage	Stage of quitting?	IF R_Plan= 1 THEN 3 ELSE IF R_Think = 1 THEN 2 ELSE IF R_Think = 2 THEN 1 ELSE 0

Feedback Variables		
Variable Name	Description	Algorithm

F_Intro	Intro to newsletter.	IF I_Addiction = 1 and I_Stage =
		  • 1 THEN 1
		ELSE IF I_Addiction = 1 and
		  I_Stage = 2 THEN 2
		ELSE IF I_Addiction = 2 and
		  I_Stage = 1 THEN 3
		ELSE IF I_Addiction = 2 and
		  I_Stage = 2 THEN 4

F_Graph	Graph of smoking effects.	IF R_CigsDay > 60 THEN 1 IF R_CigsDay > 40 THEN 2 IF R_CigsDay > 20 THEN 3 ELSE 4

entire system in place. The precision used in creating and checking the algorithms is critical to the success of the next step, creating the computer program. The next chapter discusses computer programming issues to be considered prior to implementing the program.

CHAPTER 11

Creating the Tailoring Program

For most people who are just learning about computer–tailored print communication, the most unfamiliar aspects are those having to do with the computer itself. Creating a computer program that automates the production of tailored messages can indeed be a highly technical process. In many cases, health education and health communication professionals may not have all of the necessary skills to carry it out alone. However, even when another person or organization is given the task of creating the tailoring software, it is important that those involved in planning and developing the less-technical portions of a tailored health communication program (e.g., messages, algorithms, and design templates) also have a good understanding of the software development process. This ensures that the intervention plan, message concepts, design templates, algorithms, and other content contain the information programmers need to translate this work to an automated program. As one begins to understand more about the programming process, it is often discovered that, although the programming tools and skills can be complex, the overall process that guides their use is actually quite simple.

This chapter discusses:

- What a computer program for tailored messaging should do,
- various programming strategies that can be employed,
- integrating all the parts of the tailored health communication program,
- writing the computer program itself, and
- testing the program for accuracy and completeness.

Getting Started

The Program Development Process In a Nutshell

Simply stated, creating a computer program for tailored messaging involves translating the simple verbal descriptions developed thus far into technical program logic and then translating that logic to a computer program. The first step—translating verbal descriptions to technical logic—is often referred to as program design. This task involves designing a program, just as an architect designs a building. Here the components of the program are identified and described, and the processes by which those components work together are detailed. The second step—turning this technical logic to a computer program—involves using software and programming languages to build a computer program according to this design. Building the program may involve writing program code (what is traditionally thought of as "programming") or assembling existing programs or program parts together to a larger program that performs all the functions previously designed. Usually, the process involves both activities, along with page layout and type formatting.

When to Begin Programming

The program will be based on all the planning and development work done to date, including the intervention design, data collection instruments, design templates, algorithms, message concepts, and message library. Although a tailoring program can always be modified at any time, it is important to have as many as possible of these preliminary steps completed before beginning development of the computer program. Once computer programming has begun, changes in any of these other areas can complicate and slow the process. Ideally, descriptions and content are in final form before programming begins. If future program changes are anticipated but not yet detailed, the types of changes that may occur should be described, so that those portions of the program may be developed in a way that allows easier updating at a later date.

Arranging Personnel or Contractors

Skills and resources needed for developing a computer program for tailored messaging include the ability to think in a logical, linear fashion; a general understanding of the software and programming processes to be employed (see the following), and for programmers, an in–depth knowledge of the programming languages and software to be used.

Likewise, just as it is valuable for planners and content developers to have an understanding of the programming process, it is equally valuable for those developing the computer program for tailored messaging to have an understanding of the overall tailoring process and, when possible, of the health issues and behavioral strategies driving the tailored health communication program. When computer programmers are familiar with the process and goals of tailoring, the translation of nontechnical materials into a computer program is smoother and the results closer to that intended by the project planners and developers.

In many instances, a developer from an outside agency or company or from another department in your organization is employed to create the program. Choosing and managing an outside developer can be a difficult task. Depending on the tailoring approach being employed, the availability of skilled developers may be limited in this time of high demand for such skills. Some potential sources for developers include: database development companies, custom-mailing firms, freelance programmers, design firms, and computer support departments in most organizations. The choice of developers is determined by the programming approach to be used.

When choosing a developer to work with, technical skill is only part of the equation. At least as important is the developer's ability to work with the intervention materials developed (message libraries, design templates, etc.), and to work closely with content developers. The more experience the developers have working in these ways, the less time being wasted explaining basic principles and processes to those developing the computer program for tailored messaging.

Sometimes, conducting program development in–house is the most efficient way to get the programs completed. Doing so offers the advantages of greater control, more direct oversight, potentially quick modification, and easier integration of computer program development with other development activities in a concurrent way. Depending on the programming approach being employed, you may be surprised to find that technical capacity and tools already exist in your organization. This is often the case when a merge–based or manual assembly approach is employed. If an organization presently lacks this capacity but anticipates that tailored health communication programs will become a major portion of the organization's work in the future, it is probably worthwhile to invest in building that capacity.

There are two main drawbacks to in–house development of the computer program. First, it can be frustrating fumbling through a task whose complexity exceeds the capability or experience of those in the organization. Second, an important and commonly occurring drawback is the tendency for intensive technical development and programming to draw resources from creative and content activities such that the focus of the program (or even the organization) shifts away from health and communication toward technical activities. The decision whether to arrange for outside technical assistance or to develop and use internal technical capacity is based as much on the unique characteristics, focus, and future direction of an organization as on the technical skills needed. It is important to consider these larger nontechnical issues before the program development process begins.

What Functions Will the Computer Program Perform?

The tailoring program can be designed to perform any number of different functions the designers may wish to automate. The most common of these are:

- Importing raw data from surveys or other sources into the tailoring program;
- running the raw data through algorithmic functions that determine values for intermediate and tailoring variables;
- retrieving messages from the library and laying them out in page format; and
- printing tailored pages.

In addition to these core functions, many tailoring programs add capabilities of data entry (e.g., key–punching, scanning, computer–assisted telephone interviewing, or other methods); data management (e.g., storing, searching, reporting, outputting data); message management (e.g., storing, searching, and reporting messages); or program management (automated tracking and other functions involved in managing or delivering the program). Whether these additional features are necessary in any given program varies from one project to the next. For example, if raw data from a tailoring assessment is arriving in small batches (i.e., a few subjects at a time) and quick turnaround of printed feedback is important, good data entry functions are a key part of a comprehensive tailoring program. If, however, data arrive in a single large batch or turnaround is not immediate, creating a data file from another source (e.g., an optical scanning or keypunch service) will probably be more efficient. If a program includes multiple assessments and feedback modules, it may be best served by a tailoring program with more elaborate and precise tracking and reporting capabilities. In contrast, a program that has only a single assessment and feedback module may only require tracking capabilities that find and print feedback for subjects.

Program Development Approaches and Tools

The next step in developing a computer program for tailored messaging is choosing the programming approach that most closely matches the functions needed. This decision should be made only after consulting with those who are creating the final program. However, it is important that an approach be chosen based on what will work best for the program and what functionality is needed, rather than what the programmers are most familiar with. We will discuss six main programming approaches here:

1. Merge

2. Database

3. Low–level programming

4. Authoring

5. Tailoring–specific software, and

6. Computer assisted manual tailoring.

A hybrid approach that uses two or more of these approaches is also discussed.

Merge

Creating a tailoring program using merge programs is similar to creating a mail merge using a word processor. In fact, standard word processing software like Microsoft Word® or WordPerfect® is the usual tool of choice for merge tailoring programs. A tailoring program built using this approach consists of a list of conditional statements surrounding the tailored messages. Fig. 11.1 shows an example of merge tailoring.

The conditional statements are based on the algorithms developed for the program (see chap. 9). The messages are those developed for each message block (see chap. 8). Both text and graphics messages are laid out in the merge file just as they appear when printed. When run, the merge program reads a data file containing subjects' data and then progress from the first line of merge code to the last, testing for agreement with merge instructions. When data are tested against a merge instruction and found to match, the text and graphics associated with it (i.e., the message

Figure 11.1

Example of a Merge File Page.

<<IF F_Intro = 1 THEN>> Welcome to the PRAISE Program! We have created this newsletter just for you. Even though you're not ready to start changing your diet now, we hope the information here will be useful when you are ready to make a change. <<ELSE IF F_Intro = 2 THEN>> Welcome to the PRAISE Program! We have created this newsletter just for you. Since you're thinking of starting to change your diet now, we hope the information here will be useful to you as you put your thoughts to action. Read on for information we've compiled to help you plan out the changes you're considering making. <<ELSE IF F_Intro = 3 THEN>> Welcome to the PRAISE Program! We have created this newsletter just for you. Since you're planning to start changing your diet now, we're sure the information here will be useful to you. Read on for tips and information designed to put your plans to work. <<END IF>>

version) are placed on the page in the spot where they has been assigned. The program then moves on to the next merge instruction, tests it, places the associated text and graphics if it tests true, then moves on to the next merge instruction, and so on until it reaches the end of the file. The result of running the merge program is a printable tailored page or set of pages in a file format that is readable and printable by whatever software was used to create the merge file.

Advantages. The merge approach has several advantages. First, its logical and linear format makes it easy for nontechnical people to understand. The fact that it is based on a linear structure and uses tools that are familiar to nonprogrammers makes it possible for nonprogrammers to develop. It uses inexpensive software tools that most organizations already possess. Because it uses software programs that are designed primarily for page layout, it can offer a high degree of control over text and graphic formatting. Finally, because merge instructions can often be nested within the text of the messages themselves, microtailoring is a simple task with a merge–based approach.

Disadvantages. When using a merge–based approach, a complex program can quickly become unwieldy. Because the content and algorithms are integrated so tightly, it often becomes difficult to identify and focus on specific algorithms and content, thus making updating and problem solving tedious and time–consuming tasks. Because the strength of existing software is its one–piece–at–a–time page layout functions and word processing, the merge functions can sometimes run short. A complex tailoring program may require algorithmic capabilities that are not built into the merge functions of a word processing or page layout program. Because most word processing and page layout programs have not been designed to automate the merge task, this process can be difficult and may require additional software just to run the merge program. Finally, program management functions such as tracking subjects are usually not possible using merge programs alone.

Database

The database approach to building a tailoring program also utilizes general purpose software. In this approach, two database files are created and related (i.e., linked) to one another. The first database file is the message file, and contains all text and graphic messages. Each message occupies a record in one or more fields of the database file. The second database file is the data file that contains fields that hold the raw, intermediate, and feedback data, as well as layouts that correspond to the feedback templates. This file also contains a set of instructions that when invoked by user command, find messages that match the feedback data, pull those messages to the data file, and place them on the layout to be printed.

Advantages. Because algorithms and messages are kept in separate databases, each can be changed without considerable alteration of the other. Because the algorithms and messages are kept in a database structure, the various pieces of the program (i.e., individual messages, variables) are well organized and easily found for editing and changing. Most databases have automation functionality, making it easier to build tracking functions in the tailoring program. Furthermore, database programs are built for speed. A tailoring program using this approach is faster than most merge programs.

Disadvantages. Because database software is primarily a storage and retrieval system, its capability for formatting content is sometimes limited. Databases fall short in the degree of control they allow over text and graphic formatting compared to that available using a page layout program. Finally, the inclusion of microtailored messages in a database–based program can be difficult. In many cases, it may be necessary to modify messages by creating a different version for each microtailored possibility or to split a message in multiple partial messages.

Low-Level Programming

The low–level programming language approach builds a computer program specifically for tailoring using a full–fledged programming language, such as BASIC, C, or JAVA. The end product is a program that incorporates algorithms and feedback templates in the code of the programming language used. Messages may also be incorporated in the program code or may reside in a database file that is accessed by the program.

Advantages. Creating a tailoring program from scratch using a low–level programming language offers one great advantage: It has nearly unlimited capability to perform whatever functions are needed. Formatting can be extremely precise. The most complex algorithms can be accommodated. Intervention tracking and data management functions are unlimited. If programmed well, the program is very speedy.

Disadvantages. Although this approach has many advantages, in most cases they are outweighed by its major disadvantage: Developing such programs requires considerable programming skill. Even if individuals with this skill can be hired to develop the program, making even simple modifications often requires the same or an equally skilled computer programmer. This can be very expensive, and often frustrating if those who have developed the program and those doing the computer pro-gramming do not share a common understanding of the tailoring process and program objectives.

This approach is the best choice when a skilled programmer is available and when the tailored health communication program to be developed is simple (e.g., a single–page intervention with a few dozen variables and a few hundred total messages). It should also be considered an option when the desired functionality for a program is not available through off–the–shelf software.

Authoring

Developing a tailoring program using authoring software is similar to the low–level programming approach. A stand–alone program is developed that contains algorithms incorporated into the program code itself. Messages may also be stored internally or accessed from an external database file. The difference between the authoring and low–level programming approaches is that the authoring approach employs plain–language programming languages (sometimes referred to as scripting languages) that are easier to use for nonprogrammers but more limited in capability than the low–level languages. Examples include Authorware Professional® and Macromedia Director®.

Advantages. This approach offers a great deal of functionality in handling algorithms, managing data, and other program functions. It also provides the ability to fully automate most computer functions. In effect, it offers a degree of computer functionality similar to that of low–level programming but with much simpler language.

Disadvantages. Although authoring languages offer similar functionality to low–level languages, most still fall far short on a few key functions. Most importantly, authoring software usually has limited printing capabilities. Authoring programs have been developed primarily to provide interactive on–screen displays such as multimedia, and thus most lack comprehensive formatting for printed pages. Programs created using authoring software is often much slower than those created via low–level programming. Finally, although authoring languages may use common English vocabulary and present program code in easy–to–understand schemes such as flowcharts, they can still be very complex. Five thousand lines of authoring code are simpler to understand than 5,000 lines of low–level code but can be just as difficult to write for the first time.

Tailoring Software

Using *tailoring software*—software developed specifically for the purpose of automating tailored message production—may be the future of tailored health communication programs. With such software, developing a tailoring program could be similar to, and potentially as simple as, creating a spreadsheet or a web page. Several tailoring applications have been released (Beales, 1998). Because this type of software is in its infancy, few performance evaluations have been conducted. As products become available, it is important for potential users to evaluate them carefully, just as one would evaluate a database or page layout program. Some important considerations in evaluating a tailoring program include the following:

- Is the program truly capable of tailoring? The term "tailoring" is sometimes used loosely, and is not always used to mean individual–level customization (Kreuter & Skinner, Under review).

- Does it perform all the functions that are needed for the tailoring program at hand, or simply automate one part of the process? A useful tailoring program will allow for a great deal of detailed page layout and formatting, organize messages and algorithms in a way that makes them easy to find and modify, and include data management and intervention tracking capabilities that are appropriate for a tailored intervention.

- Is it easier to use for tailoring than typical database, merge, or other software? If general purpose software can be used just as easily for creating a tailoring program, this will be easier to manage than a dedicated tailoring program that is less useful for non–tailoring functions like data tracking and analysis, and not as widely supported as general purpose software.

Advantages. Dedicated tailoring software offers the potential to create tailoring programs quickly and easily. A good tailoring application should assist users in creating and managing messages and algorithms, designing templates, and creating automated tailoring programs. For those who are new to computer tailoring, having these capabilities in a single dedicated application can help them get started quickly.

Disadvantages. It may take some time before dedicated tailoring software is used widely enough to be adequately supported by its developers. Until then, users will be left alone to figure out how to make it work for them. Dedicated tailoring applications are likely to have limited non–tailoring capabilities. Unless the program has very limited needs beyond tailoring, the difficulty of integrating dedicated tailoring software with other dedicated applications to meet multiple needs can be as difficult as simply using the general purpose software to conduct tailoring. Finally, general purpose software is becoming more tailoring–friendly with each new version and could supplant tailoring dedicated applications. Software developers are aware of the trend toward one–of–a–kind production and most are working hard to incorporate this functionality into database, page layout, authoring, and word processing applications. As general purpose applications add more and more tailoring capabilities, emerging tailoring–specific software programs may disappear quickly.

Manual Assembly

A common approach to developing a tailoring program is to skip the programming altogether and create tailored feedback using computer–assisted manual print tailoring. This approach usually involves creating:

- Page layout or word processing files that contain the messages
- spreadsheet or database files that contain the algorithms, and
- a step–by–step process for calculating messages using the spreadsheet or database, copying the specified messages from the page layout or word processing file, and pasting the copied messages on a page to be printed.

To start, two files are created in a page layout program. A template file contains an empty design template. A message file contains all of the tailored messages. A third file is created in a spreadsheet or database program. This calculation file contains the algorithms that calculate what version of each message should be printed for each person. Raw data are imported to the calculation file, which then identifies the appropriate messages. The specified messages are manually copied from the message file to the template file. The template file is subsequently printed.

Advantages. For a simple program with a small number of subjects, such as a pilot research study, manual tailoring offers a lower cost option for tailoring. Messages and algorithms can be created and edited directly in the files that contain them. Tailoring can be conducted with minimal technical skill.

Disadvantages. Manual tailoring is inappropriate for a program with more than a few dozen subjects with very complex algorithms or with an extensive message library. As the complexity of algorithms or the number of message versions increases, the risk of human error can become very high. As the number of tailored documents created increases, the amount of work involved in manual assembly begins to surpass the work required to create an automated program.

Hybrid

Given the advantages and disadvantages of the strategies aforementioned, why not combine approaches? In fact, this is what many successful tailoring programs have done. There are many ways these approaches can be combined to take better advantage of the strengths of each.

One common example is to combine a database, page layout or word processing program, and an authoring program. In this arrangement, the database manages data and calculates algorithms, the page layout program holds the messages and templates, and the authoring program "asks" the database for data, then tells the page layout program to assemble tailored pages based on that data. This approach utilizes the best of each type of application—the layout and formatting capabilities of page layout software, the data management and calculation capabilities of database software, and the automating capabilities of authoring software.

Advantages. Hybrid approaches allow users to conduct tailoring inter-ventions as a workgroup. Each of the elements in a tailoring program—the design templates, messages, algorithms, automation—can be developed by different people using the software they know how to use best.

Disadvantages. At least one person needs to know how to use all of the different applications. Even as multiple individuals use multiple applications they are familiar with, a single person capable of combining and trou-bleshooting all applications is invaluable. It may be difficult to find such a person.

Choosing the appropriate program development approach requires careful consideration of many variables. It may be that all needs are not going to be satisfied by a single approach. When this is the case, consider which needs are most important and find the approach that satisfies them. Then figure out how to modify the other needs or meet them with a combination of approaches. Figure 11.2 helps planners and programmers hone in on the most appropriate approaches.

Designing the Program

Once it has been determined which program functions are desired and which programming approach will be used, it is time to design the actual program components that make it all work. This task is performed by computer program developers. The specific components that make up the program depend on the programming approach and tools utilized. As a start, though, there are at least six basic components:

1. hardware and software environment
2. user interface
3. message library
4. database
5. layouts, and
6. assembly and automation instructions.

Hardware and Software Environment

The hardware and software environment is the collection of computer software and hardware on which the tailoring program is run. This includes all software applications that are required to run the tailoring program, the computer and operating system on which the program is run, the printer used, and any networking or other hardware required to link all of the components.

User Interface

The user interface is the set of screens, key commands, buttons, and other elements through which program staff interact with the tailoring program.

Message Library

The message library is the file where all of the messages reside. Two main issues arise in determining message library specifications: Where within the overall tailoring program does the library reside?; In what format are the messages stored in the library?

In a merge–based program, the library may be integrated with the merge instructions in a single file or may be stored externally in another file that is accessed by the merge file. In a database program, the message

Figure 11.2

Program Development Approaches.

Needs	Merge	Database	Low Level Program	Authoring	Dedicated Tailoring Software*	Manual
Data entry	Poor	**Good**	Fair	**Good**	?	Poor
Simple data management	Poor	**Good**	**Good**	**Good**	?	Poor
Complex data management	Poor	**Good**	Fair	Poor	?	Poor
Data analysis	Poor	Fair	Poor	Poor	Poor	Poor
Simple page layout	Fair	Fair	**Good**	Poor	**Good**	**Good**
Complex page layout	Fair	Fair	**Good**	Poor	**Good**	**Good**
Simple algorithm calculation	Fair	**Good**	**Good**	**Good**	?	Poor
Complex algorithm calculation	Poor	**Good**	**Good**	Fair	?	Poor
Micro tailoring	**Good**	Poor	**Good**	Fair	?	Fair
Ability to change program and content during production	Poor	Fair	Fair	Fair	**Good**	**Good**
Easy use for development (without programming skills)	**Good**	Fair	Poor	Poor	**Good**	**Good**
Fast development	**Good**	Fair	Poor	Fair	**Good**	**Good**
Low cost of development	**Good**	Fair	Poor	Fair	**Good**	**Good**
Easy use for production	**Good**	Fair	Poor	Fair	**Good**	Poor
Fast production	**Good**	Fair	**Good**	Fair	**Good**	Poor
Low cost of production	Fair	**Good**	**Good**	Fair	?	Poor
Help managing the overall tailoring process	Poor	Poor	Poor	Poor	**Good**	Poor
Integration with other software	**Good**	**Good**	Poor	Poor	Poor	**Good**

*Capabilities of dedicated tailoring software is a best guess based on descriptions of prototypes and early versions. Capabilities rated with a "?" are likely to vary considerably between different programs.

library is probably a separate database file linked to the instructions file. Where a message library resides should be determined by the need to access messages for later use or re–use. A message library that is stored externally from the rest of the program will be more accessible, but require more complex programming to be integrated into the overall tailoring program.

The format in which messages are stored is also an important consideration. Messages can be stored in an editable format (e.g., text or graphics that are editable in the program) or a fixed format (e.g., distinct objects like a PICT or postscript object that cannot be edited in the program). The format should be determined by the need to edit messages as they are used. If editing and formatting takes place as the program is used, storing messages in an easily edited format is important.

Database

The database stores and manages all data and often contains the algorithms that manipulate the raw data to intermediate and feedback data.

Layouts

The layouts are the program equivalent of the feedback templates. In the computer program, tailored messages are assembled on these electronic layouts. They are what is printed once a tailored communication for an individual has been assembled.

Assembly and Automation Instructions

The assembly and automation instructions are all part of the instructions that perform program functionality. This includes assembly of tailored feedback, data importing and exporting, and data reporting.

Building the Program

Describing the specific steps in creating the computer program is a technical issue beyond the scope of this book. However, understanding the basics of the programming process is important for program planners. Once the programming approach has been determined, spending some time becoming familiar with the specific applications to be used is useful for overseeing development and, perhaps most important of all, planning for and arranging program modifications in the future.

When the hardware and software environment has been described, reading the descriptive portions of the manuals for the applications to be used proves invaluable. Furthermore, asking the program developer who is building the tailoring program to conduct a brief training in the basics of the applications is a good way to make sure other project team members can communicate intelligently with technical staff and contractors.

Testing

The final step in developing a computer program for tailored messaging is testing. All preprogram development activities should have been tested (such as with the systems test in algorithm development) and carefully reviewed to ensure that they were complete and correct before their parts of the tailoring program were developed. Having done so prevents the need for potentially difficult content changes to the program during testing. At this point, testing should be limited to ensuring that content has been faithfully translated in the tailoring program. That said, there are some content issues that become apparent only during program testing. Expect some mistakes made long ago to become apparent at this point.

Reviewing Libraries, Algorithms, and Layouts

The programming process usually requires importing and formatting text and graphics from the message libraries, importing and translating algorithms, and assembling layout pages based on the design templates. As with translating from one language to another, mistakes are likely to be made. It is important that someone who is not familiar with each of these items have the responsibility of comparing the original nonprogram content to what is actually contained in the program.

This is a tedious and usually nontechnical process similar to any other proofreading task. The proofreader compares printed copies of the message libraries, algorithms, and design templates as they were created by the message writers, algorithm writers, and designers with on–screen or printed copies of each element as it appears in the program. Look to ensure that:

- All message versions are present
- Text content is complete
- Algorithms are correctly translated, and
- Layouts are reproduced faithfully.

Generating and Reviewing Sample Feedback

Program testing begins by creating sample cases. Create as many sample cases as time permits. One hundred is probably the minimum needed; use several hundred when possible. Sample cases may be hand–generated or generated by computer. Each case should be unique. The object is to cover as many permutations of responses as possible. Special attention should be paid to creating conflicting, inaccurate, or incomplete data—just as actual subjects are likely to do. Also, ensuring that every message appears in at least one of the sample tailored pages created from this set of sample assessments is important. Having every possible combination of messages appear would be ideal, but is impossible for all but the most simple tailoring programs. Project staff members responsible for developing the messages and algorithms are best suited for generating a comprehensive set of sample assessments.

Sample assessments are imported to the tailoring program, feedback is generated on paper or on screen, and then all of it is reviewed. Reviewers look for incorrectly assembled feedback (e.g., missing message blocks, incorrectly placed message blocks, incorrectly formatted messages) and incorrect messages. This testing offers the opportunity to see messages assembled next to each other for the first time, making conflicting or redundant messages apparent. Although these conflicts and redundancies should have been prevented with good message concepts or caught during content development, sometimes a complex set of messages only reveal such problems when messages are finally assembled at the program testing stage.

Sample assessments should be run through the program one at a time whenever possible. This way, when a problem is identified, it can be corrected immediately and the correction can itself be tested by subsequent sample feedback. The assessment–feedback generation–evaluation–correction sequence should continue until there is a long sequence of sample feedback with no problems.

Testing Program Usability

In addition to this core testing of messages, algorithms, and feedback, program instructions and interface should also be tested for functional errors. To do this, have several individuals unfamiliar with the program use it. Observe their experience and note any problems. As with sample feedback testing, problems should be corrected during testing as much as possible so that the corrections themselves can be tested.

Conclusion

On completion of program development, one should have a functioning tailoring program that carries out all of the data manipulation and feedback generation functions of the program. If so designed, it should also carry out data management tasks and automate intervention tracking. Our next step is to integrate this computer program in the broader intervention implementation.

CHAPTER 12

Implementing a Tailored Health Communication Program

In this chapter, we turn our attention to the process of implementing the tailored health communication program we have developed. Many of the steps in implementing a tailored health communication program are similar to those involved in any other type of educational or communication-based health intervention. However, the data-driven nature of tailored communication presents some unique issues. This chapter provides an outline of the overall intervention process, with particular attention paid to those aspects that are unique or especially important to tailoring. Five major components are discussed:

1. Developing an implementation plan
2. Preparing for implementation to begin
3. Collecting and managing data
4. Producing feedback
5. Delivering feedback

For each of the five components, this chapter discusses specific tasks involved. The chapter also provides recommendations for dealing with quality control issues. Quality control is a key concern during all implementation steps due to the fact that each tailored document is different from all others previously produced.

Developing an Implementation Plan

As with any intervention, successful implementation of a tailored health communication program depends on starting with a comprehensive plan. This chapter is organized around a standard implementation plan.

Setting Key Implementation Parameters

As a first step to developing an implementation plan for a specific tailored health communication program, the following questions should be asked:

- When will implementation begin? Issues related to the overall project timeline, seasonality, and timeliness of data collection should be considered.

- How will data be collected? This question will be answered primarily by the nature of the data to be collected and the population to be surveyed. Telephone and mailed surveys, in-person interviews, and interactive computer programs may be used to collect data.

- How many times and at what interval will each person be surveyed? This may range from a single-time assessment, with all tailored materials produced based on this single data set, to complex interventions with multiple assessments and each instance of tailored feedback based on the data from different assessments.

- How frequently will feedback be produced? Data may be batch-processed so that multiple individuals are batched for feedback production all at once, or each individual's feedback may be produced in a batch of one as soon as data are collected. The frequency of batches is determined by resources available.

- Are batches of feedback determined by a period of time or by a predetermined size? Batches of data may be assembled as soon as a certain period of time has passed since the last batch (for example, each day, week, or month), or once a target number of people have been surveyed (e.g., every 100 people).

- How will feedback be delivered? This may be done through the mail, in person, or through an intermediary such as a health care provider. Additionally, nonprint tailored materials (beyond the scope of this book) may be delivered through a wide range of electronic means, including the Internet, kiosks, or prerecorded audio or video tapes.

First, answer the previous questions with an eye toward the ideal. If the ideal is not feasible due to resource and time constraints, determine the most critical issues (such as whether timeliness or the method of delivery is most critical), and pare back on the ideal until it better fits the resources and time available.

When to Begin Implementation

Ideally, program implementation would begin after all development activities have been completed—in other words, after the surveys have been finalized, the algorithms and tailored messages written, and the tailoring programs developed and tested. It is common, however, for implementation to begin while some or all of these components are still being developed. For example, if a tailored health communication program contains 36 feedback modules to be delivered monthly over a 3-year period, it might be impractical to wait for final development of all 36 modules before beginning to implement the first module.

Carrying out development and implementation concurrently requires careful planning. It requires using a development process that focuses on completing the structural elements of the entire tailored health communication program first, and then filling in the details, one module at a time.

To accomplish this, a detailed intervention plan, outlines of all surveys, outlined message libraries for all modules, outlined design templates for all modules, and a shell of the tailoring software program is developed first. When all of these items have been completed, the actual surveys, messages, algorithms, and design templates can be developed one module at a time. Implementation can begin as soon as all of the structural elements and at least one survey, message library, set of algorithms, design template, and associated tailoring program module are complete. Other modules can then be integrated into the implementation process as they are completed. As long as subsequently completed modules do not deviate from the structure developed for them in the beginning and deadlines are strictly adhered to, integration should occur relatively smoothly. If deadlines are not met, subsequent modules may not be delivered to recipients quickly enough after they receive earlier modules. In general, the start of program implementation should be scheduled for at least 1 month after the expected completion of the tailoring program (or the first usable portion of the program).

Preparing for Implementation to Begin

Preintervention tasks include all activities that need to be complete prior to the program start date. These include:

- Hiring and training personnel,

- identifying and hiring outside contractors,
- producing or acquiring intervention materials, and
- promoting the program among members of the target population.

Arranging Personnel

For successful program implementation, personnel must be hired and trained to carry out the following tasks and responsibilities:

- Overall management of program implementation,
- data collection,
- data entry,
- data management,
- operation of the tailoring computer program,
- printing tailored materials,
- assembling tailored materials, and
- delivering the materials.

Although all program staff have important roles to play, the individuals responsible for overall program implementation and data management are the key players. Resources permitting, it is advisable to have employees dedicated to these tasks, rather than performing them as just one part of their many duties. The other tasks can be performed by employees dedicated to other tasks or, as later discussed, contracted to outside individuals or companies with special expertise and resources to perform these more efficiently and accurately.

Arranging Contractors

Many of the steps in program implementation can be performed by outside contractors. In fact, unless they are carrying out a very large program or several programs at once, most health agencies are unlikely to have the time, financial resources, or personnel to develop the necessary technology and carry out all the implementation steps. Likely contractors include:

- a data collection firm to survey or interview program participants,
- a keypunch or optical scanning firm to digitize collected data,
- a database programmer to develop and support a data management database, and
- a feedback production firm to produce the tailored feedback.

Look for contractors accustomed to working on tailored health communication programs. Contractors who have previously developed tools and processes for delivering generic, targeted, and personalized communication programs may initially view a tailoring program as being similar to the work they have done in the past. However, often when they attempt to carry out a comprehensive tailored health communication program for the first time, such contractors find their existing tools and processes do not apply to the unique requirements of tailoring.

When working with people who are new to tailored health communication programs, carefully explain the tailoring process and detail the work they will have to perform, taking pains to detail the differences between this intervention and the non-tailored interventions they are used to performing. In searching for appropriate contractors, follow the three basic guidelines below:

1. Look for a contractor with flexible work flows, instead of one who will simply add the project to their existing assembly line. Most contractors have developed processes for juggling multiple clients and projects that include a set of standard steps to be followed from start to finish. Ask the contractor to detail the steps they will follow, carefully consider whether the work at hand can be completed with these steps, and settle on a refined set of steps with the contractor when appropriate. If a contractor insists on strictly adhering to a predetermined process, expect frustration.

2. Look for a contractor who will allow members of the tailored health communication program staff to be involved in the initial phases of the contractor's processes. This will help to identify misunderstandings and catch mistakes early on.

3. Develop a working plan with the contractor that offers planners of the tailored health communication program some flexibility in determining deliverables and the contractor flexibility in determining charges and timeline. Although this can make contracting more difficult, it allows both parties to focus on the work at hand rather than making the product fit a bottom line of time and cost that might have been based on an initially misunderstood product.

Producing Materials

Before implementing a tailored health communication program, certain materials and supplies need to be produced or acquired. These may include:

- Printed questionnaires;

- A computer assisted telephone interviewing (CATI) program;

If data are to be collected by phone, a CATI program can be an important quality control device and will speed up data entry. If data collection is contracted out, this is the contractor's responsibility.

- A data entry program;

If data are collected on paper, a keypunch or other data entry program will be needed to assure accuracy (or a contractor to perform this function).

- A data management database;

A comprehensive database that stores and reports data about program participants, not just a statistical or spreadsheet program, is necessary for easy data management. This is discussed in detail in the following.

- Preprinted stationery for printing the tailored messages (see chap. 7 for a description);

Print at least 25 % more paper than you expect to need. Doing so will ensure that there is plenty of paper for pre-testing, reprinting misprints, and creating sample copies later on.

- Envelopes or other enclosures for packaging and delivering assessments and feedback.

Obtain at least 10 % more than you expect to need.

Promoting the Program

A tailored health communication program places one special demand on participants: the need for them to provide precise data. Any promotional activities that can get individuals excited about participating or impress the importance of participation helps ensure they make the extra effort to provide quality data.

A promotional effort designed to explain the fact that feedback is individualized helps people understand the unique aspects of the information they will be receiving, and helps to distinguish a tailoring program from other seemingly similar interventions, such as personalized direct mail appeals that have saturated most households with junk mail.

This is also a good point to assure potential participants of confidentiality. This can help pre-empt a potentially difficult issue as personal data are requested and feedback containing personal information is delivered. Finally, for research-based studies, this is the appropriate time to explain the randomization process and note that some participants receive different materials than others (or no materials at all). Potential promotional activities include:

- A postcard or letter sent to potential participants;
- promotional materials (e.g., posters) posted in recruitment areas;
- delivery of sample materials to potential participants;
- a "health fair" to provide a needed service and promote the program at the same time;
- development and advertising of incentive programs; (Examples of incentives include time off at work for participation in a program implemented at a work site, or free screening services for participants in a program implemented through a health care facility.) and,
- one-on-one promotion to gatekeepers who may encourage participation.

Collecting and Managing Data

Data collection consists of assessment(s) of individuals; entry of data into a digital (computer) format; and, management of data for analysis, tracking, and generating tailored materials. Accurate and complete data are essential to the success of a tailored health communication program. Careful consideration of data quality at each of these steps is imperative. If data are incorrect, the feedback an individual receives will not be fully individualized, or even worse, may be inappropriate or incorrect. Although many generic interventions include information that is not appropriate to a given recipient, tailored health communication programs promise personal relevance and are especially disappointing if they don't deliver on it. Implementation activities must be designed to ensure high-quality data.

Assessment

The tailoring assessment may take many forms, including a paper-based survey, telephone survey, computer-based interactive survey, or even pooling data collected previously or concurrently for other purposes (such as data from medical records). The exact method of data collection is determined as the tailored health communication program is initially planned (see chap. 5) and the assessments developed (see chap. 6). What is most important for implementation is that, regardless of how the data are collected, they must be very accurate and complete from the start.

Accuracy should be checked as data are collected. Often, data are collected with the intent of "cleaning" them at a later time — identifying missing data and response errors, correcting recording mistakes, and so forth. Because data to be used for tailoring are likely to be used soon after collection, the provisions for cleaning that might otherwise be delayed and performed on a single complete set of data at one time instead needs to be performed as data are collected, one case or one batch at a time.

Every effort should be made to collect complete data for all variables needed to create the tailored feedback. Although 100% completeness is the ideal for any data collection effort, the reality is that any single individual's data may be incomplete as a result of data points that were not collected due to participant refusal or other types of nonresponse. For tailored health communication programs, missing data can result in less individualized or even incorrect feedback. In such cases, a generic default message is inserted where a more appropriate tailored message should have been (see chap. 9). Clearly, this would fall far short of the ideal outcome.

Certain data must be provided in order for a respondent to receive complete feedback. For example, in a tailored smoking cessation program, present smoking status is essential data. Such essential data should be designated as "required," meaning that an individual's tailored feedback cannot be produced if those data are missing. Essential data usually includes personal identification information needed to personalize and deliver the feedback (e.g., the participant's name and address), as well as the most basic demographic information used throughout the algorithms (e.g., gender and age). As in the previous example, additional data may also be designated as essential if an algorithm that uses it has no provision for a default value or if it is used to determine a large number of messages. Otherwise, the recipient would receive a large number of default messages— making the tailored communication more like a generic one. Some important steps to obtaining complete and accurate data include:

- Conducting preassessment promotional efforts that include mention of the importance of providing accurate, complete responses.

- Designing surveys and interviews for easy and accurate completion.

- Conducting thorough interviews (if this is the data collection method).

- Giving essential tailoring data priority and a prominent position in surveys and interviews.

- Making the purpose of all questions clear to respondents as they complete the assessment.

- Making confidentiality a priority and assuring respondents that the information they provide is confidential. If respondents are aware of the personal nature of the feedback to be delivered, a high degree of sensitivity about confidentiality can be expected. An explanation of data confidentiality measures should be readily available to respondents.

• Making provisions for timely re-assessment of individuals who fail to provide essential data.

Data Entry

Data may be entered as they are collected (as in a CATI), entered manually after collection (as in a printed survey that is scanned or keypunched), or imported from existing data sets (as in medical records from which data are extracted). The method of data entry is generally determined by the method of data collection.

For tailored health communication programs, it is best to think of assessment data as a perishable item. As soon as individuals complete an assessment, their data begins to age and eventually may become outdated. For example, responses to questions about eating habits, although valid at the time of the interview, become less valid over time because the respondent may make significant dietary changes. Because tailored messages are data-based communication, it is imperative that assessments be quickly digitized and entered in the production process.

As previously discussed, it is also important that data be accurate from the very beginning. It cannot wait for "cleaning" later on. If manually entered in a computer from written surveys, data should be double-entered—entered twice by different data entry personnel—and compared to ensure matching. If scanned, the scanning system should be accurate and checked regularly by manual confirmation of scanned data. If imported from another data source, the accuracy of source data should be carefully confirmed.

Data Management

Because a tailored health communication program uses data intensively *during* the intervention, rather than simply collecting data and storing it for later analysis, a comprehensive data management system is key to successful implementation. The data management system should be able to:

• Store all data about each individual in a readily accessible format;

• perform automatic checking for data accuracy and completeness;

• allow for simple statistical calculations (such as frequencies and averages) of individual and grouped data to check for accuracy and completeness;

• provide at-a-glance tracking of individuals to determine their status in the data collection-feedback production-feedback delivery process;

and,

- allow for any subset of the data to be selected and exported for feed-back production.

Such a system is usually accomplished with a computerized database. For most tailored health communication programs, the technical power of the database software is not important. Common user-modifiable database programs, such as Microsoft Access (for Windows) or Filemaker (for Windows or Macintosh) offer more than sufficient capabilities for storing, retrieving, and analyzing data, and can be easily modified by nonpro-grammers. More complex database applications, such as DBASE or FoxPro, offer the ability to handle millions of records and variables and include additional advanced features, but usually require the ongoing assistance of a professional programmer to develop and maintain. Such programs are necessary for only the largest tailored health communication programs.

Developing a comprehensive database program is one of the most cost-effective and time-saving investments that can be made. The initial up-front time and cost of establishing such a database are well spent.

Producing Feedback

Some tailored health communication programs utilize complex networks of computers and high-capacity printers to produce tailored feedback. Most, however, are implemented using a single desktop computer and monochrome laser printer. As noted in chapter 7, simply preprinting the stationery, allows colorful and professional looking tailored documents to be produced using this simple technology. Still, however simple or complex the printing hardware, the process of producing tailored feedback is essentially the same. There are four basic steps:

1. Data are exported from the data management program (i.e., data-base) and imported to the tailoring program.
2. The tailoring program processes the data, choosing the appropriate messages for each person, and assembles them on a digital page.
3. The pages are printed.
4. A person (or machine) assembles the pages and prepares them for delivery.

Throughout these steps, quality control is essential. Because each piece of feedback produced in a tailored health communication program is a one-of-a-kind product, the possibility for one-of-a-kind, unexpected errors is high. Quality control is accomplished by identifying key points in the production process where errors might occur and building in assurance checks at these points.

The tailoring computer programs can be developed with functions to assist in this quality control (see chap. 11). A common example of this is a reporting function that can tell production staff exactly what should have been produced so that it can be confirmed. A good tailoring program has the capability of producing batch reports that describe the batch of subjects printed (number of subjects, number of pages, names of subjects, etc.) and case reports that describe the content of a particular subject's feedback (name, message versions, number of pages, which pages or sections should be included, etc.). In addition, the tailoring program should have the capability of saving pages digitally (rather than assembling them and immediately sending them to the printer) so that there is a permanent digital record of the feedback at each of its production points—that is, as data indicating which messages are chosen and assembled, as digital print files containing assembled messages, and finally as printed documents.

Importing Data

Raw data collected and stored in the data management database isexported from the database and imported to the tailoring program. In some cases, the data management program and tailoring program can be integrated so that this process is automatic. In most cases, however, the tasks involved in the data management and feedback production steps are so distinct that the two are not closely connected. It is not necessary to export all data collected for each individual, but only a subset containing just the data to be used for tailoring, along with any identifying variables that may help to match individual data records in the tailoring program with their parent records in the data management database (e.g., ID number, names, etc.).

Once data are imported to the tailoring program, they should be checked again for accuracy. Preferably, the tailoring program contains automatic checking functions to identify records with missing data or values that fall outside a range of acceptable values. A quick scan of the imported data also helps catch mistakes at this point. Finally, variables in the tailoring program that are calculated based on the imported data (e.g., feedback variables that indicate which version of each message an individual is to receive) should also be reviewed to ensure that all values are correct. This is accomplished by visually scanning reports (on screen) of calculated variables, and examining the variables that would contain illogical values if raw data were incorrect. Quality control at this stage confirms that:

- the correct number of records were imported;
- the correct variables from the data set ended up in the correct fields in the tailoring program;
- all required data is present for each record (no required fields are empty);
- values in fields are not out of range; and,
- values for feedback (which message is to be printed) are not out of range.

Producing Digital Feedback

A well-designed tailoring program creates digital feedback files that are saved and printed later. Doing so allows the feedback to be checked before being committed to paper and provides an electronic trail for future evaluation.

Usually, the tailoring program allows project staff members to select a subset of people in the program and then automatically assemble the pages for those people in page layout or word processing files. Once the files have been created, they are inspected. Initial production runs should include careful inspection of the pages for inaccuracies in message selection and page layout. During production of the initial sets of feedback, every page should be reviewed. Subsequent runs should require only infrequent but regular inspection, perhaps 1 in 50 pages. Reviewers should look for missing message blocks (empty spaces on the page), incorrectly placed messages (out of position or overlapping), and incorrectly formatted messages.

Printing Feedback

Digital files (aforementioned) are sent to a laser printer containing preprinted paper stock. Pages should be printed in the order in which they are assembled in the final document rather than printing page 1 for all cases, and then page 2 for all cases, then matching them up. Doing so avoids the serious error of matching Jane Doe's page 1 with John Hancock's page 2!

Pages should be printed in manageable batches that are small enough to easily sort pages and reprint as needed. Printing all 2,000 newsletters at once would be the most efficient approach but only if the printing process was perfect. Imagine, however, trying to organize and sort 2,000 newsletters if there was a paper jam or misfeed midway through the print cycle. No one would be very happy about searching out case number 987 from the stack of 2,000 printed newsletters because the printer accidentally took two sheets of paper instead of one on the 600th page and therefore printed the remaining 1,400 pages on the wrong paper. A report should be generated by the tailoring program that lists what is in each print batch. The report should accompany the printed pages to the next step: assembly.

Printed pages are inspected to ensure that errors produced when printing are caught and remedied. As with other quality control, frequency of inspection is greatest for the first few sets of feedback. However, unlike most previous steps, the printing of feedback is partly mechanical rather than entirely electronic. Therefore, even when the perfect print has been achieved 50 times, subsequent prints may be imperfect—because of mechanical failures that are a normal part of the printing process. For example, printer errors can occur when the printer jams, toner is low, the ink is not fused well (i.e., it rubs off), or pages are misfed. Misfed pages are especially important to catch. Rather than simply being ugly, they can result in incorrect feedback—with one subject's messages appearing on the page belonging to another subject. Whatever the source or result of the printing error, the printer may continue along uninterrupted, so the only way to catch the mistake is to visually spot it. To find a printing error, look for:

- messages that are printed on the wrong page or the wrong side of the page;
- different personal identification information in the multiple pages of the same document;
- messages that are out of alignment;
- faded ink or blurred ink;
- ink that rubs off the page;
- wrinkled pages; and,
- preprinted paper that contains printing mistakes (e.g., unacceptable color variations, blotches, etc.).

In this day of near-perfect printing processes, poorly printed materials stand out and reduce recipients' confidence and perception of value.

Assembly

Printed pages often require some assembly in completed documents. This may be as simple as matching a cover letter with a single-page newsletter or as complex as binding and trimming a 20-page booklet.

Errors in assembly are even more unpredictable than printing errors. Mistakes are most likely to occur in feedback containing multiple pages, particularly when one subject receives a different number of pages than another (e.g., Jane Doe's newsletter is 20 pages long whereas John Hancock's is 12 pages long). Individuals assembling the documents should follow a detailed assembly process that includes regular points of self-inspection. In addition, a regular sample of final assembled documents should be inspected. To find assembly errors, look for:

- Sloppily assembled documents;
- pages that are out of order;
- missing pages; and,
- mismatched pages (one person's pages in another person's document).

Delivering Feedback

Once the perfect tailored document has been printed and assembled, it needs to be delivered to its recipient. As with other steps in the implementation process, timeliness is important. Having spent considerable time and resources developing and producing tailored documents, it is worth it to pay the extra price of timely and personal-feeling delivery.

In the face of rapidly developing digital delivery mechanisms (e.g., the Internet) and common predictions about the end of printed media, it is easy to disregard the many creative ways that good old-fashioned hand delivery of printed materials can be employed to improve intervention outcomes. These range from methods for making a piece of first-class mail more interesting to using other delivery mechanism besides mail. The first step to delivering tailored print feedback is to think creatively about how that delivery can be carried out. Some options include:

- Well–designed, attention–getting enclosures;
- personalized (or even tailored) enclosures;
- a postcard or letter preceding the tailored document to build anticipation;
- a follow–up postcard or letter to remind the recipient to read the tailored feedback;
- distribution of tailored messages at a worksite; and,
- delivery through a respected intermediary such as a spouse, child, or health care provider.

Conclusion

Implementing a tailored health communication program, with its need for specialized skills and production resources, may seem to be a daunting task. Likewise, the special issues of timeliness and quality control, due to the data–driven nature of tailoring, add extra steps and stress to the process. A detailed implementation plan addresses these unique needs in a systematic way. Once the first few batches of feedback have passed through the system, the process seems more routine, and the problems that demand the high degree of quality control detailed here becomes rare. Program planners and staff can then begin to focus on data analysis and evaluation to determine whether, and how, the tailored health communication program is successful or could be modified in the future to become even more effective.

CHAPTER 13

Evaluating Tailored Health Communication Programs

This chapter describes the process of evaluating tailored health communication programs. A thoughtful evaluation should determine at least two things: (1) the extent to which the program was effective in meeting its objectives; and, (2) specific ways the program could be modified or fine-tuned for greater performance in the future. To get this information, four basic questions must be answered:

1. Were guidelines for program development adhered to in creating the tailored health communication program?

2. Was the program implemented in a way that maximized its chances for success?

3. Were the tailored materials well-received by the target population?

4. Was the program effective in meeting its health and behavioral objectives?

The first two questions seek to better understand how the processes of developing and implementing a tailored health communication program could have influenced the program's effectiveness. This is sometimes referred to as a process evaluation. In contrast, the third and fourth questions seek to determine how individuals responded to the tailored materials. This focus on communication, behavioral, and health objectives is an outcome evaluation. Importantly, both types of evaluation are necessary for tailored health communication programs. This chapter examines these four questions in greater detail, discussing the rationale, evaluation methods, and indicators of success that apply to each.

Question 1: Were Guidelines for Program Development Adhered to in Creating the Tailored Health Communication Program?

Have you ever accidentally left out an ingredient when cooking? The results can be disastrous—bread that doesn't rise, flat cookies, flavorless meals. If you don't follow the recipe, you may end up disappointed with the final result. The same is true for creating a tailored health communication program. If certain steps in the planning and development process are omitted or poorly executed, you may not be satisfied with the resulting product. That's why it's important for any evaluation to start with a close examination of how the program was developed. In the case of tailored health communication programs, this means examining the processes of conducting background research, and developing tailoring assessment questionnaires, message concepts and messages, algorithms, and the computer program. Like most process evaluations, an examination of these tasks should be considered an integral and ongoing part of program development, not something you do once the program is completed. At the simplest level, this might involve keeping a checklist to assure that all steps in the development process are followed. But there other, more specific, strategies that can also be used at each step along the way.

Background Research

Background research for a tailored health communication program should be comprehensive, current, and accurate. It should provide a clear and detailed description of the health problem being addressed and the population that is affected. There are at least two ways to validate background research: review by an expert panel and interviews with members of the target population.

Expert Panel Review. Experts who are knowledgeable about the health or behavioral problems being addressed in a tailored communication program can often identify gaps and point out areas that may have been overlooked. Importantly, experts will not always be scientists, researchers, or physicians. For example, if children's health behaviors are being addressed, teachers or parents might be just as likely if not more likely to have the desired expertise. Before assembling an expert panel, decide what specific knowledge and experience you need to have represented on the panel, and what role you want each member to play. Once the panel is assembled, provide clear instructions and keep tasks simple. Remember that, although panel members may have greater knowledge of the topic area than you do, they will almost certainly be less familiar with the overall project. An expert panel may be best used to answer some of the following questions:

- Is the background information that has been gathered about the health or behavioral problem the most current available? If not, where can more up-to-date information be obtained?

- Are there any important pieces of information about the problem that are missing? If so, what are they?

- Are the characterizations of the health problem and the target population accurate? If not, where do the errors lie?

- Are there any important characteristics of the relationship between the population and health problem that have been overlooked? If so, which ones?

Interviews with Members of the Target Population. In addition to consulting with experts in the field, it is also important to have a clear understanding of the problem from the perspective of the target population. The most direct way to get this information is to spend time talking with members of the population. By conducting individual or group interviews with a representative sample of population members, it is possible to get valuable feedback about the results of background research activities. Focus group interviews are particularly well-suited for this task. Focus groups typically consist of 8 to 10 individuals gathered together to exchange ideas, comments, and observations in response to questions or issues raised by a group facilitator. When using focus group interviews to evaluate the appropriateness of background research findings, the facilitator can ask the group open-ended questions such as:

- What do you see as the main causes of this problem?

- In your experience, how does this problem affect people's lives?

- What do you think would be the most effective solutions to the problem?

- What types of information might be helpful in reducing the problem?

- Who do you think is most affected by this problem?

- What, if any, characteristics are shared by those who are affected?

- If you had to reach those affected by the problem, how would you do it?

When focus group participants' responses to these questions are consistent with findings from background research activities, one can be more confident in the integrity of those findings and proceed accordingly. If the two are quite dissimilar, however, it will be necessary to go back and redo some or all background research tasks. Detailed instructions for planning and using focus group methodology are available elsewhere (Krueger, 1994; Stewart & Shamdasani, 1991).

Tailoring Assessment Questionnaires

A formative evaluation of the tailoring assessment questionnaire should consist of at least two main activities: cognitive response testing and pretesting. Each is discussed below.

Cognitive Response Testing. Cognitive response procedures are used to help understand how individuals process information. They involve intensive one-on-one interviews in which participants may be asked to think aloud about the information they just read, paraphrase the content, and respond to other planned questions and probes from an interviewer (Forsyth & Lessler, 1991; Jabine, Straf, Tanur, & Tourangeau, 1984; Sudman, Bradburn & Schwartz, 1996). Although cognitive response testing (CRT) is only one of many qualitative methods appropriate for use in formative or process evaluations, it can be especially helpful in testing questionnaires. When used in this way, CRT seeks to determine whether respondents understand the intended meaning or words or phrases in specific questions, the type of information being sought, and the desired form a response should take. When well-planned, CRT should yield answers to the following types of questions:

- How well do respondents comprehend the instructions, questions, and response choices?

- Which, if any, words or phrases do respondents find confusing or unclear?

- How accurate are respondents in judging what kind of information is being sought?

- How easy or difficult is it for respondents to retrieve the desired information?

- How frequently do respondents generate answers that have not been accounted for in the tailoring assessment questionnaire being tested?

Findings from CRT can and should be used to revise individual questions, restructure the questionnaire, or make clearer the instructions provided to respondents.

Pretesting. The term "pretesting" is used to represent a wide range of formative evaluation activities designed to generate feedback from participants about some preliminary form of a program or communication. As it relates to evaluating a tailoring assessment questionnaire, pretesting is commonly used to gather information such as:

- respondents' overall reaction to the questionnaire;

- the extent to which the questionnaire has been improved by CRT and other modifications;

- how easy or difficult the questionnaire is to complete;

- the appropriateness of the questionnaire's content;

- the appropriateness of the questionnaire's length;
- the average length of time needed to complete the questionnaire;
- which modalities (e.g., print, telephone, web) are most appropriate for administering the questionnaire; and,
- the appropriateness and attractiveness of design and layout elements of the questionnaire.

Typically, this type of pretesting involves administering the tailoring assessment questionnaire to members of the target population in the same setting in which it will be used, observing respondents as they go through the questionnaire, then interviewing them after they have completed it. By observing respondents in the process of completing the questionnaire, it is often possible to detect potential problems. For example, long delays in completing certain sections of the questionnaire, flipping back and forth between the same pages of the questionnaire, and looks of puzzlement on the faces of respondents are some of the more common signs of difficulty completing a questionnaire. Questions asked during the actual pretest interviews may be open- or closed-ended. Commonly asked pretest questions include:

- What, if anything, did you like about this questionnaire?
- What, if anything, would you change to make this questionnaire better?
- Were there any questions or any parts of the questionnaire you found confusing or difficult to understand?
- Were there any questions you did not feel comfortable answering?
- Were there any questions that offended you?
- Were there any important questions that were not asked in the questionnaire but should have been?
- How would you rate the instructions for using this questionnaire? (1 = not at all clear, 10 = very clear)
- How easy or difficult was it to follow the flow of the questions?
- Were there ever points when you weren't sure which question to go to next?
- If you received this questionnaire (in the mail/at your doctor's office/at your work place), how likely would you be to complete it? (1 = not at all likely, 10 = very likely)
- Would you say this questionnaire was too long, about the right length, or not long enough?

As with the findings from any other formative, or process, evaluation, the results of pretesting should be used to modify and improve the tailoring assessment questionnaire.

Message Concepts and Tailored Messages

The main objective of pretesting message concepts and tailored messages is to identify any ideas, information or approaches to be used that may compromise the effectiveness of the messages. By doing so, materials can be revised as needed prior to finalizing the tailored health communication program.

Pretesting tailored messages is different from pretesting other nontailored types of health information in one important way—the messages themselves are written for a person with some specific characteristic or attribute. If tailored messages are evaluated by a person to whom the messages do not apply, the messages might be rated (unfairly) as unfavorable. For this reason, we recommend an approach to pretesting that provides each pretester with the actual messages he or she would receive if participating in the tailored health communication program. This approach requires more detailed pretest planning and is more time consuming than conventional approaches, but it is the best way to assure that the pretest will yield valuable results.

The same methods used in a process evaluation of background research and the tailoring assessment questionnaire (i.e., focus group interviews, CRT, pretesting) can also be used in testing message concepts and tailored messages. By using questions like those listed in the preceding sections, messages and prototype materials can be evaluated on the extent to which they are perceived by readers as being attractive, informative, easy to understand, scientifically credible, interesting, engaging, personally relevant, culturally relevant, acceptable (i.e., not offensive), and useful in helping them meet personal health and learning objectives. Often it is not feasible to pretest all messages or combinations of messages in a tailored message library. In these instances, efforts should be made to instead pretest a representative sample of messages. This sample should always include any messages the writers are especially interested in or concerned about, any messages that use new and previously untested approaches, and any messages that have not previously been used in the target population.

Algorithms and Computer Programming

Process evaluation of the accuracy of tailoring algorithms involves conducting a system test, as described in detail in chapter 10. Likewise, procedures for evaluating the functionality of the computer program that generates tailored messages are described in chapter 11. Both of these steps are critical in determining whether program development processes have been followed and have led to an accurate, functional program.

Question 2: Was the Program Implemented in a Way That Maximized Its Chances for Success?

Even when all steps in the development process are closely adhered to, a tailored health communication program might still fail to reach its intended objectives if it is not implemented properly. An implementation error, also known as "Type III error," occurs when some problem or flaw exists in the process through which a program is delivered to its intended recipients(Basch, Slipecevich, Gold, Duncan, & Kolbe, 1985). In tailored health communication programs, implementation errors are most likely to occur in one of three general areas—recruitment and enrollment, assessment, and data processing and feedback.

Recruitment and Enrollment Errors. For any health promotion program to succeed, it must have participants. If only a small number of individuals are willing to enroll in a tailored health communication program, its impact will likely be limited. Therefore, when a process evaluation reveals that recruitment is proceeding more slowly than anticipated or enrollment is lower than expected, several follow-up inquiries must be made to more precisely identify the source of the problem. For example:

- Do the recruitment sites provide access to a sufficient number of eligible participants?

If not, a new recruitment strategy should be considered. If so, why aren't more eligible participants enrolling in the program?

- Are all eligible participants being offered the opportunity to enroll in the program?

If not, why? Are more resources or better promotion needed to assure effective recruitment?

- What are the reasons that eligible participants choose not to enroll in the program?

By identifying these reasons, the recruitment appeal can sometimes be modified to address the specific concerns an eligible participant might have.

- Do eligible participants fully understand the concept of tailoring?

Receiving personal, individualized health information is often highly attractive and motivating to potential participants, but for those who do not grasp how such information is unique or different, participating in a program holds less appeal. If this is the case, it may be that the recruitment appeal must do a better job of promoting the tailoring aspects of the program.

- Is the participation burden perceived as greater than the value of receiving tailored feedback?

If so, the program may need to modified to reduce the burden on participants. Perhaps the tailoring assessment questionnaire is viewed as too long, or there are too many assessments. Alternatively, the tailored feedback might be made more attractive and useful. Participation incentives may also be needed.

Assessment Errors. Tailoring assessment questionnaires that are not fully completed, not completed in a timely manner, or not completed at all can also be a source of implementation error. As explained in chapter 9, when a person does not answer a particular question in the questionnaire, the computer program often fills in his or her feedback with a generic default message. If a questionnaire has a great deal of missing data, the resulting feedback will likely contain many default messages. Consequently, this person's tailored feedback isn't so tailored anymore and might not have the effects we typically expect from a tailored health communication program. If incomplete questionnaires are common in your program, at least two strategies should be considered. First, re-examine the tailoring assessment questionnaire. Is it too long? Are there certain questions participants are consistently leaving blank? If so, which ones and why? The procedures described previously for process evaluation of assessments can be used to answer these questions. Second, attempt to recontact participants to obtain the missing information. This approach is more time consuming and costly but, if feasible, can help address the problem.

In programs that administer multiple tailoring assessment questionnaires and provide updated tailored feedback after each assessment, timely completion of questionnaires is essential for program success. If participants do not complete their follow-up questionnaires promptly (or do not complete them at all), they will receive a different set of tailored materials than those who do. Their materials are either incomplete, missing entire communications for which they did not return a questionnaire, or received at odd intervals because they were late completing a questionnaire. Either way, they are getting a diluted version of the optimal program, which may therefore compromise program effectiveness. If a process evaluation suggests this type of implementation error is occurring, it is important to understand why follow-up assessments are not being completed. Efforts should be made—beginning at the recruitment and enrollment stage—to more clearly inform eligible participants what will be required of them should they enroll in the program.

Data Processing and Feedback Errors. A large tailored health communication program may be serving thousands or tens of thousands of individuals at any point in time. Each of these individuals have his or her own data file in the program that may even be updated periodically. Each also receive multiple pages of tailored feedback that must be assembled, perhaps on multiple occasions. Obviously, there are many opportunities for errors to occur in this process, and any such errors could render the program less effective. Evaluation of the implementation process should assure that the systems in place to carry out these tasks are routinely checked and found to be reliable. By closely following the quality control procedures outlined in chapter 12, many potential problems in processing data and creating tailored feedback can be avoided.

Question 3: Were the Tailored Materials Well-Received by the Target Population?

According to models of communication and persuasion, the likelihood of printed materials having behavioral effects is enhanced when certain intermediate outcomes occur. (McGuire, 1991) For example, a person must be exposed to a communication, pay attention to it, like it, understand it, learn from it, remember it, base decisions on it, and then behave in accord with those decisions. Because these intermediate outcomes can be important precursors to subsequent health or behavioral change, they are often of interest when evaluating a tailored health communication program. In previous tailoring research, a wide variety of such variables have been measured, and found to be important indicators of the superiority of tailored versus nontailored communications (Brug, Glanz, Van Assema, Kok, & Van Breukelen, 1998; Brug, Steenhuis, Van Assema, & de Vries, 1996: Campbell et al., 1994; Kreuter, 1997; Kreuter, Bull, Clark, & Oswald, in press; Skinner, Strecher, & Hospers, 1994). Intermediate outcomes are typically measured at one or several points after an individual has received his or her tailored communication. These intermediate variables can be broadly classified in the following categories:

- Exposure and reading;
- reaction to appearance;
- reaction to content;
- perceived personal relevance;
- effects on communication with others;
- perceived usefulness of the information.

Exposure and Reading. Before asking individuals what they thought about the tailored communication they received, it is first necessary to confirm that they were actually exposed to the communication and to learn how thoroughly they consumed its contents. Questions such as those listed in the following have been used in previous studies (Kreuter, Brennan, Lukwago, Scharff, & Wadud, 1977) to measure recall and reading:

- In the last 3 months, did you receive any printed health information in the mail from the Change of Heart project? (yes/no)

- What kind of information did you receive? (information about quitting smoking/eating less fat/exercising more often; plus a foil—wearing seat belts)

- How much, if any, of the information did you read? (none of it/some of it/most of it/all of it)

Reaction to Appearance. Theories of information processing suggest that, under some circumstances, peripheral cues, such as the attractiveness of a communicator or a printed brochure, can increase its persuasive appeal. As with any type of printed health information, we recognize that people are generally more likely to attend to a tailored communication if their first impression of its appearance is a favorable one. The two sample measures below were used in evaluating tailored weight loss materials in a randomized trial (Kreuter & Scharff, 1999).

- Did the weight loss materials catch your attention? (7-point Likert scale: 1 = not at all, 7 = very much)

- How attractive were the weight loss materials? (7-point Likert scale: 1 = not at all attractive, 7 = very attractive)

Reaction to Content. Besides being attractive, tailored messages should also be informative, easy to understand, credible, and contain new information. These intermediate outcomes have been assessed in tailoring studies (Brug et al., 1996; Kreuter & Scharff, 1999) using questions like those listed below:

- How interesting was the health information you received? (7-point Likert scale: 1 = not at all interesting, 7 = very interesting);

- How informative was the health information you received? (7-point Likert scale: 1 = not at all informative, 7 = very informative);

- How much of the information was new for you? (none of it/some of it/most of it/all of it);

- Were you already familiar with the information? (7-point Likert scale: 1 = not at all familiar, 7 = very familiar);

- How difficult or easy to understand was the information? (very difficult/difficult/neither difficult nor easy/easy/very easy);

- In your opinion, how trustworthy was the information in the weight loss materials? (7-point Likert scale: 1 = not at all trustworthy, 7 = very trustworthy);

- How credible was the information? (7-point Likert scale: 1 = not at all credible, 7 = very credible);

- How much did you like the weight loss materials you read? (7-point Likert scale: 1 = not at all, 7 = very much);

- Do you still have the information you received? (yes/no).

Perceived Personal Relevance. As described in chapter 2, Petty and Cacioppo's (1981) elaboration likelihood model suggests that people are more likely to actively and thoughtfully process information if they perceive it to be personally relevant. Studies have shown that messages that are actively processed like this tend to be retained for a longer period of time and are more likely to lead to permanent change (Petty, 1977). Generally speaking, we would expect tailored materials to be perceived as more personally relevant than nontailored ones. This is probably the reason so many tailoring studies have sought to measure perceived relevance as an important intermediate outcome. Three different approaches to measuring this construct are shown below.

- How well did the information you received apply to you? (it didn't apply to me at all/it could have applied to anyone/it applied to me specifically);

- How much did the information in the materials apply to your life? (7-point Likert scale: 1 = didn't apply at all, 7 = applied very much); and,

- How personally relevant was the health information you received? (7-point Likert scale: 1 = not at all relevant, 7 = highly relevant).

Effects on Communication with Others. If tailored messages are effective in stimulating more thoughtful consideration of a health problem or behavior, we might expect they would also increase the likelihood of a person discussing the content of the messages with others. In fact, discussing tailored materials with others may be an indicator of greater elaboration, showing that a person is thinking and talking about the information the materials contained. Past tailoring studies have used several different approaches to measuring these effects.

- Did you show the information to any friends or family members? (yes/no);

- Did you show the information to your doctor? (yes/no);

- Have you discussed the information with others? (yes/no); and,

- How likely is it that you will show the weight loss materials to people you know? (7-point Likert scale: 1 = not at all likely, 7 = very likely).

Perceived Usefulness of the Information. The ultimate test of effectiveness for tailored health messages involves determining whether they stimulate changes in the health and behavioral outcomes they seek to influence. However, it may also be of interest to learn whether individuals perceive tailored communication to be helpful in enabling them to enact such changes. Importantly, these intermediate outcomes should not be considered a substitute for measuring actual health and lifestyle change. Several sample measures from previous tailoring research on weight loss (Kreuter & Scharff, 1999) and dietary change (Brug et al., 1996) are shown in the following.

- How useful would the materials be in helping you lose weight? (7-point Likert scale: 1 = not at all useful, 7 = very useful);
- How likely is it that you will make changes in your behavior or lifestyle based on what you read in the weight loss materials? (7-point Likert scale: 1 = not at all likely, 7 = very likely);
- As a result of the nutrition information have you changed your opinion about your diet? (yes/no);
- How encouraging were the weight loss materials? (7-point Likert scale: 1 = not at all encouraging, 7 = very encouraging);
- As a result of the nutrition information do you intend to change your diet? (yes/no);
- As a result of the nutrition information have you changed your diet? (yes/no);
- As a result of the nutrition information have you reduced your fat intake? (yes/no);
- As a result of the nutrition information have you increased your fruit intake? (yes/no); and,
- As a result of the nutrition information have you increased your vegetable intake? (yes/no).

Most of the evaluation questions listed in this section have been drawn from previously conducted tailoring studies, and most have been closed-ended so as to yield quantitative data. This is certainly not a requirement of tailored programs. In fact, we believe much valuable information can be gained by gathering more qualitative data about people's reactions to tailored messages and encourage readers to think creatively about how such measures might be employed.

Question 4: Was the Program Effective in Meeting Its Health and Behavioral Objectives?

In most cases, a tailored health communication program has as its main objective, to increase knowledge or awareness, change attitudes or beliefs, modify other psychosocial variables, or change health-related skills, behaviors, or practices. When evaluating a tailoring program, it is important to know which of these outcomes the program sought to achieve, and plan accordingly to use the appropriate follow-up measures. The specific measures in each category varies greatly from program to program depending on its focus, and many programs seek to bring about change in more than one outcome. A brief overview of each different outcome category is provided in the following.

Knowledge and Awareness

Although increased knowledge alone is seldom sufficient to bring about changes in complex health-related behaviors, it is often an important precursor to such change. Imagine a tailored health communication program for teens that has, as its goals, to increase knowledge and reduce myths about how HIV is transmitted, and increase knowledge about the ways HIV transmission can be prevented. To measure these changes in knowledge, we would likely administer an HIV knowledge test to students at baseline, provide tailored feedback based on their accurate and inaccurate responses, then re-administer the HIV knowledge test. Such a test might include questions like the following:

- You can get HIV by shaking hands with a person who has AIDS. (agree/disagree)

- Mothers can pass HIV to their babies during birth. (agree/disagree)

- Condoms made from lamb skin are just as effective as latex condoms in preventing HIV infection. (agree/disagree)

If the average student answered 14 of 20 questions correctly at baseline, we would hope for a significantly higher number of correct answers at follow-up. If an objective of the tailoring program is to increase awareness of some program or service (e.g., availability of free condoms or a clean-needle exchange), evaluation measures should seek to determine whether awareness was increased among those who received the tailored communication.

Attitudes and Beliefs

Theories of health behavior change identify a number of specific attitudes and beliefs that can directly influence health-related behaviors. For example, the health belief model (Becker, 1974) suggests that behavior change is most likely to occur when a person believes he is at risk for some health problem (i.e., perceived susceptibility) and believes that the consequences of that problem would be serious for him (i.e., perceived severity). In the absence of feeling susceptible to a problem or fearing that a severe consequence will result from it, a person is not likely to undertake preventive health actions. Under these conditions, a tailored health communication program may seek to increase perceived susceptibility and severity when they are unrealistically low and, therefore, would also evaluate changes in these constructs that occurred as a result of the program. Two measures of perceived risk and susceptibility previously used in tailoring studies (Kreuter & Strecher, 1995) are shown below.

- Compared to others your same age and sex, how would you rate your risk of getting heart disease or having a heart attack in the next 10 years? (much higher than average/higher than average/about average/lower than average/about average)

- If you continue smoking, how likely do you think it is that you will suffer serious health problems in the future? (7-point Likert scale: 1 = not at all likely, 7 = very likely)

Two constructs from Bandura's (1977) social cognitive theory—self-efficacy and outcome expectations—are also important precursors to behavior change. Efficacy expectations, or self-efficacy, are beliefs a person has about his or her ability to successfully enact some behavioral change (Strecher, DeVellis, Becker, & Rosenstock, 1986). Outcome expectations are beliefs about whether changing a particular behavior will result in a particular desired outcome. According to the theory, behavior change is most likely to occur when self-efficacy is high, and outcome expectations are positive. Many tailored health communication programs seek to influence these constructs, especially self-efficacy. Although there are specialized multi-item self-efficacy scales that can be used to evaluate program effects on behaviors like smoking, simpler measures of self-efficacy such as those following can also be used.

- How confident are you that you can do aerobic type exercise for 20 minutes, three times per week? (very confident/somewhat confident/not very confident/not at all confident)

- How confident are you that you can eat at least five servings of fruits and vegetables every day? (7-point Likert scale: 1 = not at all confident, 7 = very confident)

Other Psychosocial Variables

Still other behavioral science theories identify constructs such as behavioral intention and stage of readiness to change as important prebehavioral outcomes for evaluation. According to the theory of reasoned action (Fishbein & Azjen, 1975), the best predictor of behavior change is intention to change the behavior. This construct is especially useful as an outcome measure in tailoring studies for which the follow-up period may not be sufficient to detect actual changes in behavior. In these instances, behavioral intention can sometimes serve as a reasonable proxy measure. A recent study of tailored communication and weight loss (Kreuter, Bull, Clark & Oswald, in press) evaluated behavioral intention with the two items below.

- Do you intend to make any of the changes recommended in the weight loss materials? (yes/no)

- Which, if any, of the recommended changes do you intend to make? (open-ended)

The transtheoretical model of behavior change (Prochaska & DiClemente, 1983) identifies five distinct stages of readiness to adopt behavioral change—precontemplation, contemplation, preparation, action, and maintenance. According to the model, different intervention strategies are needed for people who are in different stages of readiness to change. Tailored or stage-matched programs and materials are particularly well-suited for this task. Importantly, Prochaska and colleagues (Prochaska, DiClemente, & Norcross, 1992) have demonstrated that movement from one stage of readiness to the next may be as important as actual behavior change. One important implication of this finding is that movement in stage of readiness may be an appropriate outcome measure in evaluating program effects. Some recent studies have found that tailored materials can facilitate positive stage movement (Marcus et al., 1998). As with self-efficacy, there are established multi-item scales available to measure stage of readiness for specific behaviors. A simpler, two-question stage measure from a tailored smoking cessation program (Strecher et al., 1994) is shown here.

- Have you seriously thought about quitting smoking in the next six months? (yes/no)

- Are you planning to quit smoking in the next 30 days? (yes/no)

Those who answer "no" to the first question are precontemplators. Those who answer "yes" to the first but "no" to the second question are contemplators. Those who answer "yes" and "yes" are in the preparation stage. Anyone indicating they are presently trying to quit smoking is classified as being in the action stage, and those who are exsmokers are considered to be in the maintenance stage.

Health Related Skills, Behaviors and Practices

Most tailored health communication programs tested have had as their ultimate objective changes in health related behaviors (e.g., cigarette smoking, diet, physical activity, medication compliance, seat belt use) or practices (e.g., getting a mammogram, getting a cholesterol test, enrolling in a quit-smoking program). Some have also been interested in building specific behavioral skills such as negotiating condom use with a sex partner, using low-fat cooking techniques, reading a nutrition label, or shopping for healthier foods at the grocery store. All previous steps in the evaluation process lead to this set of outcomes. Changes in health-related behaviors and practices are the most important outcomes to evaluate in determining whether or not the program was effective in reaching its objectives.

Although it can be very straightforward and fairly simple to evaluate changes in some behavioral outcomes (i.e., got a mammogram/did not get a mammogram), this is not always the case. Sometimes multiple measures are more appropriate. Consider the following possible outcomes from a tailored quit-smoking program (Brennan, Caburnay, & Wilshire, 1998):

- In the last six months did you make a serious attempt to quit smoking? (yes/no)

- In the last six months did you ever quit smoking for at least 24 hours continuously? (yes/no)

- Have you smoked a cigarette, even a puff, in the last 7 days? (yes/no)

Note that although only the third question measures sustained cessation (i.e., self-reported 7-day continuous abstinence), all three may be important indicators of quitting activity. Because number of quit attempts is associated with successful quitting, this is a potentially important outcome despite stopping short of actual cessation.

In evaluating behavioral outcomes, it is often necessary to obtain baseline measures of behavior in order to compare any changes that are observed after individuals are given tailored materials. For example, if a tailored health communication program seeks to reduce dietary fat consumption, it is necessary to measure each participant's level of dietary fat consumption before the program begins. Such measurement can be a part of the tailoring assessment questionnaire. In this case, a brief dietary fat screener (Block, Clifford, Naughton, Henderson, & McAdams, 1989) could be administered as part of the tailoring assessment questionnaire and serve the dual purpose of providing a baseline level of dietary fat intake, plus indicate specific areas of focus for tailored messages. Several tailoring studies on dietary change have used this approach (Campbell et al., 1994; Kreuter et al., 1997)

Reduction in Morbidity and Mortality

Although it is frequently the ultimate goal of health promotion—including tailored health communication programs—to reduce rates of death and disease and increase quality of life among program participants, these outcomes are less likely to be detected in a short-term evaluation. For this reason, most evaluations of tailoring effects have focused on more proximal outcomes such as those described previously.

How is the Information Obtained from the Evaluation to Be Used?

The information gathered from process and outcome evaluation activities should be used to continuously monitor and improve the tailored health communication program. A thorough evaluation must judge not only program effectiveness, but also the integrity of the program development and implementation processes and the appropriateness of the program's messages and materials. Successful tailoring programs is continually refined based on evaluation findings. They grow and adapt to meet changes in the needs or interests of the target population and changes in the demands required to modify health–related behaviors.

CHAPTER 14

Epilogue: The Future of Tailored Health Communication

The number of research studies and practical applications of tailored communication is exploding in a wide variety of fields. In health education and health communication, studies have already shown that tailored print materials are more effective than nontailored ones in helping individuals change health–related behaviors such as smoking, diet, physical activity, cancer and cholesterol screening, and can enhance participation in health promotion programs (Brennan, Kreuter, Caburnay, & Wilshire, 1998; Brug, Glanz, Van Assema, Kok, & Van Breukelen, 1998; Brug, Steenhaus, van Assema, & de Vries, 1996; Bull, Kreuter & Scharff, 1999; Campbell et al., 1994; Dijkstra, De Vries, & Roijackers, 1998a; 1998b; Kreuter & Strecher, 1996; Marcus et al., 1998; Prochaska, DiClemente, Velicer, & Rossi, 1993; Skinner, Strecher, & Hospers, 1994; Strecher et al., 1994). Findings from these and other tailored health communication programs described in this book suggest that computer–based tailoring has great potential as a tool for helping meet important public health objectives.

But tailored health communication is still in its infancy. Although its use is growing steadily, its methods are still relatively complex, and its applications have been limited to a handful of health problems and primarily print media. By aggressively pursuing a thoughtful research agenda in tailored communication and paying close attention to technological advancements in computerized communication, the tailoring of tomorrow promises to be simpler, more widely applicable, and a more commonplace tool for those working in the fields of health promotion and health communication. Just how this future is realized is determined by how tailoring is extended in the five key areas we describe.

New Content: Tailoring on Different Variables

Tailored health communication programs developed to date have focused on a limited set of variables drawn from a handful of behavioral science theories. In most programs, for example, messages have been tailored to a participant's stage of readiness to change (Prochaska & DiClemente, 1983), perceived barriers to changing (Becker, 1974), self–efficacy (Bandura, 1986), perceived or actual health risk, or other psychosocial variables. Although these are clearly important variables to consider (especially when behavior change is the program objective), the potential to tailor messages based on different kinds of variables is almost limitless and largely untapped.

Of particular interest in the near future will be variables that better characterize an individual's abilities, values, and preferences. These variables need not be directly related to health and behavioral outcomes to be important for tailoring. Such variables might include:

- Gender
- Age, or generation
- Cultural–based identity, values, and beliefs
- Literacy level
- Learning style

Consideration of these and related variables would extend tailoring beyond its current focus on *what* information needs to be communicated to *how* that information can be communicated most effectively to a particular individual.

New Methods: Tailoring on Multiple Variables Simultaneously

The power of tailored health communication rests in its ability to assess and address the needs of any individual. The more data that are collected from an individual and addressed in a tailoring program, the more precise the feedback can be. To date, most tailored health communication programs have tailored messages on only one or two variables at a time. This approach has been dictated by the complexity, scope, and learning curve involved in creating a comprehensive message library with unique, highly tailored, and well written messages.

However, as the technological tools for tailoring become more capable and people with message writing and software development skills join the field of tailoring, this threshold will be extended. In the future, a single tailored message might be derived from a wide–ranging collection of individual data, including demographic, cultural, cognitive, and behavioral variables. For example, a person's age, reading level, learning style, and stage of readiness to change might be combined in a single composite variable, or profile, that served to guide all other tailored messages. Using this approach, a message about overcoming a particular barrier or changing an inaccurate belief would be framed in the context of the appropriate age, reading, learning, and readiness levels. In general, we expect that this increased precision will make messages more relevant and helpful, thereby increasing their effectiveness.

New Settings: Delivering Tailored Health Communication Programs in Different Places

Tailored health communication programs implemented to date have been carried out in doctors' offices, public health clinics, work sites, churches, welfare offices, schools, and even in individuals' homes (i.e., through telephone and mailed communication). New tailoring programs are now being undertaken in communities, at senior centers, in shopping malls, and in small community–based organizations. Yet this diversity of settings only scratches the surface of potential venues for reaching the public with technology based tailored health communication. Other promising settings include:

- Grocery stores
- Public transportation facilities
- Community walking trails
- Recreation centers and health clubs
- Boys and girls clubs
- Barber shops and beauty salons
- Museums and science centers
- Sports arenas and stadiums
- Physical therapy, rehabilitation, and other specialty clinics

As described in chapter 4, thorough background research reveals specific settings in which a program might best reach its target population. Clearly, productive new venues will be discovered that are not only supportive of communication and behavior change, but also have the infrastructure to make delivery and quality assurance of tailoring programs feasible.

New Media: Developing Tailored Health Communications Programs in non-Print Media

This book has focused on tailored print materials. But not because other media are inappropriate for tailoring. Rather that nearly all tailored health communication programs developed to date have used print media. In fact, it is in nonprint media that technical advances have introduced some of the most exciting options for delivery of tailoring programs in the future. These include:

- Interactive Internet sites;
- interactive telephone programs;
- interactive computer kiosks;
- interactive video games;
- tailored e–mail;
- tailored videotapes; and,
- tailored audio tapes.

Each of these media or delivery mechanisms offer unique challenges but also opportunities for tailoring health information. Indeed, as technological innovations make modern media more accessible to developers and commonplace for users, tailored health communication will need to utilize these media in order to remain an attractive and successful method of health promotion. Although it is still quite early in the game, there is some evidence that the successes of print–based tailored health communication are reproducible in tailored interactive computer programs (Campbell, Honess–Morreale, Farrell, Carbone, & Brasure, in press).

Even in the print medium, new technologies are already increasing the capacity of program developers to create tailored materials more quickly, efficiently, and with a more polished style and design.

New Research: Continuing the Process of Discovery

Recent studies have examined if tailoring works and how tailoring works. Much is left to learn in both of these areas. For example, tailored health information has most often been compared to generic materials or to no–intervention control groups. But how will tailored health communication programs fare compared to more robust communication approaches such as targeted materials or interpersonal communication? As described in this chapter, most tailored materials tested to date have been delivered in print format. Can effects be enhanced when messages are delivered via more advanced and interactive communication technologies? Also, is tailoring more effective for some behaviors than others? For certain populations? In certain settings? What program design and development activities are most likely to improve a program's chances for success?

Perhaps most exciting is a third area of research, seeking to identify ways we can maximize the effectiveness of tailored health communication in the future. For example, what is the optimal dose model for tailoring? How many different assessments and how many sets of materials over what period of time are needed to achieve the best results? What variables are most important to tailor on?

Lastly, how cost–effective are tailored health communication programs? To date, no studies have sought to answer this important question. On the surface, it would appear that, although the development costs for a tailoring program may be high, the operating costs could be minimal. Studies are needed to determine whether one or both of these expenses can be justified by the health, behavioral, and quality of life impact of tailored materials.

These are just some of the many important and as yet unanswered questions in tailoring research. This book was written to provide students, researchers, and practitioners in health promotion and health communication with the understanding necessary to design and implement tailored programs that could be used in studies to help answer these research questions. We encourage all readers to use this new knowledge and join us in the pursuit of answers.

REFERENCES

Abad, V., Ramos, J., & Boyce, E. (1974). A role model for delivery of mental health services to Spanish–speaking minorities. *American Journal of Orthopsychiatry, 44*(4), 584–595.

Abbotts, B., & Osborn, L. M. (1993). Immunization status and reasons for immunization delay among children using public health immunization clinics. *American Journal of Diseases of Children, 147,* 965–968.

Abrams, D. B., Mills, S., & Bulger, D. (in press). Challenges and future directions for tailored communication research. *Annals of Behavioral Medicine.*

Abrams, D. B., Orleans, C. T., Niaura, R. S., Goldstein, M. G., Prochaska, J. O., & Velicer, W. (1996). Integrating individual and public health perspectives for treatment of tobacco dependence under managed health care: A combined stepped–care and matching model. *Annals of Behavioral Medicine, 18*(4), 290–304.

Aday, L. A. (1996). *Designing and conducting health surveys* (2nd ed.). San Francisco: Jossey Bass.

Akbar, N. I. (1991). The evolution of human psychology for African Americans. In R. L. Jones (Ed.), *Black Psychology* (3rd ed., pp. 99–123). Berkeley, CA: Cobb & Henry Publishers.

Annals of Behavioral Medicine (1999). *21*(3).

Anonymous. (1997). MicroMass hits market with web personalization software. *Business Marketing, 82*(1), 12.

Bandura, A. (1977). Toward a unifying theory of behavior change. *Psychology Review, 84*(2), 191–215.

Bandura, A. (1986). *Social foundations of thought and action: A social cognitive theory*. New Jersey: Prentice Hall.

Basch, C., Slipecevich, E., Gold, R., Duncan, D., & Kolbe, L. (1985). Avoiding type III errors in health education program evaluations: A case study. *Health Education Quarterly, 12*(4), 315–331.

Beale, S. (1998). Digital Presses get personal. *MacWorld*, January, 24–25.

Becker, M. H. (1974). The health belief model and personal health behavior. *Health Education Monographs, 2*, 324–473.

Becker, M. H., & Janz, N. K. (1987). On the effectiveness and utility of health hazard/health risk appraisal in clinical and nonclinical settings. *Health Services Research, 22*(4), 537–551.

Beery, W. L., Schoenbach, V. J., Wagner, E. H., Graham, R., Karon, J., & Pezzullos, S. (1986). *Health risk appraisal: Methods and programs with annotated bibliography*. Washington, DC: National Center for Health Services Research and Health Care Technology.

Bergadaa, M. M. (1990). The role of time in the action of the consumer. *Journal of Consumer Research, 17*, 289–302.

Betancourt, H., & Lopez, S. R. (1993). The study of culture, ethnicity, and race in American psychology. *American Psychologist, 48*, 629–637.

Block, G., Clifford, C., Naughton, M. D., Henderson, M., & McAdams, M. (1989). A brief dietary screen for high fat intake. *Journal of Nutrition Education, 21*(5), 199–207.

Bobo, J. K., Gale, J. L., Thapa, P. B., & Wassilak, G. F. (1993). Risk factors for delayed immunization in a random sample of 1163 children from Oregon and Washington. *Pediatrics, 91*(2), 308–314.

Boyd–Franklin, N. (1989). *Black families in therapy*. New York: Guilford.

Brennan, L. K., Kreuter, M. W., Caburnay, C. A., & Wilshire, B. L. (1998, March). *Linking smokers to smoking cessation programs: Does perceived importance of specific program characteristics predict cessation?* Paper presented at the 19th Society of Behavioral Medicine Annual Meeting, New Orleans, LA.

Brennan, L. K., Kreuter, M. W., Newton, D. L., Caburnay, C. A., Wilshire, B. L., Kunyosying, A., & Brown, T. E. (1997, November). *Using assessment–based matching to link smokers to appropriate cessation programs: Results from a randomized trial*. Paper presented at the American Public Health Association Annual Meeting, Indianapolis, IN.

Brenzel, L., & Claquin, P. (1994). Immunization programs and their costs. *Social Science in Medicine, 39*(4), 527–536.

Brinberg, D., & Axelson, M. L. (1990). Increasing the consumption of dietary fiber: A decision theory analysis. *Health Education Research, 5*(4), 409–420.

Brown, C. M., & Segal, R. (1996). Ethnic differences in temporal orientation and its implications for hypertension management. *Journal of Health and Social Behavior, 37*(4), 350–361.

Brown, D. R., & Gary, L. E. (1987). Stressful life events, social support networks, and the physical and mental health of urban black adults. *Journal of Human Stress*, Winter, 167–174.

Brownson, R. C., Remington, P. L., & Davis, J. R. (Eds.). (1993). *Chronic disease epidemiology and control*. Washington, DC: American Public Health Association.

Brug, J., Glanz, K., Van Assema, P., Kok, G., & Van Breukelen, G. J. P. (1998). The impact of computer–tailored feedback and iterative feedback on fat, fruit and vegetable consumption. *Health Education and Behavior, 25*(4), 517–531.

Brug, J., Steenhaus, I., van Assema, P., & de Vries, H. (1996). The impact of computer–tailored nutrition intervention. *Preventive Medicine, 25*, 236–242.

Bryant, C. A. (1982). The impact of kin, friend and neighbor networks on infant feeding practices. *Social Science Medicine, 16*, 1757–1765.

Bull, F. C., & Jamrozik, K. (1998). Advice on exercise from a family physician can help sedentary patients to become active. *American Journal of Preventive Medicine, 15*(2), 85–94.

Bull, F. C., Kreuter, M. W., & Scharff, D. P. (1999). Effects of tailored, personalized, and general materials on physical activity. *Patient Education and Counseling, 36*, 181–192.

Caburnay, C. A., & Kreuter, M. W. (1998). Promoting childhood immunization in urban public health centers. *Outlook, newsletter of the Society of Behavioral Medicine*. Summer.

Cacioppo, J. T., Harkins, S. G., & Petty, R. E. (1981). The nature of attitudes and cognitive responses and their relationships to behavior. In R. E. Petty, T. M. Ostrom, & T. C. Brock (Eds.), *Cognitive Responses in Persuasion* (pp. 31–54). Hillsdale, NJ: Lawrence Erlbaum Associates.

Campbell, M. K., Bernhardt, J. M., Waldmiller, M., Jackson, B., Potenziani, D., Weathers, B., & Demissie, S. (1999). Varying the message source in computer–tailored nutrition education. *Patient Education and Counseling, 36*(2), 157–169.

Campbell, M. K., DeVellis, B. M., Strecher, V. J., Ammerman, A. S., DeVellis, R. F., & Sandler, R. S. (1994). Improving dietary behavior: The effectiveness of tailored messages in primary care settings. *American Journal of Public Health, 84*(5), 783–787.

Campbell, M. K., Honess–Morreale, L., Farrell, D., Carbone, E., & Brasure, M. (in press). Effects of a tailored multimedia nutrition education program for low income women receiving food assistance. *Health Education Review.*

Centers for Disease Control. (1987). *National Health Interview Survey.* Atlanta, GA.

Chapman, S. (1985). Stop smoking clinics: A case for their abandonment. *Lancet I, 8434,* 918-20.

Converse J. M., & Presser, S. (1986). *Survey questions: Handcrafting the standardized questionnaire.* Beverly Hills, CA: Sage.

Counsel on Scientific Affairs. (1991). Hispanic Health in the United States. *Journal of the American Medical Association, 265*(2), 248–252.

Curry, S. J., Wahner, E. H., & Grothaus, L. C. (1990). Intrinsic and extrinsic motivation for smoking cessation. *Journal of Consulting and Clinical Psychology, 58,* 310–316.

Davis, S. (1987). *Future Perfect.* Reading, MA: Addison Wesley.

Davis, S. W., Cummings, K. M., Rimer, B. K., Sciandra, R., & Stone, J. C. (1992). The impact of tailored self–help smoking cessation guides on young mothers. *Health Education Quarterly, 19*(4), 495–504.

Deering, I. E. (1942). *Let's try thinking: A handbook of democratic action.* Yellow Springs, OH: The Antioch Press.

DeFriese, G. H., & Fielding, J. E. (1990). Health risk appraisal in the 1990s: Opportunities, challenges, and expectations. *Annual Review of Public Health, 11,* 401–418.

Dessart, G. (1990). The media industry perspective. In C. Atkin & L. Wallack (Eds.), *Mass communication and public health,* (pp. 170–173). Newbury Park, CA: Sage Publications.

Developing Breast Health Materials That Make a Difference. (1999). [A printed set of breast health and breast cancer materials, spanning treatment, prognosis, detection, risk and prevention, and psychosocial topic areas]. Dallas, TX: The Susan G. Komen Foundation.

Dijkstra, A., De Vries, H., & Roijackers, J. (1998a). Computerized tailored feedback to change cognitive determinants of smoking: a Dutch field experiment. *Health Education Research: Theory and Research, 13*(2), 197–206.

Dijkstra, A., De Vries, H., & Roijackers, J. (1998b). Long–term effectiveness of computer–generated tailored feedback in smoking cessation. *Health Education Research, 13*(2), 207–214.

Ditto, P. H., Druley, J. A., Moore, K. A., Danks, J. H., & Smucker, W. D. (1996). Fates worse than death: The role of valued life activities in health–state evaluations. *Health Psychology, 15*(5), 332–343.

Doorway to Recovery. (1995). [A computer tailored print intervention to support relapse among recovering alcoholics]. Wilmington, DE: DuPont Pharmaceutical Company.

Drossaert, C. H., Boer, H., & Seydel, E. R. (1996). Health education to improve repeat participation the Dutch breast cancer screening program: Evaluation of a leaflet tailored to previous participants. *Patient Education and Counseling, 28*, 121–131.

Eakin, E. G., Lichtenstein, E., Severson, H. H., Stevens, V. J., Vogt, T. M., & Hollis, J. F. (1998). Use of tailored videos in primary care smoking cessation interventions. *Health Education Research, 13*(4), 519–527.

Erickson, A. C., McKenna, J. W., & Romano, R. M. (1990). Past lessons and new uses of the mass media in reducing tobacco consumption. *Public Health Reports, 105*(3), 239–244.

Fagerstrom, K. O. (1978). Measuring degree of physical dependence to tobacco smoking with reference to individualization of treatment. *Addictive Behaviors, 3*(3–4), 235–41.

Fielding, J. E. (1989). Frequency of health risk assessment activities at U.S. worksites. *American Journal of Preventive Medicine, 5*, 73–81.

Fishbein, M., & Azjen, I. (1975). *Beliefs, Attitudes, Intention, and Behavior: An introduction to theory and research.*. Reading, MA: Addison–Wesley.

Forsyth, B., & Lessler, J. (1991). Cognitive laboratory methods: A taxonomy. In P. P. Biemer & et al. (Eds.), *Measurement Errors in Surveys* (pp. 393–418). New York: Wiley.

Fry, E. (1997). Fry's readability graph: Clarifications, validity, and extensions to level 17. *Journal of Reading*, December, 242–252.

Furino, A. (1991). Health status among Hispanics: Major themes and new priorities. *Journal of the American Medical Association, 265*(2), 255–257.

Geller, L. (1997). Customer retention begins with basics. *Direct Marketing, 60*(5), 58–62.

Gittelsohn, J., Evans, M., Helitzer, D., Anliker, J., Story, M., Metcalfe, L., Davis, S., & Iron Cloud, P. (1998). Formative research in a school–based obesity prevention program for Native American school children. *Health Education Research, 13*(2), 251–265.

Graham, R. J. (1981). The role of perception of time in consumer research. *Journal of Consumer Research, 7*, 335–342.

Green, L. W., & Kreuter, M. W. (1991). *Health promotion planning: An educational and environmental approach.* Mountain View: Mayfield.

Gritz, E. R., & Berman, B. A. (1989). Smoking and pregnancy. *Journal of the American Medical Women's Association, 44*(2), 57.

Hammond, S. L., Freimuth, V. S., & Morrison, W. (1987). The gatekeeping funnel: Tracking a major PSA campaign from distribution through gatekeepers to target audience. *Health Education Quarterly, 14*, 153–166.

Hays, W. (1973). Extended kinship relations in Black and White families. *Journal of Marriage and the Family, 35*, 51–57.

Healthy People 2000. (1991). National health promotion and disease prevention objectives. Washington, DC: Department of Health and Human Services.

Henderson J., Noell J., Reeves T., Robinson T., & Strecher V. (1999). Developers and evaluation of interactive health communication applications. The science panel on interactive communications and health. *American Journal of Preventive Medicine, 16*(1), 30–34.

Herkovits, M. (1948). *Man and his works.* New York: Knopf.

Hof, R.D., Browder, S., & Elstrom, P. (1997). Internet Communities. *Business Week, 3525*(May 5), 64–80.

Hong, B. A., Kappel, D. F., Whitlock, M., Parks–Thomas, T., & Freedman, B. (1994). Using race–specific community programs to increase organ donation among blacks. *American Journal of Public Health, 84*(2), 314–315.

Hughes, D., Seidman, E., & Williams, N. (1993). Cultural phenomena and the research enterprise: Toward a culturally anchored methodology. *American Journal of Community Psychology, 21*(6), 687–703.

Hunt, W. A., Barnett, L. W., & Branch, L. G. (1971). Relapse rates in addiction programs. *Journal of Clinical Psychology, 27,* 455–456.

Institute of Medicine. (1988). *The future of public health..* Washington, DC: National Academy Press.

Institute of Medicine. (1994). *Overcoming barriers to immunization.* Washington, DC: National Academy Press.

Jabine, T., Straf, M., Tanur, J., & Tourangeau, R. (Eds.). (1984). *Cognitive Aspects of Survey Methodology: Building a Bridge Between Disciplines..* Washington, DC: National Academy Press.

Jackson, J. S., & Gurin, G. (1987). *National survey of Black Americans, 1979–1980.* Inter–University Consortium for Political and Social Research.

Janz, N. K., & Becker, M. H. (1984). The Health Belief Model: A decade later. *Health Education Quarterly, 11*(1), 1–47.

Keane, V., Stanton, B., Horton, L., Aronson, R., Galbraith, J., & Hughart, N. (1993). Perceptions of vaccine efficacy, illness, and health among inner–city parents. *Clinical Pediatrics,* January, 2–7.

Kelsey, T. W. (1994). The agrarian myth and policy responses to farm safety. *American Journal of Public Health, 84*(7), 1171–1177.

Klonoff, E. A., & Landrine, H. (1996). Belief in the healing power of prayer: Prevalence and health correlates for African Americans. *Western Journal of Black Studies, 20*(4), 207–210.

Klonoff, E. A., Landrine, H., & Scott, J. (1995). Double jeopardy: Ethnicity and women's health. In H. Landrine (Ed.), *Bringing cultural diversity in feminist psychology: Theory, research, practice* (pp. 335–360) . Washington, DC: American Psychological Association.

Koop, C. E. (1995). A personal role in health care reform. *American Journal of Public Health, 85*(6), 759–760.

Kreuter, M. K., Vehige, E., & McGuire, A. G. (1996). Using computer–tailored calendars to promote childhood immunization. *Public Health Reports, 111,* 176–178.

Kreuter, M. W. (1997, November). *Towards more effective health communication: comparing effects of tailored, personalized, and untailored messages in a randomized trial.* Paper presented at the American Public Health Association Annual Meeting, Indianapolis, IN.

Kreuter, M. W., & Scharff, D. P. (1999). The role of health assessment in planning health promotion programs. In G. C. Hyner, K. W. Peterson, J. W. Travis, J. E. Dewey, J. J. Foerster, & E. M. Framer (Eds.), *Society of Prospective Medicine Handbook of Health Assessment Tools* (pp. 101–109). Pittsburgh, PA: The Society of Prospective Medicine.

Kreuter, M. W., & Skinner, C. S. (Under review). What's in a name? (editorial). *Health Education Research, Theory and Practice..*

Kreuter, M. W., & Strecher, V. J. (1995). Changing inaccurate perceptions of health risk: Results from a randomized trial. *Health Psychology, 14*(1), 56–63.

Kreuter, M. W., & Strecher, V. J. (1996). Do tailored behavior change messages enhance the effectiveness of health risk appraisals? Results from a randomized trial. *Health Education Research, 11*(1), 97–105.

Kreuter, M. W., Brennan, L. K., Lukwago, S. N., Scharff, D. P., & Wadud, E. (1997, November). *Using computer tailored educational materials to promote nutrition label reading.* Paper presented at the American Public Health Association Annual Meeting, Indianapolis, IN.

Kreuter, M. W., Bull, F. C., Clark, E. M., & Oswald, D. L. (in press). Understanding how people process health information: A comparison of tailored and untailored weight loss materials. *Health Psychology.*

Kreuter, M. W., Lezin, N. A., Kreuter, M. W., & Green, L. W. (1998). *Community Health Promotion Ideas that Work.* Boston: Jones & Bartlett.

Kristeller, J. L., Merriam, P. A., Ockene, J. K., Ockene, I. S., & Goldberg, R. J. (1993). Smoking intervention for cardiac patients: In search of more effective strategies. *Cardiology, 82*(5), 317–324.

Krueger, R. A. (1994). *Focus Groups: A practical guide for applied research..* Newbury Park, CA: Sage.

Landrine, H., & Klonoff, E. A. (1994). The African American Accultration Scale: Development, reliability, and validity. *Journal of Black Psychology, 20*(2), 104–127.

Landrine, H., & Klonoff, E. A. (1995). The African American acculturation scale II: Cross–validation and short form. *Journal of Black Psychology, 21*(2), 124–152.

Landrine, H., & Klonoff, E. A. (1997). Traditional African American family practices: Prevalence and correlates. *Western Journal of Black Studies, 20*(2), 59–62.

Langkamp, D. L., & Langhough, R. (1993). What do parents of pre–term infants know about diphtheria, tetanus, and pertussis immunizations? *American Journal of Perinatology, 10*(3), 187–189.

Lannon, C., Black, V., Stuart, J., Caplow, M., McNeill, A., Bordley, W. C., & Margolis, P. (1995). What mothers say about why poor children fall behind on immunizations: A summary of focus groups in North Carolina. *Archives of Pediatrics and Adolescent Medicine, 149,* 1070–1075.

Last, J. M. (1988). *A Dictionary of Epidemiology* (2nd ed.). New York: Oxford University Press.

Leshan, L. L. (1952). Time orientation and social class. *Journal of Abnormal and Social Psychology, 47,* 589–592.

Levine, D. M., Morisky, D. E., Bone, L. R., Lewis, C., Ward, W. B., & Green, L. W. (1982). Data–based planning for educational interventions through hypertension control programs for urban and rural populations in Maryland. *Public Health Reports, 97*(2), 107–112.

Lieu, T. A., Black, S. B., Ray, P., Chellino, M., Shinefield, H. R., & Adler, N. E. (1994). Risk factors for delayed immunization among children in an HMO. *American Journal of Public Health, 84*(10), 1621–1625.

Lozoff, B., Wolf, A., & Davis, N. (1984). Cosleeping in urban families with young children in the United States. *Pediatrics, 74,* 171–182.

Mandansky, D., & Edlebrock, C. (1990). Cosleeping in a community sample of 2– and 3–year old children. *Pediatrics, 86*(2), 197–203.

Marcus, B. H., Emmons, K. M., Simkin–Silverman, L. R., Linnan, L. A., Taylor, E. R., Bock, B. C., Roberts, M. B., Rossi, J. S., & Abrams, D. B. (1998). Evaluation of motivationally tailored vs. standard self–help physical activity interventions at the workplace. *American Journal of Health Promotion, 12*(4), 246–253.

Marlatt, G. A. (1985). Relapse prevention: Theoretical rationale and overview of the model. In G. A. Marlatt & J. R. Gordon (Eds.), *Relapse Prevention* (pp. 3–70). New York: Guilford Press.

McCombs, M., & Shaw, D. (1972). The agenda setting function of mass media. *Public Opinion Quarterly, 36,* 176–187.

McGuire, W. J. (1991). Theoretical foundations of campaigns. In R. E. Rice & C. K. Atkin (Eds.), *Public Communication Campaigns,* (2nd ed.) (pp.43–65). Newbury Park: Sage.

McKenna, J. W., & Romano, R. M. (1989, October). *Using media for tobacco control: What works.* Paper presented at the American Public Health Association annual meeting, Chicago, IL.

McLaughlin, G. H. (1969). SMOG grading — a new readability formula. *Journal of Reading, 20,* 242–252.

Meldrum, P., Turnbull, D., Dobson, H. M., Colquhoun, C., Gilmour, W. H., & McIlwaine, G. M. (1994). Tailored written invitations for second round breast cancer screening: A randomized controlled trial. *Journal of Medical Screening, 1,* 245–248.

Mishra, S. (1992). Leisure activities and life satisfaction in old age: A case study of retired government employees living in urban areas. *Activities, Adaptation & Aging, 16*(4), 7–26.

Morgan, G. D., Noll, E. L., Orleans, C. T., Rimer, B. K., Amfoh, K., & Bonney, G. (1996). Reaching mid–life and older smokers: Tailored interventions for routine medical care. *Preventive Medicine, 25*(3), 346–354.

National Cancer Institute. (1994). *Clear & Simple: Developing Effective Print Materials for Low–Literate Readers* (NIH Publication No. 95–3594).

National Vaccine Advisory Committee. (1992, May). [Standards approved by U.S. Public Health Service and endorsed by American Academy of Pediatrics].

Nobles, W. W. (1991). African Philosophy: Foundations for Black Psychology. In R. L. Jones (Ed.), *Black Psychology,* (3rd ed., pp. 47–63). Berkeley, CA: Cobb & Henry Publishers.

Novello, A. C., Wise, P. H., & Kleinman, D. V. (1991). Hispanic Health: Time for data, time for action. *Journal of the American Medical Association, 265*(2), 253–254.

Oeffinger, K. C., Roaten, S. P., Hitchcock, M. A., & Oeffinger, P. K. (1992). The effect of patient education on pediatric immunization rates. *Journal of Family Practice, 35*(3), 288–293.

Orenstein, W. A., Atkinson, W., Mason, D., & Bernier, R. H. (1990). Barriers to vaccinating preschool children. *Journal of Health Care for the Poor and Underserved, 1*(3), 315–330.

Orleans, C. T., Boyd, R. N., Noll, E., Crosette, L., & Glassman, B. (1996, March). *Intervening through a prescribed benefit plan for nicotine patch users.* Paper presented at the Society of Behavioral Medicine Annual Meeting, Washington, DC.

Paisley, W. (1989). Public Communication Campaigns: The American Experience. In R. E. Rice & C. K. Atkin (Eds.), *Public Communication Campaigns* (pp. 15–38). Newbury Park, CA: Sage.

Parker, K. D., & Calhoun, T. (1996). Predictors of life satisfaction among black Americans. *The Western Journal of Black Studies, 20*(3), 134–139.

Partners in Women's Health. (1997–1998). [A computer tailored program to facilitate medication compliance among pre–, peri–, and post menopausal women at increased risk for heart disease and osteoporosis]. Montvale, NJ: Merck Medco Managed Care and Innovative Health Solutions.

Pasick, R. J. (1997). Socioeconomic and cultural factors in the development and use of theory. In K. Glanz, F. M. Lewis, & B. K. Rimer (Eds.), *Health Behavior & Health Education: Theory, Research & Practice,* (pp.425–440). San Francisco: Jossey–Bass.

Pathways to freedom: Winning the fight against tobacco. (1992). Philadelphia: Fox Chase Center.

Patterson, R. S., & Roberts, D. J. (1951). *Community health education in action.* St. Louis, MO: Mosby Publications.

Patton, M. Q. (1980). *Qualitative evaluation methods..* Beverly Hills, CA: Sage.

Peppers, D., & Rogers, M. (1993). *The One to One future: Building relationships one customer at a time.* New York: Doubleday.

Peppers, D., & Rogers, M. (1997). *Enterprise One to One: Tools for competing in the active age.* New York: Currency Doubleday.

Petty, R. E. (1977). The importance of cognitive responses in persuasion. *Advances in Consumer Research, 4*, 357–362.

Petty, R. E., & Cacioppo, J. T. (1981a). Epilog: A general framework for understanding attitude change processes. In Petty & Cacioppo (Eds.), *Attitudes and Persuasion: Classic and Contemporary Approaches*, (pp. 255–269). Dubuque IA: William C. Brown Company.

Petty, R. T., & Cacioppo, J. T. (1981b). *Attitudes and persuasion: Classic and contemporary approaches*. Dubuque, IA: William C. Brown Company.

Petty, R. T., Cacioppo, J. T., Strathman, A. J., & Priester, J. R. (1994). To think or not to think. Exploring two routes to persuasion. In S. Shavitt & T. C. Brock (Eds.), *Persuasion. Psychological Insights and Perspectives*, (pp. 113–147). Boston: Allyn and Bacon.

Pine, J. (1993). *Mass customization: the new frontier in business competition.* Boston: Harvard Business School Press.

Prochaska, J. O., & DiClemente, C. C. (1983). Stages and processes of self–change for smoking: Toward an integrative model of change. *Journal of Consulting and Clinical Psychology, 51*, 390–395.

Prochaska, J. O., & DiClemente, C. C. (1988). Measuring process of change: Applications to the cessation of smoking. *Journal of Consulting and Clinical Psychology, 56*, 520–528.

Prochaska, J. O., DiClemente, C. C., & Norcross, J. C. (1992). In search of how people change: Applications to addictive behaviors. *American Psychologist, 47*(9), 1102–1114.

Prochaska, J. O., DiClemente, C. C., Velicer, W. F., & Rossi, J. S. (1993). Standardized, individualized, interactive and personalized self–help programs for smoking cessation. *Health Psychology, 12*(5), 399–405.

Ramirez, T. (personal communication, January 21, 1999)

Raphel, M. (1996). Customer specific marketing. *Direct Marketing, 59*(2), 22–27.

Rimer, B. K., & Glassman, B. (1998). Tailoring communications for primary care settings. *Methods of Information in Medicine, 37*(2), 171–177.

Rimer, B. K., & Orleans, C. T. (1994). Tailoring smoking cessation for older adults. *CANCER Supplement, 74*(7), 2051.

Rimer, B. K., Orleans, C. T., Fleisher, L., Cristinzio, S., Resch, N., Telepchak, J., & Keintz, M. K. (1994). Does tailoring matter? The impact of a tailored guide on ratings and short–term smoking–related outcomes for older smokers. *Health Education Quarterly, 9*(1), 69–84.

Rogers, E. M. (1983). *Diffusion of innovations.* (3rd ed.). New York: The Free Press.

Rohner, R. P. (1984). Toward a conception of culture for cross–culture psychology. *Journal of Cross–Cultural Psychology, 15*(2), 111–138.

Ryan, W. (1971). *Blaming the Victim.* New York: Vintage.

Salsberry, P. J., Nickel, J. T., & Mitch, R. (1993). Why aren't preschoolers immunized? A comparison of parents' and providers' perceptions of the barriers to immunizations. *Journal of Community Health Nursing, 10*(4), 213–224.

Schoenbach, V. J. (1987). Appraising health risk appraisal. *American Journal of Public Health, 77*(4), 409–411.

Scutchfield, F. D., & Keck, C. W. (1997). Concepts and definitions of public health practice. In FD Scutchfield and CW Keck (Eds.), *Principles of Public Health Practice,* (pp. 3–9). Albany, NY: Delmar.

Shiffman, S., Gitchell, J., & Strecher, V. J. (1997, August). *Real–world efficacy of computer–tailored smoking cessation material as a supplement to nicotine replacement.* Paper presented at the 10th World Conference on Tobacco or Health, Beijing, China.

Skinner, C. S., & Kreuter, M. W. (1997). Using theories in planning interactive computer programs. In R. L. Street, W. R. Gold, & T. Manning (Eds.), *Health Promotion and Interactive Technology: Theoretical Applications and Future Direction* (pp. 39–65) Mahwah, NJ: Lawrence Erlbaum Associates.

Skinner, C. S., Campbell, M. K., Rimer, B. K., Curry, J., & Prochaska, J. O. (in press). How effective is tailored print communication? *Annals of Behavioral Medicine.*

Skinner, C. S., Siegfried, J. C., Kegeler, M. C., & Strecher, V. J. (1993). The potential of computers in patient education. *Patient Education and Counseling, 22*(1), 27–34.

Skinner, C. S., Strecher, V. J., & Hospers, H. (1994). Physician recommendations for mammography: Do tailored messages make a difference? *American Journal of Public Health, 84*(1), 43–49.

Skinner, C. S., Sykes, R. K., Monsees, B. S., Andriole, D. A., Arfken, C. L., & Fisher, E. B. (1998). The Learn, Share, and Live program: Breast cancer education for older, urban women. *Health Education and Behavior, 25*(1), 60–78.

Snoddy, R. (1996). Name dropping junk mail treats us all like burkes. *Marketing, 9,* 10.

Stein, A. D., Lederman, R. I., & Shea, S. (1993). The behavioral risk factor surveillance system questionnaire: Its reliability in a statewide sample. *American Journal of Public Health, 83*(12), 1768–1772.

Stewart, D. W., & Shamdasani, P. N. (1991). *Focus Groups: Theory and Practice.* Newbury Park, CA: Sage Publications.

Strecher, V. J. (1998, March). *Using advanced communication technologies to improve health related behaviors.* Paper presented at the 19th Society of Behavioral Medicine Annual Meeting, New Orleans, LA.

Strecher, V. J., & Kreuter, M. W. (1999). Health risk appraisal from a behavioral perspective: Present and future. In G. C. Hyner, K. W. Peterson, J. W. Travis, J. E. Dewey, J. J. Foerster, & E. M. Framer (Eds.), *Society of Prospective Medicine Handbook of Health Assessment Tools* (pp. 75–82). Pittsburgh, PA: The Society of Prospective Medicine.

Strecher, V. J., DeVellis, B. M., Becker, M. H., & Rosenstock, I. M. (1986). The role of self–efficacy in achieving health behavior change. *Health Education Quarterly, 13*(1), 73–92.

Strecher, V. J., Kreuter, M. W., Den Boer, D. J., Kobrin, S., Hospers, H., & Skinner, C. S. (1994). The effects of computer–tailored smoking cessation messages in family practice settings. *Journal of Family Practice, 39*(3), 262–270.

Strecher, V. J., principal investigator. (1994). *Developing a tool for evaluating the quality of print–based health education materials.* U.S. Department of Health and Human Services, Public Health Service, Centers for Disease Control and Prevention, Atlanta, GA.

Strecher, V. J., Rimer, B. K., & Monaco, K. D. (1989). Development of a new self–help guide—Freedom from smoking for you and your family. *Health Education Quarterly, 16*(1), 101–112.

Street, R. L., & Rimal, R. N. (1997). Health promotion and interactive technology: A conceptual foundation. In R. L. Street, W. R. Gold, & T. Manning (Eds.), *Health promotion and interactive technology. Theoretical applications and future directions* (pp. 1–18). Mahwah, NJ: Lawrence Erlbaum Associates.

Sudman, S., Bradburn, N., & Schwartz, N. (1996). *Thinking about answers: The application of cognitive processes to survey methodology.* San Francisco: Jossey–Bass Inc.

Thomas, P. R. (Ed.). (1995). *Weighing the Options: Criteria for evaluating weight–management programs.* Washington, DC: National Academy Press.

Thomas, R., Cahill, J., & Santilli, L. (1997). Using an interactive computer game to increase skill and self–efficacy regarding safer sex negotiation: Field test results. *Health Education and Behavior, 24,* 71–86.

Triandis, H., Lambert, W., Berry, J., Lonner, W., Heron, A., Brislin, R., & Draguns, J. (Eds.). (1980). *Handbook of Cross–Cultural Psychology* (Vols. 1–6). Boston: Allyn & Bacon.

Turshen, M. (1989). *The Politics of Public Health.* New Brunswick, NJ: Rutgers University Press.

U.S. Bureau of the Census. (1997). *Statistical Abstract of the United States: 1997,* (117th ed.). Washington, DC.

U.S. Department of Health and Human Services. (1992). *Making Health Communication Programs Work.* Washington, DC: National Cancer Institute, Office of Cancer Communication, NIH Pub. No. 92–1493.

U.S. Department of Transportation. (1987). *Fatal Accident Reporting Systems (FARS).*

U.S. Dept. of Health and Human Services. (1989). *Reducing the health consequences of smoking: 25 years of progress.* A report of the Surgeon General. Atlanta, GA: U.S. Department of health and Human Services, Centers for Disease Control and Prevention, Center for Chronic Disease Prevention and Health Promotion, Office on Smoking and Health.

U.S. Preventive Services Task Force. (1996). *Guide to clinical preventive services: report of the U.S. Preventive Services Task Force* (2nd ed.). Baltimore: Williams & Wilkins.

Wadud, S. E., Kreuter, M. W., & Clarkson, S. (1998). Risk perception, beliefs about prevention, and preventive behaviors of farmers. *Journal of Agricultural Safety and Health, 4*(1), 15–24.

Wagner, E. H., Beery, W. L., Schoenback, V. J., & Graham, R. M. (1982). An assessment of health hazard/health risk appraisal. *American Journal of Public Health, 72,* 347–352.

Wallack, L., Dorfman, L., Jernigan, D., & Themba, M. (1993). *Media advocacy and public health: Power for prevention.* Newbury Park, CA: Sage.

Warner, K. E. (1987). Television and health education: Stay tuned. *American Journal of Public Health, 77*(2), 140–142.

Weese, C. B., & Krauss, M. R. (1995). A "barrier–free" health care system does not ensure adequate vaccination of 2–year–old children. *Archives of Pediatrics & Adolescent Medicine, 149,* 1130–1135.

Weinstein, N. D. (1988). The precaution adoption process. *Health Psychology, 7,* 4.

White, J. L., & Parham, T. A. (1990). *The Psychology of Blacks: An African–American Perspective.* (2nd ed.). Englewood Cliffs, NJ: Prentice–Hall.

Wileman, R. (1993). *Visual Communicating.* Englewood Cliffs, NJ: Educational Technology Publications.

Winefield, H. R., & Cormack, S. M. (1986). Regular activities as indicators of subjective health status. *International Journal of Rehabilitation Research, 9*(1), 47–52.

Wood, D., Halfon, N., Sherbourne, C., & Grabowsky, M. (1994). Access to infant immunizations for poor, inner–city families: What is the impact of managed care? *Journal of Health Care for the Poor and Underserved, 5*(2), 112–123.

Yankauer, A. (1987). Hispanic/ Latino– What's in a name? *American Journal of Public Health, 77*(1), 15–17.

Zimmerman, R. K., Ahwesh, E. R., Mieczkowski, T. A., Block, B., Janosky, J. E., & Barker, D. W. (1996). Influence of family functioning and income on vaccination in inner–city health centers. *Archives of Pediatrics & Adolescent Medicine, 150,* 1054–1061.

Zimmerman, R. S., Vega, W. A., Gil, A. G., Warheit, G. J., Apospori, E., & Biafora, F. (1994). Who is Hispanic? Definitions and their consequences. *American Journal of Public Health, 84*(12), 1985–1987.

Index